T0114625

Jezebel

Jezebel

The Untold Story of the Bible's Harlot Queen

Lesley Hazleton

DOUBLEDAY

New York London Toronto
Sydney Auckland

⊂D

DOUBLEDAY

Copyright © 2007 by Lesley Hazleton

All Rights Reserved

Published in the United States by Doubleday, an imprint of The Doubleday
Publishing Group, a division of Random House, Inc., New York.
www.doubleday.com

A hardcover edition of this book was originally published in 2007 by Doubleday.

DOUBLEDAY is a registered trademark and the DD colophon is a trademark of
Random House, Inc.

Book design by Ralph Fowler / rlf design
Map illustration by Jeffrey L. Ward

Library of Congress Cataloging-in-Publication Data
Hazleton, Lesley, 1945–
    Jezebel : the untold story of the Bible's harlot queen / Lesley Hazleton.
      p. cm.
    Includes bibliographical references.
    1. Jezebel, Queen, consort of Ahab, King of Israel. I. Title.
    BS580.J45H39 2007
    222'.5092—dc22

                                2007005339

ISBN 978-0-385-51615-0

First Paperback Edition

147028622

for Dorothy Pantanowitz

and forty years of friendship

Contents

Contents

Jezebel

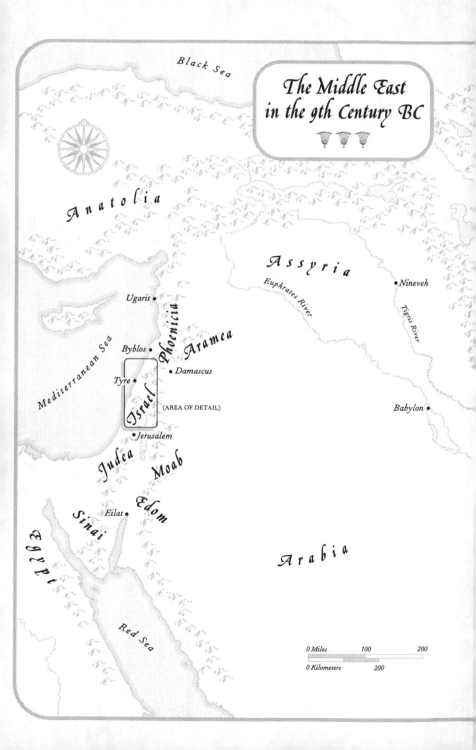

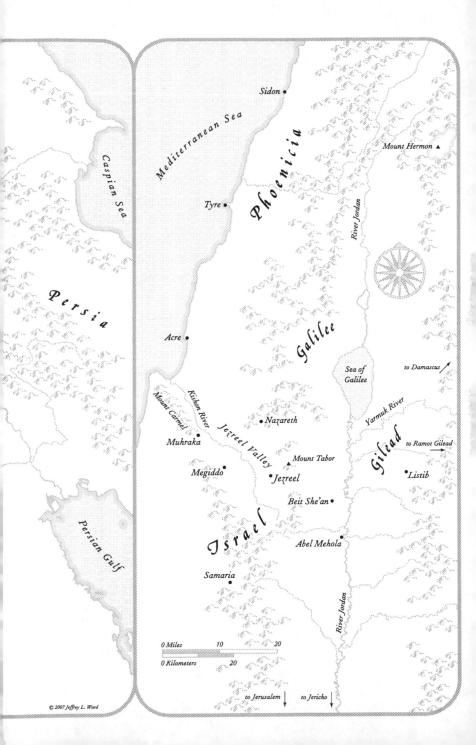

Sidon •

Mediterranean Sea

Caspian Sea

Phoenicia

Mount Hermon ▲

River Jordan

Tyre •

Persia

Galilee

Acre •

Sea of
Galilee

to Damascus ↗

Yarmuk River

Mount Carmel

Kishon River

Nazareth •

Gilead

to Ramot Gilead
→

Muhraka

Jezreel Valley

Mount Tabor ▲

Listib •

Megiddo •

Jezreel •

Beit She'an •

Israel

Abel Mehola •

Persian Gulf

Samaria •

River Jordan

0 Miles   10   20

0 Kilometers   20

© 2007 Jeffrey L. Ward

to Jerusalem ↓   to Jericho ↓

Introduction

in which Jezebel has gained a reputation

Jezebel, Jezebel, fornicating under the walls of God's holy city!"

The words intruded into what had been, until that moment, a beautiful Jerusalem spring morning. I'd been walking peaceably along when I was suddenly confronted by this irate, shabbily dressed stranger who seemed to have appeared out of nowhere. My imagined fornication lit him up with righteous indignation. It energized him, even delighted him. To judge by his grandiose phrasing, I was being denounced to both heaven and earth—or at least as far as the walls of the Old City, where he trailed me, ranting and raving all the way. At Zion Gate, he finally gave up and turned back, doubtless to pounce on another harlot deserving of denunciation.

Never mind that the real Jezebel had never set foot in Jerusalem. No matter either that any resemblance between myself and her could at best be said to be entirely coincidental. This true believer had seen a secular woman whose long-sleeved shirt and jeans hid nothing from his righteous vision. I was flaunting myself in public, a shameless hussy inflaming his basest desires by my mere presence. In his mind, I could only be another Jezebel out to pollute holiness.

He was mad, of course—yet another victim of what psychiatrists call "the Jerusalem syndrome," where biblical history acts as the tipping point into schizophrenia for the unstable mind. But no madness takes place in a vacuum. The form it takes is a distorted reflection of the culture. The enormous cultural weight of the Bible projects three-thousand-year-old stereotypes deep into modern consciousness, and none so deep, it seems, as the name Jezebel.

There is a magic in names. A power sometimes of enchantment, sometimes of curse. They can be cooed, whispered, murmured between lovers. Chanted and intoned in worship. Invoked in oaths. Hurled and spat in anger. Jezebel's name is always hurled, always spat. In fact it has been distorted to invite just such a reaction.

Her real name was Itha-Baal, which means "woman of the Lord" in her native language, Phoenician. But in a pun worthy of the craftiest modern spinmeister—the kind of wordplay common in the Hebrew bible—this was changed in Hebrew to I-zevel, or "woman of dung," which was later written as Jezebel in Greek and so also in English. The change kept the same three-consonant Semitic root, but gave it the opposite meaning. What it lacked in subtlety, it gained in effectiveness.

The Hebrew meaning is the one that has persevered, molding

the various forms Jezebel has taken in the imagination. She is the prototype of the evil woman, the original femme fatale, "a creature both forceful and bold" in the words of the first-century historian Josephus, who described her as going to "great lengths of licentiousness and madness." An aura of treachery and perfidiousness enshrouds her. She's the harlot queen, the shameless fornicator, the painted hussy, the scheming seductress enticing the innocent into the depths of wickedness. Hollywood visions of female perversity all play on various aspects of her image: Theda Bara's dark-eyed, bloodsucking vamp; Bette Davis's scheming southern belle in her scarlet ballgown; Marlene Dietrich's ruthless manipulator in *The Blue Angel*; Sharon Stone's cold seductress in *Basic Instinct*. But as novelist Tom Robbins put it: "In the Bitch Hall of Fame, Jezebel has a room all her own—nay, an entire wing."

Cleopatra was a prude by comparison, Catherine de Médicis an upstanding citizen. In historical novels purportedly based on Jezebel's life, she becomes an Orientalist fantasy of dangerous eroticism. On the first page of *Jezebel* by Denise Robins, she is stark naked "except for a single ruby glittering in her navel." By the third page, her wardrobe is augmented by "a black and yellow python coiled obediently around her ankles." She is a woman of "almost insatiable desire" in Frank Slaughter's *The Curse of Jezebel*, first seen naked "save for a tiny golden girdle about her hips and golden paint covering the nipples of her full breasts." The effect on the novel's hero is "a surge of desire so great it made him tremble." Such overheated prose is the norm. In Israeli playwright Mattitiyahu Shoham's *Tyre and Jerusalem*, merely to lay eyes on Jezebel is to come under her sexual spell. Only the prophet Elijah summons up the superhuman ability to resist, and even then, according to one stage direction, "he turns to gaze at her for yet another moment, to saturate his eyes with the pleading glory of flesh, to set his blood ablaze and seething with maddened lust."

As you surface for breath, you realize you can hardly blame a madman for latching on to Jezebel, when so many seemingly sane people have done exactly the same. Her name is so potent that nearly three thousand years after she lived—and died one of the goriest deaths in a book not known for eschewing gore—the very mention of it calls up a kind of forbidden allure. In the United States, it is still used to condemn women seen as sexually promiscuous. "That little Jezebel," someone will murmur spitefully. And it has an especially pernicious history as the stereotype used to stigmatize and exploit black women in the era of slavery, when it acted as a rationale for sexual abuse by white slaveowners.

This vast accumulation of condemnatory baggage is solidly rooted in the Bible, where Jezebel gets more ink than any other woman, Eve and Mary included. In the two books of Kings—two books simply because of the standard length of the papyrus scrolls on which they were first written—this foreign princess who became the queen of Israel is called a harlot, a sorceress, a liar, and a murderer. She seems eminently worthy of Elijah's terrible *fatwa*—"Jezebel shall be eaten by dogs by the walls of Jezreel"—and is indeed eventually thrown down from her palace walls, torn limb from limb by dogs, devoured by them, and finally, for good measure, excreted by them. She becomes literally a woman of dung. And even then, the Bible was not done with her. Nine hundred years later, the level of biblical vitriol was further ratcheted up when she was held up as the epitome of evil, the partner-in-crime to the Whore of Babylon in the terrifying vision of Saint John of Patmos known today as the last book of the New Testament, Revelation.

Despite all this—or, rather, because of it—few people today know much about who Jezebel really was. The harlot image has taken over to such a degree that it comes as a surprise to many that she was the princess royal of the most sophisticated civilization of her time: the Phoenician city-state of Tyre, on the coast of what is now Lebanon. Or that she was the great-aunt of Dido, the founder of Carthage, the same Dido whom Virgil made the lover of his legendary hero Aeneas. Or that her dramatic confrontation with the great Israelite prophet Elijah would be the pivotal point in the battle between polytheism and monotheism.

On this grand stage, Jezebel takes her place front and center. A magnificent, sweeping saga plays out, and it is told in Kings with flair and flourish. It includes terrifying public oaths and curses as well as pillow talk between Jezebel and her husband, King Ahab. It features evil schemes and underhanded plots, war and treason, false gods and falser humans, and all with the fate of entire nations at stake. A grand opera, in short. And at its center, one man and one woman: Elijah, whose Hebrew name Eliyahu means "Yahweh is my God," and Jezebel, the "woman of the Lord."

The two were well matched: equally proud, equally arrogant, equally committed to their principles and their faiths. They were a dramatic clash of opposites: her sophistication versus his stark puritanism; her polytheism versus his monotheism; her policy of cosmopolitanism and détente versus his of absolutism and confrontation. Their epic conflict was to pit tolerance against righteousness, pragmatic statesmanship against divine dictates, liberalism against conservatism. It would become far more than the story of two people, for this is the original story of the unholy marriage of sex, politics, and religion. It traces the defeat of pragmatism by ideology, and the disastrous consequences for all involved, which is why it rings uncomfortably close in the modern ear. It is, in fact, the foundation story of modern radical fundamentalism.

When your story is written by those in passionate opposition to everything you believe in, it will be, to put it mildly, warped. Everything becomes twisted; every action, every gesture, becomes not only suspect but turned on its head. The wildest rumors are passed off as fact. Inconvenient facts are ignored or edited out, relegated to oblivion, until all we are left with is not a real person but an image, a morality-tale character, which is how Jezebel would become a kind of wicked witch of the east.

Her story was first written three centuries after she reigned and met her gruesome death, and it was written by her enemies. If we are to have any idea of the real woman behind the feverish legend, we need to bear this solidly in mind. Whether or not we believe the Bible was divinely inspired, we tend to think of it as something that has simply always been. Given the reverence in which we hold it, it is easy to forget that it was written by specific men in specific times and places, for specific reasons. Nowhere is this more evident than in the aptly named Kings, which is the saga of the rise and fall of the Israelite monarchy from its inception under David and Solomon in a golden age that never really was, through its split into two kingdoms—Israel in the north and Judea in the south—to its disappearance in exile.

The split came shortly after the death of Solomon. The north, resentful of control from the Judean capital of Jerusalem, seceded and quickly became a regional power, leaving Judea as a kind of isolated and impoverished country cousin. Yet just two hundred years later, the northern kingdom had vanished. It was swallowed up by the Assyrian empire, and its population deported to become what would be known as "the ten lost tribes of Israel." Soon after, the southern kingdom came under a similar threat from another powerful empire to the east, in Babylon. It was the perfect time to write a polemical history, one that would explain why the north had collapsed, and act as an object lesson for the south.

The argument made by the authors of Kings was that the north, led by evil kings but "none more evil than Ahab, incited by his wife Jezebel," had been unfaithful to the national god, Yahweh. The collapse of the Kingdom of Israel was thus divine punishment for this infidelity. But polemics alone would never play. A good story was needed to grasp the imagination, and the Kings account reads so well precisely because it is a great story, loaded with attitude. Its Judean authors nursed centuries of resentment against the fallen northern kingdom, and as Gibbon would discover vis-à-vis Rome, the fall is inevitably a lot more interesting than the rise. There is always that element of what the Germans call *schadenfreude*—of delight in the misfortunes of someone you envy or resent. Sure enough, in Kings the authors' delight is palpable. They seized on the opportunity to settle old scores, expressing their resentment of the renegade kingdom and righteous satisfaction at what they saw as its well-deserved end.

There is a certain joy in bias. It is almost a luxury to be able to take out all your resentments and frustrations on a specific target, and all the better when your target is personified. Find one person who will represent everything you want to fulminate against—arrogance, vanity, luxury, cosmopolitanism, all the false gods of those who worshipped anyone other than Yahweh—and you are on a roll. All the better when the personification of such sins is not just a woman, but a powerful foreign woman. Foreign influence was subverting the purity of the Yahwist state, and Jezebel was the embodiment of it. The Kings authors must have counted their blessings for her very existence. If she had never lived, they would have had to invent her. And in a way, they did.

Reveling in their bias, they painted a huge bull's-eye on Jezebel's back, a metaphorical *H* for harlot as big as the crimson *A* of adultery in Nathaniel Hawthorne's *The Scarlet Letter*. Inevitably, that *H* would overtake the real woman, because we still have a lot invested in the harlot image of her. As pernicious as the image of the evil sexy woman may be, it is also fun. As any talk radio host can tell you, bias may be cruel, but people enjoy it. We need the "bad guys" of our stories as much as we need the good guys; otherwise there would be no story to tell. Every hero needs an antihero, just as Elijah needed Jezebel; without her to oppose, the great prophet would never even have been called into being.

But this is the logic of stories, not of real life. The confrontation between good and evil is never as absolute in reality as it is in the later retelling. In hindsight, everything seems more clear cut, and so the story adapts, expanding and contracting to accommodate that vision as it simplifies over time. With Jezebel, we have taken our cue from Kings, mixed in a dash of Revelation, and spun an image that by now has little relation to the proud queen who actually existed. And we have done this because we create the myths and images we need. The idea of Jezebel as the manipulative seductress satisfies both men and women, in different ways—men as the hapless victims of female sexuality, women as powerful temptresses, holding sway over men. Both images have great payoffs: both are sexy, both the stuff of soap opera, even pornography. But more to the point, both reduce vitally important political, cultural, and social issues to sex and so direct our attention away from what really matters.

How do you destroy a woman's reputation? The tactic is familiar in today's world of spin. You sexualize her. You spread innuendo. You do a smear job. And you do so repeatedly, to the point of nausea, so that it no longer occurs to anyone to ask what is really going on beneath the surface. When Pakistani premier Benazir Bhutto was called "the virgin ironpants" by Salman Rushdie, when Hillary Clinton was rumored to be lesbian by Edward Klein, when Golda Meir was referred to as "the only one with balls in the Israeli cabinet"—all were being sexualized. Even when apparently praised (attributing gonads to Meir was intended as the highest compliment), they were being demeaned. Their sexuality was distorted to appeal to public prejudice. Their power could not be seen distinct from their gender, and both power and gender were debased as a result.

This is what we have done, over three thousand years, to Jezebel. The grandeur that was this ancient queen has been reduced to a tawdry stereotype. So it is quite startling to realize that nowhere in the Kings account does Jezebel behave sexually. There is only that one word of accusation—"Harlot!"—thrown out just before her assassination and destined to echo through the millennia.

Given the vitriol lavished so abundantly on her by the Kings authors, it is clear that if Jezebel had acted in any way close to her reputation, they would have leaped on even the most minor sexual peccadillo. But either she acted with the greatest discretion, in which case the word "harlot" can hardly be said to apply, or she was the image of sexual fidelity to her husband. She behaves like a foreigner, clearly. Like a queen, most definitely. But she certainly never plays the harlot. If anything, in fact, she plays the overly loyal wife, so devoted to her husband's well-being that the Kings writers accuse her of being willing to murder for it.

And yet she is indeed a harlot. In biblical terms, that is. The sexualized image has made us overlook what the Bible makes patently clear. In the biblical mind, harlotry was not a matter of sexual promiscuity or of sex for sale; it was a matter of religion. You prostituted yourself to false gods—the very gods that Jezebel brought with her from Phoenicia to Israel. Sex was the metaphor and, as we'll see, a well-chosen one. The same rule applied three thousand years ago as today: sex sells. The biblical writers wanted to get their message across, and they knew how to sell a story as well as any modern romance writer.

As so often, sex is the smokescreen. Jezebel's transformation into a byword for lewdness and lasciviousness is a distraction, masking the real import of her life. Strip away the seven veils, and what we find is a startlingly contemporary story, so much so that it sometimes seems as though the three thousand years that have passed between her time and ours had never taken place at all.

Jezebel was framed, that much is certain. The deed was done for political and ideological reasons, centuries after she was literally thrown to the dogs. She was made the fall girl, as it were, for the decline and fall of the Kingdom of Israel. But the fact that she was framed does not necessarily mean she was innocent.

When I first began to research this book, I imagined that it would be a rehabilitation of Jezebel, even choosing "a rehabilitation" as my working subtitle. But the deeper I went into her story, the more I realized that to do this would be merely to replace one stereotype with another, that of "the good woman wronged." And Jezebel was far too interesting to be pigeonholed in this way. If she was not the total villain Kings makes her out to be, she was no angel either. It may be tempting to see her as one or the other because we tend to underestimate those who lived in what we think of as antiquity. We imagine things were simpler then, as though people were somehow less intelligent and less emotionally complex than we are now. In fact, what we are doing is the historical equivalent of looking through a telescope the wrong way round, so that everything becomes smaller, devoid of the kind of detail we need to see real people and real dilemmas.

Are we ready to see a female protagonist who is arrogant and ambitious yet also admirable? We can accept ruthless, ambitious men; we think of them as charming rogues, perhaps, or as captains of industry. Even though we may not like them, we tend to admire them, however grudgingly. But an unacknowledged need to see women as "good" still lingers, along with the tendency to condemn women for the very qualities that we find acceptable in men. One man's strategic planning, for instance, becomes another woman's underhanded manipulation. Even the most secular among us may well be more biblical than we imagine when it comes to women in power.

Jezebel was a queen in the ninth century B.C., and that meant that she was proud, arrogant, dictatorial, and as ruthless as she needed to be. If she had been none of these things, she would never have survived to hold power for thirty years. But survive she did, and thrive. Despite the *fatwa* against her, she would outlive the man who placed it on her, Elijah. She would help guide Israel to the height of its power in the region, an unrivaled era of prosperity and security. And when the dogs were finally unleashed on her, her death would mark the moment when the kingdom itself began to die, finally to disappear under the Assyrian onslaught a hundred years later.

We need to shift the weight of almost three thousand years of opprobrium to see Jezebel whole: not just her pride and even her ruthlessness but also her intelligence and her vision. Her story is too important to relegate to the soft-core prison of sex.

Behind all the Orientalist fantasies, the real woman called Jezebel was as dedicated to her many gods as Elijah was to his one. She was a powerful, complex woman whose courage and dignity even her fiercest detractors would have no option but to acknowledge. Her fatal flaw was the arrogance that led her to underestimate the dangers posed by the ascent of radical fundamentalism—the same dangers we face in today's world, with the same disastrous potential.

The story of her clash with Elijah and his followers is the story of what happens when humans believe they have a direct line to the divine; how that belief can be manipulated by the politically ambitious; and how it finally destroys not only its perceived enemies but also itself. We need to see Jezebel whole not only out of a sense of historical reality but because her story is the founding template for the clash between pluralism and tolerance on the one hand and fundamentalist fanaticism on the other. In the twenty-first century, we ignore her real story at severe risk.

If Jezebel's pragmatic pluralism had held sway, it may well have saved the Kingdom of Israel from being swallowed up by the Assyrians. It may also have averted the consequent fall of the Kingdom of Judea into exile. But of course if that had been the case, most of the Hebrew bible as we know it would never have been written. Whether this is a matter of irony or of justice I leave to the reader to decide.

How a story is told is as important as the content of the story itself. For all its drama, the Kings account is still only the bare bones of reality, and one that hides as much as it reveals. My aim here is to re-create Jezebel's life, to take it out of the realm of legend and back onto the solid ground of history, using the major advances of the past four decades in archaeology, Middle East history, and the history of religion. To this end, my own background of thirteen years in Jerusalem as a psychologist and Middle East reporter has served me well; when you have lived and worked in a place with so ancient a history, and when that history is so integral a part of its modern identity, it seems far less daunting to reach back into time and uncover the reality behind the veil of legend. And though this is a nonfiction book, I occasionally use what the great Oxford historian R. G. Collingwood called "the historical imagination" in order to re-create Jezebel's point of view.

Just as important, I have gone back to the original Hebrew of the Kings account. We think of the Bible as gorgeous high-flown language, which in the King James translation it is. But in the Hebrew, it more often uses the earthy language not of princes but of peasants. It had to be, to hold in the imagination and the memory through all the years before the legends it was based on were written down and codified. The vivid, even lurid, language of Kings is completely at odds with the decorous tone of most translations. The story seems to leap off the page. Curses and oaths are fulsome and imaginative, the wordplay is downright outrageous, and at times the text takes on a startling, almost sacrilegious quality that makes Yahweh seem altogether too real in human terms.

Here and there, you can certainly find passages that achieve their own glory in English, especially the King James English, but most of the time the translators seem to have been shackled by their own piety. They "cleaned up" the text, masking its vivid imagery and directness. The Hebrew uses puns to defame and denigrate, as in the play on Jezebel's name, or the transformation of the god Baal-Zebul—"Lord-Prince" in Phoenician—into the Hebrew Beelzebub, meaning "Lord of the Flies." It invites the kind of booing and hissing from the audience that would become standard in Shakespeare's time, when theater was a participatory sport and those who stood in the pit at the Globe Theatre responded with drunken enthusiasm. And it leaves little room for decorous circumlocution. For instance, where the standard translation of the prophetic curse on Ahab and all his heirs reads "I will cut off every man and every man-child," the original Hebrew does not. That reads, word for word: "I will cut down every one that pisses against a wall." Which is what I mean by vivid detail.

The story was written this way for good reason. Hebrew is quite capable of saying "every man-child." It does so elsewhere in the Bible. But the writers had no intention of using such polite language here. This was a curse. It was pronounced not in stately pomp but in anger, indeed in white-hot divine fury. The Kings authors deliberately used the bluntest possible language—the street language of insult, the ancient Hebrew equivalent of Anglo-Saxon four-letter words. How else achieve the force of curse? The crudeness is deliberate, its effect both startling and terrifying.

All quotes from Kings in this book, then, are my own translations from the original Hebrew, as close as possible to both the spirit and the letter of the text. This includes all the dialogue, none of which has been invented—at least not by me. The places where Jezebel's story transpired are not invented either. I spent several weeks back in the Middle East seeking out those I did not already know, some of them now only unmarked ruins far from any beaten track. As you might expect from such a grand saga, the narrative ranges far and wide. It encompasses ancient names still vibrant in the imagination like Carthage, Babylon, Megiddo, and Tyre; capital cities such as Jerusalem and Damascus; and places whose names would have been long lost if not for the Bible, like Jezreel, Gilead, and Samaria.

Jezebel stepped into recorded history as a young bride-to-be newly arrived in the Israelite capital of Samaria from her home in the Phoenician city-state of Tyre. It was the year 872 B.C. She was at the very beginning of her thirty years in power, and if there was ever a moment when she could be said to be innocent, this was it. She had no idea yet of what she would be up against. Or perhaps she was just beginning to realize it. And so her story begins . . .

I.

Tyre

in which Jezebel is homesick

She is not conventionally beautiful. She is, rather, utterly striking. The long aquiline nose, the heavy shaped eyebrows, the proud, almost disdainful set to her mouth, all speak of a young woman born to wield authority, used to being obeyed. Except by sleep.

She wakes in the night with her throat parched and dust in her nostrils. It's been just a few hours since her attendants sprinkled the floor with citron-scented water to freshen the air, but the relief hasn't lasted. The heavy tapestries on the walls hold the heat, and now it seems to close in on her. She needs to get out into the open air. Perhaps there she can breathe free.

The truth is she has not slept through the night since she arrived in this landlocked kingdom, though it would be beneath her to complain of it. She was born a princess royal, after all, the leading daughter of the first great maritime empire in the world, and everything about her declares her status. The regal carriage of long neck and straight spine, the head held high so that she seems tall even by modern standards, the fluid motion as she rises and drapes a deep purple robe over her shoulders—she is every inch the aristocrat.

This is Jezebel at age fifteen, newly arrived in Samaria for her wedding to Ahab, the king of Israel. The week-long celebration of her marriage is nearing its end. In the morning she will be crowned queen, and she and Ahab will become husband and wife. She is not sure if this is something she wants or dreads.

A peacock's cry, that's what woke her. She hears it again, the long mournful high-pitched sound echoing through the stone courtyards, as though the creature had to pay for being so beautiful to look at by being so discomforting to listen to.

She steps carefully, barefoot. If she is quiet, she can have this time to herself and be alone for the first time since she left Tyre. The maidservants lying on the floor at the foot of her bed stir but don't wake. The sleeping eunuchs outside the doors guard a chamber empty of royalty as she heads for the stairs to the tower of the western gate. In the light of the full moon, perhaps she can catch a glimpse of the sea.

She can never let anyone know how much she misses that great expanse of water. Her lungs long for the rhythmic breath of it, her ears for the sounds of seabirds wheeling above it. Tyre was an island city, surrounded by water, and only now, in its absence, does she realize how the sea has cradled her life. There are sea people and there are hill people, she thinks, and she is a sea person marooned in a country of hill people. Even the way they speak reflects the harshness of the hills—the Phoenician and the Israelite languages so close, essentially different dialects of the same tongue, yet so different to the ear. Where the Phoenician is soft and sibilant, like lapping water, the Israelite Hebrew carries the harshness of stone and dust. It is the dialect of a warrior people.

She took water for granted in Tyre. It splashed in fountains in the palace courtyards and the temple forecourts; idled mirrorlike in ornamental pools planted with lotus, the flower of the great goddess Astarte; was poured gracefully from silver jugs into glass goblets filled with fresh mint. The sweetest water to drink, soft and refreshing. Yes, she thinks, even the water was gentle.

Here in Samaria it tastes hard, like the stone it comes out of. Here, nobody can take water for granted. They live in constant fear of its absence, in terror of drought and the starvation that accompanies it. How not, when their god Yahweh seems to use it as a weapon, threatening to withhold it? He is so like and yet so unlike Phoenicia's Baal Shamem, the Lord of the Skies, who rises anew each year with the first rains, willingly giving the gift of water when he is rescued by his sister Anat from the jaws of the death god Mot. Both Yahweh and Baal Shamem ride the storm clouds. Both carry lightning bolts in their chariots. Both speak in thunder. They could be brothers, even twins. But no, this Yahweh of Israel turns his back on all the other gods and rules alone in this land—the one and only Israelite god, at least according to his prophet Elijah, who claims to hear his voice and to speak for him. Jezebel thinks it all very strange. Surely the more gods you acknowledge, the safer you are in the world they rule. How could there ever be too many gods? But she is willing to respect the Israelites' choice. When you believe in many gods, you respect those of other people, even if they only have one. It has never occurred to her before that the tolerance might not be mutual.

She feels almost sorry for Yahweh. A god with no family is surely lonely; no wonder he is so jealous of all the other gods. Still, she is intrigued by the awe he provokes, and by the way people whisper the name of his prophet Elijah as though in fear. They say he lives in the wilderness, this prophet, and rarely appears in the city. When he does, he seems to come out of nowhere, and the drama of such sudden apparition makes his declarations all the more dreaded. He sounds fierce and harsh and unforgiving, the opposite of everything Jezebel holds dear, yet the more she hears, the more she wants to see him for herself. Her advisers warn that the last thing she should want is to attract his attention, but at this she just laughs. She has already attracted his attention, simply by being here. Besides, she is a princess, now to be a queen; what threat can such a man pose to her?

The peacocks settle down as she passes. Tiny white monkeys—a wedding gift from the Egyptian pharaoh—chatter softly in their cage, as though speaking in their sleep. Hidden in the moon shadows by the dark purple of her robe, she slips past the sentries and climbs to the topmost level of the tower. The air here is so clear, it seems to ring with silence, a pure bell-like sound that will last only another couple of hours, until dawn wakes the city below. She leans against the parapet and looks down through the hills of this landlocked kingdom, this strange land in which she is to be queen. She looks down past the stones and thorns, past the marshy coastal plain, and there she sees the faint glimmer of the sea in the distance and her eyes fill with tears—moisture at last.

Only sixty-five miles separate Samaria from Tyre, as the crow flies. But humans are not crows, not now and not then. Culture shock is too mild a term for what Jezebel must have experienced on arrival in this hilltop city. So far as she was concerned, she was in the boondocks. In one stroke, she had been cut off from the most sophisticated culture of her time, never to return. But no one who had laid eyes on Tyre, let alone lived there, could ever forget it.

Physically, the island city was simply stunning. Its name means "The Rock"—*Tsor* in both Phoenician and Hebrew—and the legend is that it was formed when two rocks were joined together by the roots of a sacred olive tree. But in this case, not even legend could match reality. It made such an impression not only because it was so magnificent that even its enemies sang its praises, but because it was so utterly improbable. There was nothing like it in the world of the time. There still is not.

From the mainland, Tyre seemed to float in the middle of the sea, a white city rising straight up out of the water with marble walls a hundred and fifty feet high—the glass skyscrapers of its time—and inside the walls, the ornate gilded roofs of the royal palace and the great temples. The jewel of the Mediterranean, they called it: an island half a mile long and almost as wide, reached by a six-hundred-yard-long arched viaduct that looked as though it were riding the waves like a line of white dolphins.

It seemed incredible that men could have built this vision of splendor, and yet it was indeed man-made. A century before Jezebel was born, King Hiram I of Tyre and Sidon ordered his masons to join two small islands on the rocky coastal reef into one and to build a city that would express Tyre's new status as the most powerful of all the Phoenician city-states up and down the coast of what is now Lebanon. He commissioned three gem-studded temples—the first dedicated to Melqart, literally "King of the City," whose titles included Baal-Zebul or "Lord-Prince"; the second to the great mother Astarte, the consort of El, the father of all the gods; and the third to their son Baal Shamem, "Lord of the Skies," the god of rain and fertility. These temples would become so renowned that biblical writers would later claim that Hiram then sent his masons to King Solomon to build a still more resplendent temple to Yahweh in Jerusalem.

People wrote in praise of Tyre throughout the known world, from the Greek historian Herodotus to the Hebrew prophet Ezekiel, who detailed its grandeur all the better to savor its eventual fall. "Haughty Tyre," he called it, "swollen with pride," yet even he seemed to delight in its splendor:

> *You were an exemplar of perfection.*
> *Full of wisdom,*
> *Perfect in beauty,*
> *You were in Eden, in the garden of God,*
> *And a thousand gems formed your mantle.*
> *Sard, topaz, diamond, chrysolite, onyx,*
> *Jasper, sapphire, ruby, emerald,*
> *The gold of your flutes and tambourines—*
> *All were prepared on the day of your creation.*

This glittering ostentation was the result of Tyre's mastery of the sea. The real heart of the island city was the source of its

wealth: two deep-water harbors hewn out of the rock and pro-
tected by fifty-foot-wide breakwaters in a feat of engineering that
would be unparalleled for hundreds of years. One harbor faced
north, the other south. Whichever way the wind was blowing, the
square-sailed Phoenician trading ships could always make it
safely into port. No waiting offshore for the wind to change, no
danger of foundering on the rocky reefs—Tyrian captains were
so expert that they took their ships right into harbor with
sails aloft. Their skill was as legendary as the island itself, their
wealth so great that rumor had it their anchors were made of solid
silver.

The city that rose up out of the sea lived by the sea. The
Phoenicians didn't just control the maritime trade routes of the
Mediterranean; they created them. They were the first to chart
the currents and gain speed by them; the first to navigate by the
North Star so that they could sail by night; the first to use trian-
gulation, taking readings off headlands and mountains to estab-
lish their exact position and progress. They ventured where no
ships had ever dared set sail before, beyond the Mediterranean
and into the open Atlantic through the narrow mouth of the
Mediterranean known first as the Pillars of Melqart, then by the
Greeks as the Pillars of Hercules, and in the end, placidly secular-
ized, as the Strait of Gibraltar.

This is how a tiny island state with few natural resources
makes its fortune and its name: it creates the first great maritime
trading empire. It brings down cedars from the mountains to
build huge round-hulled ships, then sends those ships out to
trade. It picks up gold in Africa and works it into jewelry. Brings
in raw silk and linens and dyes them exquisite shades of red and
purple. Buys rare spices and resins and sells them on. It bases its

wealth on the principle of added value: import raw materials, export luxury goods. And it becomes a brilliant exception to the conquer-and-enslave policy of other empires of its time, conquering by trade instead of by force. A very modern kind of empire.

In short, the Phoenicians were the world's first capitalists. And Tyre was a trading hub, the meeting point of east and west, north and south. The whole downtown area between the two harbors was alive with the sights and smells and sounds of merchants from different cultures. Anatolians, Hittites, Damascenes, Assyrians, Egyptians, Cypriots, Greeks—these and dozens of others mingled in the squares and along the piers. The Phoenicians defined the word "cosmopolitan" before the Greeks had even invented it. But it was the Greeks who would give them their name.

The people we now call Phoenicians were the original Canaanites. That was how they referred to themselves. They became Phoenicians, as it were, thanks to the Greek name for the most famed of all their exports: the dye known as "the Tyrian purple." Extracted from the glands of a spiny spiral-shaped sea snail, it was said to be the color of the flashing wings of the phoenix, the legendary bird reborn from its own ashes. The dye was so coveted through the centuries that it came to be worth three times its weight in gold, and so admired that the Roman emperor Nero would eventually declare that only he could wear robes steeped in this dye, thus beginning the tradition of what was to become "the royal purple."

Jezebel had left behind the most sophisticated civilization of her time, and Israel inevitably suffered by comparison. It cannot have been an easy transition. As proud and arrogant as the glittering city she came from, she may have been about to become queen, but with the sea only a distant shimmer in the light of the dying moon, she surely felt more like a hostage of politics.

This was not a marriage of love on Jezebel's part, or even one of choice. No such thing existed for a princess of her time. Like all royal marriages, this was an alliance between rulers, between her father Ithbaal, the king of Tyre, and her husband, Ahab, the king of Israel. As the princess royal, her hand in marriage was a gift to be bestowed by her father. She was the foremost sign of his friendship with Israel, and the most valuable token of his esteem. Her body would be the seal on the alliance; her presence in Samaria—hers, and that of the priests and courtiers, diplomats and merchants, artisans, eunuchs, and servants who formed her entourage—would be the presence of Tyre.

She had known all along that she would be married to a foreign king, and that both country and husband would be her father's decision, not hers. She may have been young by today's standards, but she had no illusions. She was the senior princess of the realm, and thus well trained in how power worked, in the subtleties of persuasion and manipulation, of veiled threats and backroom dealing. Even, if necessary, in the use of force. Now she would be her father's chief representative in this strange Israelite enclave, his political and cultural ambassador. Whatever she felt about his decision was not important. What was important was to make the arrangement work.

And Ahab seemed a wise choice on Ithbaal's part. The Kingdom of Israel had become a force to be reckoned with. Thanks to its dominance over its weak southern sister, Judea, it controlled not only the main east-west trade route from Damascus to the Mediterranean but also vital sections of the two north-south trade routes of the region: the Via Maris north out of Egypt along the coast, and the King's Highway on the east bank of the Jordan River, from Damascus to the Red Sea. Through Jezebel's marriage to Ahab, Tyre would gain the most valuable thing of all to a merchant trading state: access to as yet untapped markets. Now Tyre would develop the Red Sea port of Etzion Geber, giving it the Phoenician name that was then adopted in the Hebrew: Eilat, meaning "the goddess"—the great mother Astarte. Tyrian ships—"the ships of Tarshish," as Isaiah would call them—would ply the coasts of Arabia and east Africa, going as far as India in their search for spices and silk. And for the privilege of access, Tyre would pay Israel handsomely in tolls and fees. It was, in modern terms, a win-win situation.

In acknowledgment of the significance of the marriage, Jezebel would be crowned the queen consort. Like all rulers of the time, Ahab was polygamous, but she would be the highest-ranked of his many wives and the only one to be named in Kings. She would have her own residence within the palace and her own seal, and most important, her children would be the heirs to the throne. She and Ahab would create a dynasty, combining Phoenician brain and Israelite brawn in what was planned as the perfect alliance.

The people of Samaria certainly saw it that way. Though you would never imagine so from the Kings account, the marriage was popular. In fact it was fulsomely welcomed. One court poem written for the occasion was addressed to the king and to the "daughter of Tyre, the richest of people." It praised her beauty and the richness of her dowry, and blessed the union with the hope for male heirs:

All glorious is the king's daughter within the palace,
Her raiment fine brocade inlaid with gold.
She shall be led to the king in rich embroidery,
Her virgin companions shall be brought unto you.
They shall be led with gladness and rejoicing,
They shall enter into the king's palace.
Instead of your fathers shall be your sons,
And you will make them princes in all the land.

If the words sound familiar, it is because they would survive only to be reinterpreted as a messianic hymn—the hymn we now know as Psalm 45—which means that Jezebel's wedding song is still sung in synagogues and churches around the world, her marriage unknowingly celebrated within the very traditions that excoriate her. If she were alive today, she would not be able to resist a certain wicked glee at the idea.

The irony inherent in Psalm 45 is compounded by the fact that the whole of the Bible could never have been written if not for Jezebel and her people. All the purple dye and all the gold filigree and cedarwood in the world would never match the Phoenicians' greatest contribution to history: they invented writing as we know it. And they did so for the most pragmatic of reasons—they needed it for trade.

The Sumerian cuneiform and Egyptian hieroglyphic systems in use until then were horribly clumsy, with thousands of icons and symbols. They were just too cumbersome and time-consuming for the everyday business of recording cargoes and destinations. Instead, the Phoenicians developed a new stripped-down system of notation, using a simple twenty-two-letter alpha-bet—the script that would become the basis of every modern Western and Middle Eastern language, adopted first by Phoenicia's neighbors, and then by all the lands it traded with.

The Israelites were among the first to use the new script, which is why ancient Hebrew writing is virtually identical to Phoenician. But the dimensions of the cultural debt become even greater when we realize that we would not even have the word "bible" if it were not for the Phoenicians, since it comes from *Byblos,* the Greek name for the city of Jibail twenty miles north of modern Beirut, which once imported vast quantities of raw Egyptian papyrus reeds and refined them for export, thus becoming the main distribution center for the very stuff of writing. And in perhaps the ultimate sign of cultural borrowing, even the biblical name for Israel—"a land flowing with milk and honey, the place of the Canaanites" as it's called in Exodus—came from Phoenicia, where the white-frothed Nahr al-Leban, literally "the River of Milk," still tumbles down to the Mediterranean from its source, the Spring of Honey.

The Greeks would expand the alphabet slightly, adding vowels to adapt it to their language. Either more gracious than the biblical writers in their sense of indebtedness or more secure in their separate identity, they created a beautiful myth in acknowledgment of the European debt to Phoenicia. It is the story of Cadmus, son of the legendary Tyrian king Phoenix, who himself was said to be the son of the sea god Poseidon. When Cadmus' sister Europa is abducted and carried over the sea to Crete by Zeus, who has turned himself into a bull for the purpose, Cadmus goes in search of her and brings to Greece the alphabet—the *aleph bet,* or *alpha beta*—of his native land. He never finds his sister, but he does find and marry the nymph Harmony, with whom he founds the city of Thebes.

It was a good name, Harmony, given by her mother Aphrodite, the goddess of love and beauty who was the Greek manifestation of the Phoenician Astarte, the great goddess carried across the sea by Tyrian merchant ships, so that the legend developed that she was born out of the seafoam, perfect on her famous half-shell. Her choice of Harmony for her daughter's name spoke of nations open to each other's influence, living in peace with each other, sharing their strengths. It spoke of mutual respect and tolerance and exchange. It spoke, that is, of the principles on which Tyre was based, the very principles that led to the marriage of Jezebel with Ahab, and whose defeat would lead to the ultimate in disharmony.

When the sun rises, Jezebel's attendants will cluster around to paint her with henna for beauty and fertility. Intricate patterns of leaves and lotus blossoms will unfold over her forehead. Vines will twine around her ankles and wrists, their tendrils reaching down to loop around each toe and each finger. On her feet, dolphins will leap over her arches, as though she were walking on water. But on this last night as a bride-to-be, as the moon sinks below the western horizon and the glimmer of sea dissolves into darkness, she knows that these dolphins are lost to her. The one comfort left in sight is the distant gleam of snow-capped Mount Hermon far to the north, standing high above all the other peaks. The home of Baal Shamem, it dominates even this land where they deny him, as clear from here as from Tyre or from Damascus. It will become Jezebel's Pole Star, she determines—her point of reference, of identity and belonging. Whatever happens in this strange land, the Hermon will always be there for her, beckoning of home.

Her courage renewed, she goes down from the tower, passes by the massive gates to the Yahwist temple, and turns instead into the small but perfectly proportioned temple of Astarte, built for her by Ahab as a wedding gift. The face of the goddess gazes calmly out at her from the finely carved ivory plaques set into the altar. They show just her head, framed in a temple window, with a smile so enigmatic that it will be twenty-three hundred years until Leonardo da Vinci manages to reproduce it on the lips of the woman he'll call the Mona Lisa. Truly, thinks Jezebel, a divine smile.

She remembers the moment in the Phoenician saga of the gods when Astarte comes to visit her husband, the great god El:

> *As soon as El spied her*
> *He unfastened his scabbard and laughed.*
> *He put his feet on his footstool,*
> *And wiggled his toes.*

How could one not adore a god who wiggles his toes in anticipation of sex? How not want to emulate El and Astarte in the bridal chamber, to take off Ahab's scabbard and make him laugh with pleasure? Jezebel senses Astarte's smile on her own lips as she refreshes the scented oil in the lamps, first to the great mother and then to Gula, the goddess of healing, whose giant dogs guard the territory between health and sickness, life and death. She pours wine into libation bowls, with their delicately inscribed prayers spiraling down from the rim, then slowly pours them out on the altars. There is comfort in the ritual. Comfort, and resolve.

Soon enough, her maidservants will bathe and perfume her with the musky scents of cassia and sandalwood. They'll part her hair into heavy braided tresses, then catch the tresses up in gold chains and loop them through a gem-studded diadem until her head is as dressed as her body. They'll paint her brows into high arches, rim her eyes heavily in kohl, whiten her face into a regal mask. They'll place her finest gold-embroidered robe over her shoulders; hang heavy gold loops in her ears; tighten a wide choker of gold and gems around her neck; slip on anklets and bracelets, toe rings and finger rings—heavy, chunky jewelry that will weigh her down, and so force her to stand all the taller in defiance of gravity, raising her head high to appear weightless. And if there is an anxious teenage girl behind the mask of makeup and finery, no one will see it. If all she wants is to flee this stark place and return to her element, the sea, that is something no one will ever know. No matter how she may wish she had never left Tyre, here in this landlocked kingdom is where the gods have determined she must be. What her father envisaged—the two nations bonded, strengthening each other—this will be her marriage. She will make it work. She is young enough to imagine that everything is possible. That alliance can replace separatism. Pragmatism replace ideology. Trade replace bloodshed.

The oracles have all been consulted. The innards of sacrificed animals, the alignment of the stars, the colors and patterns of the sunsets—all have been deemed propitious. The gods look down in approval, both her many gods and Ahab's one. And when the final day's psalms of praise have been sung, the orations delivered, the processions and the libations and the receptions completed, even as the banqueting still continues in the great hall of the palace, Jezebel will be led to her new bridal chambers like a kind of human sacrifice, her body the pledge of alliance. Her attendants will disrobe her and take down her hair, and then they will leave her. Ahab will enter. Alone together for the first time, they will begin to find out whom each has married.

2.

Samaria

in which Ahab is a peaceable warrior

It might be tempting to imagine the romantic ideal of love at first sight. Jezebel certainly knew she was marrying a soldier, not a courtier, so she would have been prepared for Ahab's dark skin, tanned by sun and wind, his eyes etched deep around with the lines of hard experience in the field, his long warrior's hair, never cut as a sign of virility. She would have appreciated the way he carried himself with the loose confidence of well-earned authority—authority earned not by force but by the genuine respect of his men. Would have sensed, perhaps, that this was a man who could ride as one with his horse, scorning the chariots usually used by kings in battle.

Ahab carried with him the scents of his world, of dust and leather, horses and sweat, and beneath them the suggestion of the sharp acrid tang of steel. But if we imagine that he had the irresistible attraction for a sophisticated woman of a man of battle, a man who knows death intimately and whose taste for life has been honed by that knowledge, that is only because we have been influenced by too much romance fiction. The truth is that Ahab was more likely to have shocked Jezebel at first. Repelled her, even.

That stink of horse sweat and leather, the weather-beaten face and arms, the jagged scars on his legs from enemy swords, all would have revolted her. He'd have seemed wild and savage, brutal compared to the smooth-skinned men of the Tyrian court. She was used to men who were barbered and perfumed, their beards primped and curled and oiled, their bodies wafting scents as rare and expensive as her own. Men whose voices were soft, whose eyes, like hers, were ringed with kohl. Here she saw a hard man who would far rather be among horses in a military camp than in a palace with ivory and lapis lazuli for ornament, carpets underfoot, and hangings on the walls. Whose sense of music was the trumpets of his charioteers, not the flutes and lyres and tinkling bells of her musicians. Whose language, though so close to hers that she could make out most of it, sounded harsh and guttural in her ears. If she had known the fairy tale of Beauty and the Beast, that is what she would have thought of. And remembered that Beauty transforms the Beast.

Though Ahab was famed in his own time, his name is remembered today mostly thanks to Herman Melville, who chose it for the doomed whaling captain in his Bible-haunted novel *Moby-Dick*. Given his source, Melville chose well. Captain Ahab sells his soul in his obsession with the white whale, which he makes into a kind of false god, leading him on to his inevitable destruction. He earns his name because in Kings, Ahab is accused of selling his soul to the false gods of Jezebel, abandoning Yahweh for her polytheistic pantheon and so ensuring his own destruction. He built a temple for her god, after all. Never mind that this was the standard practice when a foreign princess was taken in diplomatic marriage; Solomon had done the same for his foreign brides. The Yahwist ideologues who opposed the marriage of Ahab and Jezebel saw the newly expanded acropolis of Samaria as a symbol of foreign encroachment on the culture, identity, and god of Israel.

In fact, far from abandoning Yahweh, Ahab reigned in his name, just as all kings of the time reigned in the name of their national gods. Some even incorporated the divine name into their own, like Ben-Hadad of Damascus—literally "son of the god Hadad"—as a means of establishing a divine right to the throne. Ahab made no such claim to filial divinity, but he was crowned in Yahweh's name, as England's kings and queens still are. He fought his battles and celebrated his victories in the name of Yahweh, sought the advice and blessings of the priests of Yahweh, and would name all three of his children by Jezebel in praise of Yahweh: two sons, Ahaziah, meaning "he who holds Yahweh close," and Joram, "Yahweh is exalted," and a daughter, Athaliah, "Yahweh is on high." The biblical portrait of Ahab, it turns out, is as distorted as that of Jezebel.

Strange as it may sound in terms of contemporary Middle East politics, the authors of Kings were virulently anti-Israel. Their version of history was the product of theology as much as politics—of theopolitics, that is. Writing nearly three centuries later in the southern kingdom of Judea, they so denigrated and downplayed the northern kingdom that its existence would come to be all but forgotten. It wouldn't be until the late twentieth century, when Near East archaeology finally shook off the yoke of traditional biblical archaeology and its aim of "proving" the Bible rather than investigating it, that researchers began to appreciate the dynasty of Omri and Ahab as the golden age that the era of David and Solomon never was.

In their book *The Bible Unearthed* archaeologist Israel Finkelstein and historian Neil Asher Silberman laid down the parameters of the new archaeological vision: "Had the biblical authors and editors been historians in the modern sense, they might have said that Ahab was a mighty king who first brought the kingdom of Israel to prominence on the world stage, and that his marriage to the daughter of the Phoenician king Ithbaal was a brilliant stroke of international diplomacy. They might have said that the Omrides built magnificent cities to serve as administrative centers of their expanding kingdom. They might have said that Ahab and Omri, his father before him, succeeded in building one of the most powerful armies in the region, with which they conquered extensive territories in the far north and in Transjordan."

The real story of the Omrides—the dynasty founded by Omri—was one of stability established out of near chaos. The succession of coups d'état in the northern kingdom had reached such absurd proportions that Omri's predecessor, the corrupt chariot commander Zimri, lasted exactly seven days on the throne until Omri cornered him in his capital of Tirza, burned it to the ground, and built a new capital on the hill of Samaria. Over the next twelve years, until he died of natural causes—by then a refreshingly different style of death for an Israelite king—Omri set about establishing his legacy to his eldest son, Ahab: a newly stabilized kingdom with expanded borders, achieved by the judicious use of military might.

Even Israel's enemies would acknowledge the military prowess of the Omrides. They did so on the principle that the greater your enemy, the greater you must be. The power of your foes was a measure of your own power, and both Omri and Ahab were eminently worthy foes.

One densely chiseled stone document of the time records the military campaigns of Shalmanezer III, the ruler of the dangerously expansionist Assyrian empire in what is now northern Iraq and Syria. Known as the Monolith Inscription, it lists "Ahab the Israelite" as fielding the largest force—two thousand chariots and ten thousand infantry—in a coalition that held off the Assyrian army at the Battle of Qarqar on the Orontes River. Another, a black basalt stele known as the Moabite Stone, found in Jordan but now in the Louvre, recounts in the voice of Moab's King Mesha that Omri and Ahab "oppressed Moab many days," building border strongholds there to consolidate their control of the King's Highway caravan route, which ran from Arabia and the Red Sea through Edom, Moab, and Gilead to Damascus. Even after the Omride dynasty had been destroyed, Assyrian records would continue to refer to Israel as *bit-Humri*—the House of Omri—and to its kings as the sons of Omri. Thanks to these stone documents and other archaeological evidence, we now know that Ahab, the king the Bible would call "the most evil of all the kings of Israel," was probably the most gifted, the most respected, and the most powerful. As would be his new queen.

The marriage to Jezebel was especially important to Ahab because this alliance with Tyre would mark a major turning point in Israelite policy. Like his father before him, Ahab had a reputation based so far on his military accomplishments, extending Israelite control north to Mount Hermon and east almost to Damascus. He had proved himself a great warrior, leading his men into battle instead of giving orders from the rear because he knew it would inspire them. In the process, he established a military legacy that nearly three thousand years later would be the making of the modern Israeli army, with its officers' battle-cry of *aharai* ("follow me"), the extraordinary cohesiveness of its ranks and officers, and the legends of military derring-do on the part of generals like Moshe Dayan, Yitzhak Rabin, and Ariel Sharon—legends that played a large part in propelling their political careers.

Like his modern successors, Ahab had fought more wars than anyone should ever have to fight. Now he was ready for the fruits of victory. Not the usual long lines of chained and shackled prisoners, the orgies of massacre and decapitation, the sadness of royal harems incorporated wholesale into his own; these were the spoils of victory, not its fruit. The fruit was peace, and the prosperity that would come with it. Like Rabin, even like Sharon, the experienced soldier eventually realizes that all the bloodshed is for nothing if it does not ensure that he and his people can live without constant fear of retaliation. Only those so young that their idealism is untainted by humanity, or those armchair warriors who speak out loud and bravely to send others off to be killed, think there is glory to be found in other people's blood.

Tyre dominated through trade, not weapons, and had proved—as it would for hundreds of years to come—that commerce was a far more effective keeper of the peace than the sword. Ahab may have lacked the surface sophistication that

Jezebel was accustomed to, but he had a soldier's sense of strategic pragmatism. This Tyrian princess represented the prosperity he wanted for his kingdom. If she worshipped other gods than Yahweh, that was no great matter. Her gods might be powerful in their own territory to the north, but they could be no threat to him on Israelite soil, no matter what a prophet like Elijah might think.

Throughout the week leading up to their wedding night, as he watched Jezebel will herself to self-control and noted the awed excitement in his court at this apparition of refinement and culture, Ahab must have congratulated himself on his choice. If this princess was indeed repelled, she gave no sign of it. The whole principle of this alliance was a marriage of opposites; each needed the other. Jezebel was not to be deterred by the whiff of sweat and bloodshed. Though perhaps she should have been.

What remains of the royal city of Samaria is still haunted by the ghosts of battle. Just getting there turns out to be a journey fraught with tension and uncertainty. Driving north from Jerusalem, you go through a long succession of Israeli military checkpoints. The soldiers are hot and tired, and this is the last place they want to be, on a Palestinian road where Israeli civilians are forbidden to drive. They are the most visible signs of the heavily resented military occupation of the West Bank, and this makes them irritable, curt, and rude. If you travel as I did with Palestinian archaeologists, all conversation inside the car stops at each checkpoint. You bite your tongue, wait patiently while the soldiers make a show of examining documents, answer their questions as briefly as possible. Both sides are all too aware of the potential for sudden violence.

A landscape interrupted by barbed wire and concrete barricades can hardly be considered beautiful, but as you make your halting way from the high desert reaches of the Judean hills and into the northern part of the West Bank, the hills seem to round out and lose some of their harshness. The landscape begins to feel a bit softer, more inclined to human settlement.

You don't realize how steep the hill of Samaria is until the car's engine moans in protest on the narrow winding road through the hillside village of Sebastiya. People stare with a mix of curiosity and resentment as you go past the dry fountain in the village square, past the dilapidated mosque where John the Baptist's head is said to be buried, and on up to the top of the hill, fourteen hundred feet above sea level. The parking lot is empty; half a dozen restaurants and coffeehouses surround it, but all are closed. Nobody comes here any longer. No buses full of tourists or schoolchildren, not even most archaeologists. The trip is too unpredictable; it can take hours or even days to drive the forty-five miles from Jerusalem, depending on the security situation, or you may never arrive at all. Israelis think it too dangerous; Palestinians, too difficult.

Yet once you are up here, the daily misery of the political situation seems to fall away. The hill rises in solitary splendor, surrounded by deep valleys setting it off from the rest of the highlands so that in every direction you have the heady sense of space and height. A soft breeze blows, erasing the heat of the dusty roads you've traveled. There's the illusion of peace, of being above it all.

The most impressive ruins are the most recent: the Roman-era

colonnaded street, the temple to Augustus, the tiered stone theater, the huge gateways that are the work of Herod, the tyrant
puppet king of the Romans who imagined he could build himself
into history. It would have been a bitter irony for him to realize
that his main claim to historical fame would come thanks to an
impoverished peasant preacher from the Galilee. But Herod is a
latecomer in biblical terms. He built on top of ruins from nearly
nine hundred years earlier: Omri and Ahab's city.

What's left of Ahab and Jezebel's palace is magnificently sited
on the southwest side of the acropolis, at the very edge of the hill.
The view is stunning, as though a grand penthouse had been built
where eagles nest. My companions tell me that on a clear day you
can see the Mediterranean glimmering twenty-five miles to the
west, but there are very few clear days anymore; the haze of pol-
lution has muddied the horizon, confusing the once clearly per-
ceptible geography of the land. I have to take the Mediterranean
on trust.

Only the foundations remain, the bare supports of what were
once magnificently finished walls. Made of giant ashlar blocks
with chiseled edges, they were cut so straight by Phoenician master masons that they fit together with perfect precision. Just an occasional ornate capstone indicates what the walls once enclosed:
the massive columns, the covered walkways, the stairways of the
palace called "the house of ivory" in Kings, so that many people
still think, against all probability, that the whole place was made of
ivory. In much the same way, would-be immigrants once believed
that the streets of Manhattan were literally paved with gold.

But ivory there certainly was, and in abundance. In the 1930s,
archaeologists found large caches of delicately carved bas-relief
and fretwork ivory plaques inside the palace walls—plaques used

as decorative inlays on thrones, altars, and feasting couches. Shaded with blue faience and highlighted with gold leaf and precious stones, they were clearly the work of Phoenician craftsmen. Some show ibex feeding from the branches of the palm tree that represents the great mother goddess Astarte—the tree that would be known in Genesis as the Tree of Life. Others show the goddess herself framed in a triple-recessed window, her hair arranged like the branches of the Tree of Life. Still others depict lions hunting deer, and banquets, and ornamental motifs like doves and lotus blossoms, the motifs themselves evidence of their Phoenician origin, since the semidesert highlands of Samaria are not exactly lotus land.

Close by the palace are the remains of what was probably an ornamental pool with a fountain in its center and peacocks strutting around it, fanning their tails in gaudy display. There's no water in the pool anymore, of course; the tunnels and shafts that brought spring water within reach of the acropolis are long gone, and the only water the hill gets now is what falls in winter. But as you walk around the perimeter of the palace, shaded by wild fruit trees, you can still quench your thirst. White mulberries hang overhead, heavy and luscious with moisture. You reach up and pick one here and there and let the luxury of sweetness flood your mouth. It's like drinking fruit. You pick an unripe apricot and split it open to savor the seeds, fresh and green-tasting like tender young almonds. You look around at the olive and fig trees growing on the steep slopes and the patches of wheat planted among the ruins, and these combine in your mind with everything you know about the palace that was once here—its sounds, its furnishings, its temples—and you find yourself thinking that ancient Samaria might have been a rather pleasant place to live. Unless, that is, you happened to be from Tyre. And had brought your Tyrian gods with you.

Jezebel had traveled in style. Her entourage included not only courtiers and servants, emissaries and traders, but also, according to Kings, no less than four hundred priestesses and four hundred and fifty priests to serve in her new temple. Given the large number of priestesses, this temple was almost certainly dedicated to the goddess Astarte, but the Kings authors nevertheless called it "a temple of Baal." Refusing to accord any foreign deity the honor of his or her full name, they instead adopted a kind of speak-no-evil shorthand by referring to all foreign gods as "baals," meaning "lords." But much as they might abhor Astarte's presence in the Samarian acropolis, she was not nearly as foreign as they wished. As Jezebel was yet to discover, Yahweh did indeed have a consort—a lesser version of Astarte known as Asherah.

We know of her from ancient inscriptions calling down the blessings of "Yahweh and his Asherah" as well as from the Bible itself. In Jeremiah she is known as "the queen of heaven," and her image—a stylized Tree of Life—was placed beside the main altar in the temples of Yahweh. Pilgrims "dressed" it with ribbons and hangings, and made ritual offerings of fertility cakes: folded pastry triangles brimming over with poppy seeds in clear symbolism of female genitalia. Like most Israelites of the time, they saw no contradiction between worshipping the national god Yahweh and seeking intercession from his consort. They were practicing what historian of religion Mark Smith called "polytheistic Yahwism." In much the same way, animistic beliefs and practices have been absorbed into modern Christianity in Asia, Africa, and the Caribbean, creating a hybrid often called "folk religion." But in ninth-century B.C. Israel, Asherah as an adjunct of Yahweh was one thing; Astarte as a powerful goddess in her own right was quite another. For the Yahwist purists, the new temple quickly became a flashpoint of resentment.

Beneath the surface of Jezebel's official welcome in Samaria lay a potentially explosive combination of cultural rancor with religious absolutism, one that had been brewing long before her arrival. So long as Israel had been at almost continual war with its neighbors, this rancor had been kept bottled up, external enemies being an excellent means of keeping internal dissent under control. But now that the kingdom had achieved stability, it was merely waiting for the spark to set it into play.

The presence of the exquisite temple to Astarte in the heart of the Samaria acropolis had something of the same effect as that of McDonald's in Paris or of Starbucks inside the walls of the Forbidden City in Beijing—highly visible, immensely popular, and therefore all the more provocative to ideologues concerned with maintaining separate national identity. It was a piece of Tyrian territory in the very heart of Samaria, much as a foreign embassy in a national capital today is an independent presence within its host country. And just as American embassies in Islamic countries would be perceived as bastions of wealth and privilege threatening the cultural integrity of their host nations, so too Jezebel's temple would become the focus of those opposed to Ahab's policies of alliance and détente.

What these opponents feared was cultural dominance, and they had a strong argument. It was not just a matter of the alphabet or of the exact borders of "the land of milk and honey." The similarities between Yahweh and Baal Shamem were too close for monotheistic comfort, as we know from the hundreds of clay tablets found from 1929 on at Ras Shamra, the site of the northernmost Phoenician city-state of Ugarit. Among these tablets were the magnificent series of religious epic poems known as the *Baal Cycle,* in which we see Baal Shamem riding the clouds with thunder and lightning in his hands—the very same imagery later used in the biblical portrayal of Yahweh. We see Astarte called "the queen of heaven" and the consort of the great god El, as Asherah would be the consort of Yahweh. And we realize that many of the customs we think of as uniquely Israelite were in fact adopted from Phoenician practices, including the festivals of Matzot at the beginning of the barley harvest and Succot at the grape harvest.

Such a degree of influence does not inspire gratitude. As in Islamic countries today, it inspires a mix of envy and resentment, a mix that finds its most volatile expression in the form of religious principle. The Yahwist ideologues saw Jezebel's new temple as a clear and present danger to the purity of the Israelite kingdom, but they needed more than a temple to brand the king an infidel. Now they would find the perfect opportunity in the very arena that had made him such a formidable opponent: the battlefield.

To the modern mind, what happened next sounds like the story of an extraordinarily successful end to hostilities. But to the biblical mind, it was a tale of shameful apostasy. To invert Shakespeare's phrase about Julius Caesar, it was told not to praise Ahab, but to bury him.

The story, told as a stand-alone chapter in Kings, begins with a declaration of war. Just when it seems that stability has been achieved, Israel's traditional enemy Damascus, the leading city-state of Aramea, renews hostilities. It's a surprise move on the part of Ben-Hadad, the king of Damascus, and a well-timed one. Ahab is relatively new to the throne, a battle-tested warrior but still untested as commander in chief, and history has already proved that young, inexperienced kings tend to fall more easily than older, wilier ones.

Ben-Hadad demands that Israel cede the territory of Gilead on the east bank of the Jordan, and declares that he'll pummel Ahab's kingdom into dust if he does not comply. In a classic formulation of the time, he invokes his own gods to back up his threat. "So may the gods do to me, and more," he says, "if Samaria be anything but handfuls of dust compared to my strength." He even makes outrageous demands for tribute. "Your gold and silver are mine," he declares, "and your wives and children too."

Your wives and children too? Though it was standard procedure of the time for a victorious king to take a defeated opponent's wives into his harem, the reaction of Ahab's newest wife, Jezebel, had to be quite spectacular. Forget rage and indignation; this was pure unadulterated insult. If such a word had existed at the time, one can almost hear her saying, "The chutzpah!" But there will be no Cleopatra-like asp at hand in case Ben-Hadad succeeds, not for Jezebel. The queen who in thirty years' time will taunt her assassin in the moments before her death is hardly to be intimidated by pompous threats from Damascus. Neither is a warrior as experienced as Ahab.

Ben-Hadad has underestimated the young Israelite king. Not only does Ahab not give in, but he responds with epigrammatic wisdom:

"It is not the man who puts on armor who should boast," he says, "but the one who takes it off."

It is an amazing reply. Any modern antiwar activist would be proud of it. And it could come only from a stance of supreme confidence. In this one statement, we see the man Jezebel married: a warrior sure of his abilities in the field, but also a farsighted politician who realizes that though military action may be effective in the short term, it will only prolong the cycle of violence. He wants to put a stop to the vicious series of attacks and counterattacks, the kind of tribal warfare that has weakened every kingdom in the Near East and made them all vulnerable to incursions by the Assyrian empire to the east, in the vast valley of Mesopotamia. Ahab will be neither deterred by Ben-Hadad's opportunism, nor bullied into submission.

Ben-Hadad foolishly chooses to see Ahab's unwillingness to fight as a sign of weakness instead of strength. He consults his priests, who are essential to the business of warfare, since every kingdom fights under the banner of its national god. War is pursued only after the priests of the royal court consult the oracles and assure the king that his god favors him and will ensure victory. But as in every time and place, courtiers, by the nature of their profession, aim to please the king. Since a bad sign from the national god is bad news for the king, they tend to interpret the signs as the king wants, which is exactly what Ben-Hadad's priests do now. If he can lure Ahab's army across the Jordan River, they tell him, then the Damascene god Baal-Hadad will prevail over Yahweh, whose power will be weakened beyond his own territory.

By the time Ben-Hadad takes the field, his army is so big that the Israelite one looks "like two herds of goats against them." It is an unlikely imbalance given other rulers' tributes to Ahab's military prowess, but a vivid turn of phrase. Seeing that war is inevitable, Ahab consults his own priests, who urge him to take the initiative, cross the Jordan, and take Ben-Hadad by surprise. Yahweh will avenge the Damascus king's insult, they say. In the name of Yahweh, Ahab will be victorious.

And so it turns out. In an eerie foreshadowing of the 1967 Six-Day War and Israel's sudden preemptive attack against the massive Arab forces surrounding it, the Damascene king is decisively defeated in a week-long battle, and his forces decimated.

In desperation, Ben-Hadad's generals now advise throwing themselves on Ahab's mercy. "We have heard that the kings of Israel are merciful kings," they tell him. "If we dress in sackcloth, put ropes around our necks, and go out to the King of Israel, perhaps he will spare your life." Once again, we learn more of Ahab from his enemies than from his own people; a reputation for mercy would make a great warrior all the more legendary.

The Damascus generals strip naked except for sackcloth around their waists, then place ropes around their own necks as though they were already captive. You can see lines of near-naked captives roped this way on commemorative plaques of the time, often with hooks through their noses. If that is not gruesome enough, these are the lucky ones compared to those shown impaled on long staves or being stabbed through the eye. Ben-Hadad's generals may hope for the best, but on the natural assumption that their enemy will do what they would have done in his place, they fear the worst. So when they reach Ahab's tent, they throw themselves on the ground before him.

"Your servant Ben-Hadad begs you, spare my life," they say, only to be completely taken aback by the reply:

"What, he is still alive?" says Ahab. "He is my brother. Go bring him to me."

Considering Ben-Hadad's bloodthirstiness of just a week earlier, this declaration of brotherhood—as in brothers-in-arms—is extraordinary even by today's standards. By ancient standards, it was all but unprecedented. "Your brother?" the generals stutter, barely able to believe what they're hearing. But Ahab demonstrates that he means what he says. When Ben-Hadad himself arrives, rope, sackcloth and all, Ahab literally extends the hand of peace: he reaches down from his chariot and brings the defeated king up to stand beside him, not as a conquered enemy but as a brother and ally.

It is a magnificent gesture, both dramatic and subtle. At the same time as it shames Ben-Hadad's previous belligerence, it forgives him. Ahab takes off his own armor and, in so doing, proves his point about who should boast. A Zen master could not have done better.

Ahab was now in a position to dictate terms: Transjordanian cities like Ramot Gilead, the fortress on the King's Highway to Damascus, would remain under Israelite control; Israel would have an embassy in the huge oasis of Damascus, the nerve center of the caravan trade from the east; the two kingdoms, Israel and Damascus, would sign a mutual defense pact. It was a peace treaty on the most advantageous terms possible, sealed in the unshed blood of the Damascene king who now owed his life, let alone his throne, to Ahab.

But by the same stroke, Ahab had also played into the hands of the Yahwist purists in his own kingdom. What looks like far-sighted statesmanship to us was heresy and treason to them, for the king had contravened the most basic principle of war as they understood it. This war, like all wars of the time—indeed, like many wars today—was a holy war. It had been fought for the glory of Yahweh, and the victory had been granted by Yahweh. The fruits of victory—the enemy captives—thus belonged to Yahweh and had to be sacrificed in his name.

Deuteronomy, compiled not long before Kings and probably by the same group of scribes, would be quite clear on this: "When Yahweh your god gives them over to you and you defeat them, then you must utterly destroy them. You shall make no covenant with them, and show no mercy to them." There is no room for human compassion or compromise; the divine claim is seen as absolute, and it is terrifying in its absolutism.

This was not the first time an Israelite king had failed to make the required sacrifice. Some two hundred years earlier, King Saul had been ordered by the prophet Samuel, speaking for Yahweh, to "smite Amalek" in these words: "Utterly destroy all that they have, and spare them not, but slay both man and woman, infant and suckling, ox and sheep, camel and ass." When Saul nevertheless spared the Amalekite king in return for tribute, Samuel announced the divine punishment—"Because you have rejected the word of Yahweh, he has rejected you as king of Israel"—and anointed a true warrior king to take Saul's place. David, described as "a man of blood," took the throne, leaving Saul to descend into despair and madness. The message was clear: deprive Yahweh of his due at the risk of your sanity, and possibly your life.

Not that Yahweh was the only god who claimed the lives of his enemies. The practice applied throughout the Middle East. Whether the god in question was Moab's Chemosh or the Damascene Baal-Hadad or the Assyrian Assur, the sacrifice of prisoners to the god who granted victory was a sacred duty. On the Moabite Stone, King Mesha recorded that "I seized and killed everyone—seven thousand native men, foreign men, native women, foreign women, concubines—for I devoted them to my god Ashtar-Chemosh." The sign of devotion was destruction.

The term for this practice was *herem*, a concept as complex in its interpretation as *jihad* would later become in Islam. It means "set apart" for the god, or consecrated to him. Thus Mount Hermon, the magnificent snow-covered landmark that is the highest point in the Middle East, is literally "the consecrated mountain." It belongs to god and is *haram*, forbidden to humans. So too the Haram al-Sharif, the Arabic name for the Temple Mount in Jerusalem with its two magnificent domes, the gold of the Dome of the Rock and the silver of El-Aksa mosque, is in principle set apart for Allah and those who follow him, off limits to infidels. But in the context of battle, *herem* was quite clear: it demanded the sacrifice of those who had been conquered. When Ahab flouted this divine law by sparing Ben-Hadad, he had been revealed as an infidel—one who was literally unfaithful to his god. He had acted not like an Israelite warrior but like a godless foreigner. Or rather, a foreigner with too many gods. He had acted, that is, like a Phoenician.

Much as they may have scorned it, the Kings writers were certainly familiar with Phoenician mythology; it was too widespread to ignore. They would have known the legends of the *Baal Cycle*, and specifically what happened when the god Baal Shamem defeated his enemy, Yam, and made to kill him. The great Astarte herself intervened, pleading that it was dishonorable to kill a prisoner, and her woman's words softened Baal's wrath. He spared Yam, and they made peace, each agreeing to rule his respective sphere—Baal the skies, Yam the sea. Now the Kings writers insisted that another Phoenician woman's words had intervened to spare a life. Ahab, they said, had "sold himself into evil in the eyes of Yahweh, incited by Jezebel his wife."

The language is that of pure demagoguery. The implication of prostitution in that phrase "sold himself" is deliberate, tying in perfectly with the theme of harlotry that still haunts the image of Jezebel. Just as deliberate is the use of the word "incited." Most translations use the far milder phrase "stirred up by Jezebel his wife," but the Hebrew *hasat* has the clear political meaning of illegal or subversive agitation. It implies deliberate and malicious intent. But where today we talk of incitement to riot or to murder, in this case it was incitement *not* to murder.

Jezebel did indeed influence Ahab, as the Kings authors maintained. But he did not "sell himself into evil" in Jezebel's bed, as implied by that hint of prostitution. Her influence was not sexual, but political: Ahab had sold his warrior's soul for peace.

As the Yahwist purists saw it, only an Israelite king under the sway of Phoenicia would even conceive of sparing a captive's life in order to make peace. They saw it as a sign of weakness. Not only did it undermine the harsh military ethos of a warrior state; it was a dangerous infiltration of foreign values into the highest echelon of Israelite society. It was, in fact, a betrayal of both god and country at a time when there was no perceived difference between the two.

The battle lines had been drawn: divine law on the one hand, pragmatic statesmanship on the other. There was no room for compromise, and the law of *herem* would now be invoked in full. Because he had denied the divine claim on his enemy's life, Ahab would have to pay with his own. "Thus says Yahweh," declared a strangely unnamed prophet. "Because you have let go the man who was consecrated to me for destruction, your life shall be forfeit for his life, and your people for his people." In other words, "Die, infidel!"

From here on—from the moment of what should surely have been his greatest victory—Ahab was a marked man. And the stage was set for Elijah to make his grand entrance and unleash his awesome fury on Jezebel.

3.

Gilead

in which Elijah is surrounded by harlots

Word of the prophet's arrival had spread like wildfire through the city. The reception chamber was packed, and a huge crowd had gathered outside, waiting for word of what was happening to be passed back by those in front. You could sense the tension in the mass of subdued voices. Many doubtless reveled in the anticipation of confrontation. The very fact of Elijah's appearance, let alone the suddenness of it, was a guarantee of drama; the prospect of a face-off between two great authorities, royal and divine, was just too good to be missed. Others, more sophisticated, quailed. If Elijah appeared out of the blue like this, it could bode nothing good. They feared the moment of divine punishment for Ahab's transgression.

Yet the minute she laid eyes on the man, Jezebel's first impulse was to break out into mocking laughter. This was the great Israelite prophet whose name she'd heard spoken with such fear and trembling? All she saw was an emaciated wreck of a man whose clothes—if clothes they could even be called—were mere pelts, still ripe with the blood of the animals they'd come from. His long matted hair was tangled with filth, his beard a mass of knots, his teeth stained brown by the carobs she'd heard he lived on—honey and locusts, they'd say in centuries to come, not realizing that carobs were the fruit of the honey-locust tree.

She took in the gnarled fingers clenched around a coarse wooden staff; the long jagged fingernails curled and yellowed with neglect; the eyes burning with fever, or perhaps fervor—they were, after all, much the same thing. What kind of man would do this to himself? A delusional man, surely. A creature to be sorry for, to turn gently away with scraps from the table. A pitiable creature, teased by young boys and stoned by adolescent bullies.

She didn't laugh, of course. She had far too much self-control to give in to such an impulse. But she gathered the silk folds of her robe close about her with a slight shudder, as though the prophet's very presence could contaminate her. He didn't belong here, in her court, her domain. He was an intrusion, an apparition from a world that was the antithesis of hers. And she could see in his eyes that he knew it. That this was precisely why he was here.

Not even the king's guards had dared deny him entry into the main reception hall of the Samarian palace. If there was an element of derision in the way they looked at him, there was also awe. They may have wanted to snicker at his looks and his garb, at his uncouth speech and unkempt hair, but it seemed there was a power in him that they dared not challenge. He had the aura of a man appointed by the divine, one who heard the voice of their god and transmitted it to them. And his wretched appearance worked only to strengthen this charismatic aura. His primitive clothing was the sign of holiness not in the sense of modesty and humility—no barefoot Franciscan, this—but as a deliberate and calculated slap in the face of all human authority and custom.

Jezebel took her cue from her husband, who sat stoic and blank-faced beside her. There was no way to deny Elijah access, she could see that. Not even as popular a king as Ahab could close out this fearsome a prophet. The court priests could be appointed and fired; they were courtiers first and foremost, their livelihoods dependent on telling those in power what they wanted to hear. Those who had dared criticize Ahab for sparing Ben-Hadad's life had been dismissed. Rumor had it they were living in caves in the wilderness, on bread and water smuggled to them by sympathetic supporters. Those who were left were the ones who had learned how to balance the dual prerogatives of the royal and the divine. They had been tamed. But Elijah was downright feral.

There was no such thing as compromise for him, no recognition of any authority other than Yahweh. He was the *Navi*—literally, one who is called. Called, that is, to defend the divine law. And this calling made him untouchable by human law, as he made quite plain. He stood unbending before the king—not so much as a nod of the head, let alone a deep bow or full prostration in the royal presence. It almost seemed that he expected the king to bow to him. He'd walked into the reception chamber with the stride of a man half his age, as though he were the true king of this palace and Ahab a mere imposter. That unyielding back, that stiff neck permitting not so much as a nod of deference, that fierce unblinking stare out of reddened dust-rimmed eyes—all spoke of supreme confidence. Though Jezebel was loath to admit it, he unnerved her. So if her first impulse had been laughter, her second was fury. How dare he! How dare he bring the stink of the wild into this small haven of civilization? How dare he present himself at court filthy and unkempt? How dare he flaunt his disrespect?

And then those fierce eyes focused on her, and she saw not just the hatred in them—that, she'd expected—but a delight in that hatred, in the blood-pumping, energizing urgency of it. And this took her off guard. What had she ever done to him, she thought, to attract such intense animosity? What strange kind of world did he inhabit in which he was brought to life by this hate-fueled zeal? What stark and cruel land had he come from?

The image of Elijah is indeed that of a stark man from a cruel land. Yet compared to the west bank of the Jordan Valley, his native Gilead on the east bank of the river is the image of fertility. Today it is part of the Kingdom of Jordan, but it still has what the hills of Samaria do not: water. Ahab knew what he was doing when he spared Ben-Hadad in return for continued control of this area. In the arid Middle East, water is life.

In only fifteen miles, the land rises sharply from the River Jordan at five hundred feet below sea level to pine-forested hills three thousand feet above. After that, it gives way to the great desert steppes that run five hundred miles east into Mesopotamia. For these first few miles, however, it is a rare haven of greenness, home to vineyards and olive groves and fig orchards. Perennial rivers, from the Yarmuk in the north to the Zarqa in the south, rush white-watered through deep chasms. Peer over the edge and you can see the lush tangle of reeds hundreds of feet below, and hear the water roaring through as though it were cutting the gorge deeper even as you stand there. Come here as I did across the Jordan, and you can't help thinking how absurd it is that there is so much conflict between Israelis and Palestinians over the dry and barren west bank of the river, when these lush hills are just a few miles away on the east bank. The air itself seems fresh and fragrant compared to the perennial dust of the other side. But first impressions are not always the best.

"Go up unto Gilead, and take balm," Jeremiah would write, only to taunt his listeners: "Is there no balm in Gilead?" He knew the answer, of course. There is indeed no balm in Gilead, not in his time and not today either. Wherever I asked in the markets, nobody had even heard of Gilead—that's the ancient biblical name, so it doesn't appear on modern Jordanian maps—and the only balm I could find was Indian tiger balm.

I was there in May, when a strong but soothing breeze rises out of the west, just as the late afternoon heat begins to wear on you, and lasts into the evening. Natural air-conditioning, you think appreciatively. But this early summer comfort is deceptive, people told me. Imagine it here in winter, they said, when that refreshing breeze becomes a relentless biting wind, funneled up through the gorges with bitter cold and even snow for weeks at a time, until it feels like the whole land is howling at you. Come back then, they said, and you'll see how harsh it can be. But the harshness was already waiting for me when I set out to find the place where Elijah was born.

I was lucky to have a guide. De'eb was born and raised in Gilead, an amiable and generous man whose name—"wolf" in Arabic—seemed quite incongruous. When he heard that I was going to Tel Mar Elias—the *tel* of Master Elijah—he laughed at the very idea that I might be able to find it myself, and insisted on coming with me. He was right; signposts are all but nonexistent on Jordan's back roads, and if I'd found the place at all, it would have been only after hours of misdirection. And even then, as often happens in the Middle East, I'd have been in the wrong place.

Tel Mar Elias is on one of the highest hills in Gilead, and the view west over the Jordan Valley and into Palestine and Israel is stunning. The whole of the hilltop is covered with the remains of a large Byzantine church, and many of the mosaic floors are still intact, so that you look down to find fourteen-hundred-year-old pictures of grape arbors and wine goblets beneath your feet. On the western side, a magnificent oak overhangs the entrance to a deep well, its shade a perfect place to sit and reflect that this site has the peace and the grandeur that seem appropriate to a place where a great prophet was born and raised. It's easy to see why the Byzantines declared that this was Elijah's birthplace and chose to build their church here and not on the lower hill of Listib just to the west, a small mound crisscrossed with dirt tracks that today is home to a half-dozen mud-brick hovels.

Listib is only a few hundred yards away from Tel Mar Elias, yet you can stand on the Byzantine ruins and never even notice it unless you know to look. Even then the eye wants to skip over it, to rest on the wheat fields and orchards and gorges surrounding it, not on this ungainly little blot on the landscape. Yet this is the leading candidate for the honor of being Tishbi, Elijah's actual birthplace. If, that is, there ever was such a place.

The biblical identification of Elijah reads *Eliyahu ha-tishbi mitoshvei Gil'ad*, a phrase that can be read two ways: either as "Elijah of Tishbi from the residents of Gilead," or as "Elijah the settler from the settlements of Gilead." Which translation you opt for may depend as much on modern politics as on linguistics; the latter reading certainly seems appropriate when you consider that one of the anthems of Israel's modern settlement movement in Palestinian territory is a hymn celebrating Elijah. All that can be said for sure is that although no place called Tishbi survives, those who appreciate the word games so rife in the Hebrew bible point out that Listib—*el-Istib* in Arabic—contains the consonants of Tishbi, and is therefore an excellent candidate for Elijah's birthplace.

So when De'eb and I got back to my rental car at Tel Mar Elias, I took the narrow asphalt lane leading toward Listib. I didn't think to check with my passenger. To come so far and not stand on the place where Elijah was born was inconceivable to me. But not to De'eb. So far as he was concerned, the view from the Byzantine ruins was as close as anyone would ever want to get. "No way," he said with alarm when he realized where we were heading. "There are dogs there, and I'm afraid of dogs."

It seemed absurd that a man named for a wolf should be afraid of dogs, but De'eb was deadly serious. We negotiated. "Okay, but I'm not setting foot outside this car," he said, and on that understanding, I turned onto a dirt track and started up the hill. Which was when the dogs appeared.

They seemed to come out of nowhere, five or six of them—in the panic of the moment there wasn't really time to count. Some were pure white, others mottled, and it was immediately clear that they were built and they moved like wolves, not mere dogs. They were wild wolf-dogs, that is, and clearly more wolf than dog.

They blocked the track, snarling ferociously, wild-eyed and jittery. It needed no imagination to see those teeth ripping an arm from your body and coming back for more. Then without warning we were surrounded by them. They launched themselves at the car—at the wheels, onto the hood, at the windows, which I managed to get closed just in time. They yelped as they bounced off the sheet metal and then hurled themselves back into the one-sided fray, claws searching for purchase. The car shuddered under the assault. In front of me, open jaws spattered drool on the windshield. To one side, fangs loomed inches from my eyes. To the other, De'eb was bent double, his head buried in his hands.

I looked for someone to call off the attack, but there didn't seem to be a single person around. No washing hanging out to dry, no chickens or donkeys or any of the other signs of human habitation. So far as I could tell, the mud-brick hovels were abandoned, and the wolf-dogs owned the hill.

The car's metal casing suddenly seemed very fragile. With no room to turn on the narrow track, I finally regained my senses and backed down from the fray and off that hill as fast as I dared while I still had air in the tires. The wolf-dogs kept up the attack as far as the asphalt, then ranged themselves in a row at the threshold of the dirt track, barring it. They were snarling and panting but no longer attacking, their pose that of zealous guardians who had successfully defended their territory.

De'eb just stared at me, eyes wide open with fear, shaking his head. I only started shaking as I drove away, when I realized I no longer had any doubt that this was where Elijah was born.

Zeal and jealousy are kissing cousins. In Hebrew they come from the same root, *qana,* and the doubleness survives in English: both words derive from the Greek *zelos,* which indicates both "attack" and "defense." You can be jealous *of* a person and zealous *for* a cause; you can still hear of a man being jealous for his honor, while the Hebrew bible speaks of men being zealous for Yahweh. And no one more so than Elijah. Like the wolf-dogs of his birthplace, he was jealous of his territory and zealous in guarding it. In his devotion, he would prove himself the great progenitor of zealotry.

This is certainly a harsh description of him, but just as certainly one in which he would have taken great pride. His other side—the caring intercessor, the protector of the poor, the downtrodden, and the falsely accused—would be created far into the future, when rabbinical legend would give him an afterlife that was the complete reversal of his ninth-century B.C. self, almost as though some universal karma were at work to transform him into the antithesis of what he had been as an eternal lesson in atonement.

The Elijah who actually lived would have scorned such an idea. Gentleness was not for him. In his mind, there could be no tolerance of what he saw as Jezebel's evil influence on Ahab and Israel. There was no room for compromise or negotiation when the laws of Yahweh himself were at stake. And in the face of such absolutism, Jezebel would find herself trapped in the quandary that faces every modern liberal. On the one hand, to tolerate intolerance is to give silent assent to its destructiveness, and to allow it to fester and grow; on the other, if you are intolerant of it, you risk becoming what you oppose. How much simpler the world is when there is only one hand, and that is the hand of God.

Jezebel could hardly be blamed if she initially underestimated her opponent. There was no way for her to know that she was face-to-face with the prototype of the fire-and-brimstone prophet, the original model for every "pro-life" minister applauding the killing of doctors, every extremist imam praising the attack on Manhattan's Twin Towers, every fanatical rabbi calling for all Palestinians to be deported or killed. Elijah embodied a new level of radical intolerance. He was the founder of what scholars now call "militant" or "opposition" prophecy, the obsession with subsuming the kingdom of human beings to the kingdom of God.

It is indeed obsession, and an immensely rewarding one. In his book *Under the Banner of Heaven* Jon Krakauer notes that "the zealot may be outwardly motivated by the anticipation of a great reward at the other end—wealth, fame, eternal salvation—but the real recompense is probably the obsession itself . . . As a result of his infatuation, existence overflows with purpose. Ambiguity vanishes from the fanatic's worldview; a narcissistic sense of self-assurance displaces all doubt. A delicious rage quickens his pulse, fueled by the sins and shortcomings of lesser mortals, who are spoiling the world wherever he looks. His perspective narrows until the last shreds of proportion are shed from his life. Through immoderation, he experiences something akin to rapture."

That delicious rage is what Jezebel must have seen in Elijah's eyes. And what unnerved her may have been the realization that it was her doing. That is, it was she who had brought him to life. If not for Jezebel, Elijah would never have appeared. The Kings account brings him into being only because of her arrival in Israel. Her very existence was the call for the warrior of Yahweh to report to duty, rousing him out of his hilltop hideout and sending him across the river to the royal palace in Samaria.

By the time he came to a halt in front of Ahab's and Jezebel's thrones, Elijah had seen all he needed to know to render his sentence. Not just the new temple to Astarte with its Tyrian priests and worse still, priestesses, though they were bad enough, but the ostentatious luxury that was all around him. The gold leaf, the ivory panels, the gems, the silks, the scents—all were everything he had expected. Everything, that is, that both tempted and disgusted him. He saw a whole city of well-fed satisfied faces, of people smug in their newfound prosperity, unaware of the depths of degradation into which they had been led by their king and queen. Even as they called themselves loyal Yahwists, they placidly accepted and adopted foreign norms and values. Everywhere he looked he saw a weakening of the moral fiber, a threat to the stern values he held dear, even a mockery of the whole tradition of Yahwist law. Ahab's sparing Ben-Hadad's life had been only the most visible symptom of the divine will thwarted by human arrogance. Israel's rulers had betrayed Yahweh and led the people astray, and the sickness had reached into the core of every Israelite. They were selling their souls for profit, for the material benefits of those ill-begotten alliances with Damascus and Phoenicia. The influence of this Phoenician-born queen had led them into evil and decadence.

Perhaps the closest modern equivalent to how Elijah saw Samaria can be found, with discomforting irony, in the writings of Sayyid el-Qutb, the Egyptian ideologue whose book *Milestones* would become what Jonathan Raban has called "the essential charter of the Jihad movement—its *Mein Kampf*." Analyzing Qutb's writings, Raban notes that "he exhibits an intense, prurient disgust at the fallen morals of the modern city . . . and holds up religion as the purifying force in a contaminated world." The letters Qutb sent home from his two years in the United States as a student in the early 1960s "show him wading fastidiously, a lone pilgrim, through 'the filthy marsh of this world.'"

"The Believer from his height looks down at the people drowning in dirt and mud," Qutb wrote. "Humanity today is living in a large brothel! One has only to glance at its press, films, fashion shows, beauty contests, ballrooms, wine bars, and broadcasting stations! Or observe its mad lust for naked flesh, provocative gestures, and sick suggestive statements in literature, the arts, the mass media!" In the Arab world too, Qutb saw decadence everywhere he looked. His own people were worshipping the false gods of materialism, seduced into a state of *jahaliyyah*—the dark ages of ignorance and barbarism before the advent of Islam. They had become infidels.

If Qutb's holy book had been the Hebrew bible instead of the Koran, he would have used the same word as the Israelite prophets for what he saw all around him: harlotry.

The word "harlot" still has the power to hurt. There is a degree of willfulness to it that goes beyond simple sex for sale. It implies lasciviousness, a certain lewd delight in decadence. Yet the unspecified "harlotries" that Jezebel would be accused of just before her eventual assassination meant something very different in ninth-century B.C. Israel than in the twenty-first-century West. They had nothing to do with sexual prostitution. In fact—and this may be far more shocking to a modern reader than any degree of moral decadence imagined by the most fervent preacher—they had little if anything to do with sex at all.

Fundamentalists may choose to be literal when they read the word "harlot" in the Bible, but those who originally wrote it did not. They consciously used harlotry as a metaphor. And they were fully aware that metaphors are not neutral. On the contrary, they color our whole way of thinking and behaving.

Take one example given by linguist George Lakoff in his analysis of the power of metaphor. Think of argument as war, and that will influence how you argue—aggressively, with the intent of "beating" your "opponent." But think of it as dance, and you will argue in a very different way, playfully instead of antagonistically, constructively instead of destructively. The choice of metaphor, that is, is crucial.

Harlotry and infidelity are two of the most powerful metaphors ever invented. The fact that they have maintained their impact over three thousand years is testament to their strength. Young women can still be put down with the words "slut" and "whore" or with their personification, "Jezebel." Writers are accused of prostituting their talents by "selling out" to Hollywood. In the Middle East, Palestinian women opposing the policies of the fundamentalist Hamas movement are called prostitutes; men doing the same are called infidels. Biblical metaphor still determines the way we think.

"You have polluted the country with your harlotry and your vices," said the prophet Jeremiah, railing against the worship of idols and false gods. "Have you seen what unfaithful Israel had done? How she has made her way up to every high hill and to every spreading tree, and has whored herself there? . . . She committed adultery with lumps of stone and pieces of wood." Hosea, Isaiah, and Ezekiel all joined Jeremiah in accusing not only Samaria and Jerusalem but the whole of Israel of "playing the harlot" with foreign gods and "whoring themselves" to false deities. The Israelites had become, said Isaiah, "sons of a sorceress, seed of an adulteress and a harlot."

"You have offered your services to all comers," Ezekiel railed. "You have prostituted yourself to the Assyrians; you have played the whore and not been satisfied even then. You have piled whoring on whoring with Canaanite and Chaldean, and even then not been satisfied." Where Jeremiah made do with describing Jerusalem as "a lustful she-camel running around in heat," Ezekiel became so carried away with his own rhetoric that it devolved into lurid pornography. In the kind of explicit detail generally fudged in translation, he had Judea "infatuated by profligates with penises as big as those of donkeys, ejaculating as violently as stallions"— a phrase delicately rendered in the King James Version as "doted upon her paramours, whose flesh is as the flesh of asses, and whose issue is like the issue of horses."

The fear of foreigners—foreign influence, foreign power—is palpable. They are the stallions and the Casanovas. They are irresistible, dominant, all-consuming. The implication that Israelites are weak and effeminate by comparison is intentional. The insult is not to women but to men, since the members of the covenant with Yahweh were exclusively male—those who underwent circumcision, the sign of the covenant. To depict them as promiscuous women was to attack them where it would hurt most, in their sense of masculinity. Jeremiah and Ezekiel knew what they were doing: they were grabbing the attention of their audience, using insults, taunts, and the coarsest imagery in an attempt to shock people into awareness. Sexualize religion—cast religious infidelity in sexual terms—and you have made your point with desperate intensity.

Indeed, much of the Hebrew bible seems obsessed with the

idea of infidelity. How not, when the same word is used both for sex with someone other than your spouse and for worshipping a god other than the "true" one? The double meaning becomes startlingly intense when Yahweh is shown not just as the one true god of Israel but also as its husband. Hosea saw the covenant as a contract between Yahweh the groom and Israel his bride, and so the wronged husband curses his adulterous wife:

> *Let her rid her face of her whoring,*
> *and her breasts of her adultery,*
> *or else I will strip her naked,*
> *expose her as on the day she was born . . .*
> *I mean to make her pay for all the days*
> *when she burnt offerings to the Baals*
> *and decked herself with rings and necklaces*
> *to court her lovers,*
> *forgetting me . . .*
> *She will call me "my husband,"*
> *No longer will she call me "my Baal."*
> *I will take the names of the Baals off her lips,*
> *their names shall never be uttered again.*

The violence of the betrayed god ramps up in Ezekiel when Yahweh threatens to exterminate his own people rather than have them worship other gods. The parallel that comes inevitably to mind is a husband who kills his wife out of jealousy. Insecure in his status as the one true god, Yahweh demands absolute loyalty, and so imposes an equally absolute penalty. Infidelity is fatal. Israel will belong to Yahweh or to no god at all. Ezekiel shows Jerusalem stripped naked in front of her foreign lovers, then dismembered, stoned, stabbed, and burned: "They will level your mound and demolish your high places. They will uncover you, take your jewels, and leave you completely naked. They will whip up the crowd against you. You will be stoned and run through with a sword. They will set your houses on fire . . . I will put an end to your whoring. No more paid lovers for you. I will exhaust my fury against you."

But to take Ezekiel literally is to entirely miss his deeper meaning, which involves perhaps the most poignant and painful play on words in the whole of the Hebrew bible. His word "uncover"—*gala* in Hebrew—also means "exile," the ultimate condition of being without cover, without protection. To be in exile is to be naked, vulnerable, abandoned. It is Israel deserted by her lord and protector, Yahweh, and at the harsh mercy of foreigners. It is the prophet's worst nightmare come true.

Barely more than a century after the northern kingdom was at the height of its power under Ahab and Jezebel, it would be destroyed, in 720 B.C., and its population dispersed throughout the Assyrian empire. Just over a hundred years later, Isaiah and Jeremiah would see the same fate looming for the southern kingdom of Judea. But for Ezekiel, the worst had already happened: he was writing in exile, in Babylon. Yahweh was no longer threatening to desert his people; he had done it. Israel stripped and raped, outcast and dismembered, represents the experience of exile, the bitterness and violence of it. For Ezekiel, the inexorable penalty for harlotry and adultery—for infidelity, that is—was already in effect.

We tend to assume that as moderns we are more sophisticated than the ancients—an assumption one might say borders on hubris if it were not well beyond that. Jezebel's reputation as a harlot survives only because we have become hopelessly literal in our reading of the Hebrew bible, stuck to the most superficial meanings of deeply metaphorical writings. The question, then, is why we should be so blind to what the ancient writers and their audience grasped quite clearly.

Ancient myths are often seen as rather naïve but entertaining systems of belief, but in the twenty-first century we can be just as naïve. We have created our own modern myths about antiquity, generally under the guise of questionable scholarship. And as the leading polytheist given the role of the heavy in a monotheistic morality tale, Jezebel has been a kind of myth magnet. The so-called "pagan queen" is subject to the wholly untested complex of beliefs in which monotheism is the key to high moral values, while polytheism is a cesspool of immorality. She is defined, that is, by what can only be called the myth of orgy.

This myth centers on the existence of the "sacred prosti-tute"—the usual English translation for the word *qdesha*, literally "a sanctified woman," which appears in all ancient Semitic lan-guages. Sacred prostitutes were supposedly employed in pagan temples, particularly in the ones dedicated to the great mother goddess, to act out fertility rites with worshippers, and this was clearly an entrancing idea for the late-nineteenth- and early-twentieth-century European scholars who gave it academic re-spectability. It matched their image of the sensuous, seductive, belly-dancing Orient, full of harem girls and odalisques experi-enced, as they used to say, "in the ways of pleasuring a man."

The very use of the term "pagan," which comes from the Ro-man word for a peasant as opposed to an urbanite, is a measure of the prejudice against polytheism. It calls up images of primitives living benighted existences—as in Conrad's *Heart of Darkness*—much given to exuberant naked dancing, strange sexual practices, and unimaginable cruelties. The deeper the moral darkness of their existence, the purer and more morally enlightened the Western monotheism of its proponents by comparison. The myth of orgy thus served a most satisfying double purpose: on the one hand, those who promoted it felt upright and superior by comparison, while on the other, they indulged a palpable prurient delight in retailing the myth.

"The temples of the Semitic deities were thronged with sacred prostitutes," declared William Robertson Smith in his famed *Religion of the Semites*, published in 1889 and still given pride of place in nearly every bibliography on ancient religion. Karl Budde followed suit ten years later, describing Canaanite religion as "voluptuous and dissolute" and adding that "debauchery and excesses went with it hand in hand." In 1911, Franz Cumont elaborated further: "Immorality was nowhere so flagrant as in the temples of Astarte, whose female servants honored the goddess with untiring ardor . . . transforming the temples into houses of debauchery." The same year, Sir James George Fraser completed *The Golden Bough*, an extraordinary collection of myths about mythology that is still a perennial seller, not least due to its insistence that from Babylon to Heliopolis and from Baalbek to Armenia, "all girls were obliged to prostitute themselves in order to earn a dowry" and "all women were obliged by custom to prostitute themselves to strangers at the sanctuary of the goddess." Even archaeologists would prove vulnerable to the myth of orgy: "Sacred prostitution was apparently an almost invariable concomitant of the cult of the Phoenician and Syrian goddess," wrote William Albright in 1946. "The erotic aspects of their cult must have sunk to extremely sordid depths of social degradation."

Since these are some of the most respected names in their fields, it is no surprise that the sacred prostitution charge lived on, repeated and embroidered despite the absence of any substance to the idea. A few terms of qualification did begin to creep in—an "apparently" here, a "there can be little doubt" there, even a strictly correct "it is generally assumed." But as Harvard historian Robert Oden put it as recently as the year 2000, "There is, to be sure, a mounting hesitancy to claim clear unambiguous testimony for the existence of sacred prostitution among several Near Eastern religions. But this hesitancy hardly prevents scholars from asserting repeatedly that the rite must have existed."

The closer you look, the more sacred prostitution emerges as a kind of academic urban legend—a fiction that, because it satisfies the preconceived ideas of those who hear it, gets passed on ad infinitum as fact. But even an urban legend begins somewhere.

This particular one began, not in Jezebel's time, but four centuries later in the person of Herodotus, the fifth-century B.C. Greek historian often referred to as "the grandfather of history"—a title many historians today regard as a libel on the very idea of history. One single paragraph of his on Babylon and Cyprus turns out to have become the sole basis for the delirious fantasy of sacred prostitution.

"The foulest Babylonian custom," he wrote, "is that which compels every woman of the land once in her life to sit in the temple of Aphrodite and have intercourse with some stranger." Never mind that Aphrodite was a Greek goddess unknown to the Babylonians—a later incarnation of the once-powerful Ishtar and Astarte. Herodotus described women lining up to have sex with strangers, and ended with perhaps the earliest known version of a crude locker-room joke: "So then the women that are fair and tall are soon free to depart, but the uncomely have long to wait because they cannot fulfill the law; some of them remain three years, or four."

Bad enough that this is the sole source for the whole legend, to be repeated, with various rhetorical flourishes, by classical authors from Strabo and Lucian up to modern venerables such as Fraser and Mircea Eliade, creating fact by dint of sheer repetition. But there is also an increasing realization that Herodotus probably never saw what he claimed to have seen, for the simple reason that he was never in those places. As Robert Oden points out, the "observations" of Herodotus were at best fanciful, his interpretations superficial, and his knowledge apparently reliant on an unnamed source who may or may not have existed.

A few basic questions would have exploded the myth of orgy very quickly. If every woman was expected to lose her virginity to a stranger at the temple, why then did ancient Semitic cultures insist on female virginity at marriage? Since virginity was essentially a guarantee of paternity—it ensured that the identity of the father of the firstborn child was beyond doubt—and since paternity was key to the whole system of inheritance, how could such cultures have determined inheritance if sacred prostitution existed? And why did they impose the death penalty for marital adultery or for premarital sex if at the same time they required it in the temples? The more questions one asks, the shakier the whole foundation of the myth of orgy becomes. But until the late twentieth century, there was little interest in asking such questions. It wasn't until women began to rise in the ranks of religious studies that the myth of orgy would be seriously scrutinized.

Their work has made it quite clear that the *qdesha* as sacred prostitute was not merely a mistranslation, but a major misunderstanding of the role of women in ancient religion. It was, in fact, an unconscious projection onto ancient times—or, as Columbia University's Edward Said would have seen it, a Western projection onto Middle Eastern society.

Sacred prostitution is one of the oldest and most flagrant symptoms of the syndrome Said identified as Orientalism. Essentially, he reasoned, the Western image of the Middle East was skewed by a conglomeration of fantasies and assumptions, based on a solid streak of anti-Semitism—not anti-Jewishness, specifically, but prejudice against all Semitic peoples. "The Orient" or "the Levant"—from the French for "rising" since the sun rises in the east—was seen as sensuous, dangerous, and devious, especially as compared to what was assumed to be the rational, logical, developed mind of the West. The more degenerate the Orient appeared to be, the more enlightened the West was by comparison. As it had been for Herodotus and the Greeks, so too for the nineteenth- and twentieth-century Orientalists the myth of orgy was an act of cultural self-promotion, one made all the more powerful by its capacity to titillate the sexual imagination. The Orient became the repository of everything that both tempted and dismayed the Western scholar. It was not just exotic, erotic, and mysterious; it was subversive of all decent Western order. In essence, the Orientalist perception of the Middle East would serve as almost a mirror image of Sayyid el-Qutb's perception of the degenerate influence of Western culture on decent Islamic order.

The old-style gentlemen scholars, hampered by Orientalism and blinkered by misogyny, simply could not conceive of women as priests. To them, there was only one possible explanation for the presence of women officiating in the temples of the Middle East: a consecrated woman could only be consecrated to sex.

Elijah himself would have thrown up his hands in despair at the astonishing literalness of the myth of orgy. He saw Jezebel as a harlot, certainly, but he saw every Israelite that way. Israel was selling its soul, not its body. This was abomination. This was treason. This was harlotry. The strumpet foreign queen with her Baalite priests and priestesses had seduced the king and his people into faithlessness. But if you had suggested to Elijah that by this he meant that Jezebel was available for sex, he'd have spat in your face and cursed you, convinced that you were laughing at a matter of the utmost seriousness. And a curse in the mouth of Elijah would have shaken you to the very roots of your being.

This was a man who knew how to curse. A man who could call down the infinite power of the divine to give his words the force of inescapable fate. And that is exactly what he now did in the great reception chamber of the Samarian palace. Standing tall before Ahab and Jezebel and the throng of people massed tightly around him, he did what he had come to do: he pronounced the punishment for harlotry, loud and clear and with an absolute certainty that left no room for illusions of mercy.

"As Yahweh the god of Israel lives, before whom I stand, there shall be neither dew nor rain these years, except by my word."

The words rang out with terrifying clarity in the silence of the packed chamber, echoing off the walls and penetrating with a force stronger than steel into the hearts and minds of every Israelite. In a country constantly teetering on the edge of drought, this was the worst imaginable fate. Drought would mean the slow strangulation of the whole country. The soil would harden and crack, the plants wither and dry. First the crops would die, then the herds, starving with nothing to feed on, then the people. Children would cry in the night for moisture and then, worse still, as they lost the strength to cry, fall into a terrible silence, their bellies distended, their limbs wasted, their eyes grown huge as the flesh around them retreated into the skull.

Elijah's words fell like blows, each one hammering home the terrible fate he was dictating. Not one drop of rain, he made clear. Not so much as a hint of dew. Nada. Nothing. Nil.

4.

Carmel

in which the gods have a showdown

Curses are still chilling. Anyone who's been cursed at by another driver on the road knows it. The very fact of having engendered such rage in someone else is discomforting. You drive on, telling yourself that whatever was said, they were just words, but still, a pall seems to have descended on the day. You know that the words were impersonal, that they were a manifestation of the other driver's problem, not yours, yet you can't help but take them personally. They reverberate, because curses carry force even in the twenty-first century. In the ninth century B.C. they carried far more. They were a direct invitation to the gods to do their worst. Or rather, a direct promise *by* the gods.

The Bible is full of curses. They haunt its stories, populating them with foreshadowings of a dire and terrible future. In the mouth of someone speaking in the name of the divine, they were literally awesome—full of awe. Call down a curse in the name of your god, and that god's power was behind the curse. Call down a curse as a prophet of Yahweh, and that was Yahweh's curse.

Many of the most stunning curses in the Hebrew bible come directly in the voice of Yahweh himself at the end of Deuteronomy, which codifies his covenant with Israel. Structured in a format familiar from other vassal treaties and covenants of the time, the book defines the parties, their history, the obligations of both sides, the benefits of the treaty, and the penalties for breaking it. The first fourteen verses of the twenty-eighth chapter are devoted to the benefits in the form of blessings; the remaining fifty-four—four times as much space—list the penalties, in the form of curses. And what curses! This is where Deuteronomy achieves its full grandeur, in the munificence of its punitive imaginings.

"You shall be cursed in the city, and cursed in the field . . . Cursed in the fruit of your womb, and cursed in the fruit of your soil . . . Cursed when you come in, and cursed when you go out." Plague, pestilence, fever, madness, blindness, hunger, thirst, poverty, slavery, cannibalism, exile, all are fulsomely predicted. The Deuteronomic imagination ranges from the inclusiveness of verse 61, a kind of catch-all that reads "Also, every illness and every plague that is not written in this book of the law, Yahweh will bring upon you until you are destroyed," to the existential despair of verse 67, a definition of chronic misery that even Kierkegaard would not better: "Your life will hang suspended before you, and you will be in terror night and day, and have no confidence in your life. In the morning you will say 'Would that it were evening,' and in the evening you will say 'Would that it were morning.' "

But of all the curses possible, the worst by far was drought.

The Israel highlands were almost totally dependent on rainwater, and the winter rains were as variable then as they still are today in any semidesert area. Human settlement had become possible only a mere two or three centuries earlier thanks to the advent of iron tools, which allowed farmers to dig cisterns into the limestone to collect and hold winter rain, and to build stone terraces on the hillsides to hold in both soil and moisture. But all the iron in the world was of no use if there was no rain. It was a resource that could never be taken for granted.

Rain was beyond human control. It was the province of the gods. In the absence of science, theology provided the explanation of nature and served as both the physics and the meteorology of the time. Everything was either the result of divine actions that merely happened to impact human beings, which is how the Phoenicians saw the world, or the demonstrative will of God, which is how the Yahwists saw it. You might say that where the Phoenicians were at the mercy of their gods, who were neither benevolent nor malign, Israel determined the actions of its god by its behavior, and he could be both benevolent and malign. When pleased, he granted rain; when displeased, he withheld it. And never, according to Elijah, had he been as displeased as he was now.

"Take heed that your heart be not deceived and you turn aside and serve other gods and worship them," Deuteronomy would warn, "for Yahweh's wrath will be kindled against you and he will shut up the heavens and there will be no rain and the land will not yield her fruit." Hosea would repeat the threat in Yahweh's own words to his unfaithful nation: "I will make a wilderness of her, turn her into arid land, and leave her to die of thirst." But the threat of drought was one thing, its implementation quite another. Never before had drought actually been imposed as divine punishment. Never had it been announced beforehand. And never with such devastating thoroughness, as though Elijah were savoring each detail.

"There shall be neither dew nor rain, except by my word"— and that word unavailable, for no sooner had Elijah passed sentence than he turned on his heel, strode out of the court, and disappeared.

Jezebel must have doubted her own ears as Elijah's words rang out through the palace. Surely no prophet could call down such suffering on his own people. And not only with such relish, but with such utter self-righteousness. To maintain that they must die for their own good? No, this was intolerable. Impossible. Yet the echoing silence in the reception chamber told her that she had heard perfectly. She saw the blood drain from her husband's face; watched, dumbfounded, as Elijah strode out of the chamber, the crowd making way for him as though afraid of the merest contact; listened with only half an ear as Ahab finally stirred himself, called his counselors, and began to issue orders to secure stores of grain.

How did these Israelites stand for it? How had they not risen up and killed this prophet, silenced the words of doom in his mouth? How could they not see that this was an act of treason, and he a false prophet? But even her husband hadn't lifted a finger against Elijah. Ahab was bound as tightly as the most pious of his subjects into the Yahwistic idea of human responsibility for the actions of their god. In his ashen face, what Jezebel saw was guilt, the conviction that his own actions had brought this about—marrying her, building the new temple to Astarte, sparing the life of Ben-Hadad. Never had Ahab seemed more foreign to her, more distant from everything in which she believed.

How could humans think themselves so important in the divine scheme of things that their actions could determine drought and bounty, life and death? The very idea of the divine as a system of reward and punishment was abhorrent to Jezebel. For a god to be jealous of humans—jealous for their praise and their loyalty— seemed a terrible diminution of the whole idea of the divine. Baal Shamem played in the sky regardless of what humans did below. He didn't need their worship and devotion to assure his existence. He was beyond such reassurance; that was the essence of his divinity. But this Israelite brother of his, Yahweh, was possessed by such a fierce jealousy, and was so dependent on human loyalty, that he was driven to extraordinary wrath if crossed. It was sheer madness, Jezebel thought, to imagine that any god's behavior was dependent on human behavior, as though the gods were mere puppets of humanity instead of the other way around. Either it was a self-aggrandizing delusion, or Yahweh was so petty that he had nothing better to do than demand the absolute loyalty of mere humans and punish them if he thought it was withheld.

Yet her reaction was precisely what Elijah had planned: shock and awe. Shock at the severity of the punishment, and awe at his power to pronounce it and at the power of Yahweh to make it come true. To him, Yahweh was a political god, a proactive god deeply involved in human affairs. A historical god, that is, who would help shape the story of his people. That story would be determined by Israelite obedience to the covenant originally made with Abraham in which Yahweh had promised this land in return for loyalty. No human treaties or covenants could compare. Yahweh's power was supreme. Merely to recognize the existence of other gods was to question that supremacy, while to tolerate this foreign queen with her foreign gods and her foreign values was an abomination.

As Elijah saw it, Israel was selling its soul for the material benefits of trade with Phoenicia and Damascus. This harlotry had to be punished, and the punishment had to be a collective one—one in which everyone would suffer, guilty and innocent alike. For in Elijah's mind there were no innocents. Every Israelite was part of the covenant, and every one was thus responsible. Only collective punishment could rouse them into action, wake them from their heathen state of well-being, and shock them back into the true faith.

Twenty-eight centuries later, Ayman al-Zawahiri, the second in command of Al Qaida, would redefine this stance as "internal jihad." Shock tactics were needed to rouse the Islamic masses into awareness, he declared. Muslim unbelievers were not merely heathens but worse than heathens, since their betrayal came from inside. Religious warfare against them was thus a legitimate means to protect the purity of Islam. As Harvard's Jessica Stern, a leading scholar of religious terrorism, put it, "because the true faith is in jeopardy, emergency conditions prevail, and the killing of innocents becomes religiously and morally permissible."

Any strategy was valid to break what Zawahiri called "the spell" of foreign influence, impurity, and corruption. Like Sayyid el-Qutb before him, he saw himself as fighting an epic battle against an evil empire. Foreign ideas were corrupting Muslim minds, values, and society; once corrupted, people were no longer true Muslims and so could be killed. The terror thus created would shock others into rising up and overthrowing Western-influenced regimes. Violence would become what

Frantz Fanon called "a cleansing force" restoring pride and dignity. It would become redemptive.

Radical Islam's most bitter criticism was reserved not for the West but, as Stern noted, for Arab leaders. "Arrogant, corrupt, westernized princes and autocrats," Sayyid el-Qutb called them. In Egypt, President Anwar Sadat's assassin saw him as a traitor to Islam and to the Islamic people. So too in Israel, Prime Minister Yitzhak Rabin's assassin saw him as betraying Yahweh and the Jewish people. Paradoxically, radical fundamentalism bridges religious differences. Extremist Jews and Muslims may hate one another, but they are mirror images. They subordinate the core values of Judaism and Islam to their radical view of the world until extremism itself becomes a separate faith all its own.

The Kings authors never show the effects of the drought on Israel. There is no mention of the devastation and the suffering or the number of deaths, though it must have been well into the thousands. We know that the kingdom as a whole was organized enough to withstand the drought; without constant warfare with neighboring states draining his resources, Ahab had been able to focus on strengthening his country's infrastructure. The huge underground grain silo uncovered by archaeologists at Megiddo was certainly one of many. But as the drought stretched into the second year, and then into the third, the country was inevitably weakened. With no surpluses, trade suffered; with reduced provisions, the military was weakened; with emptying grain silos, people starved. A fourth year was unthinkable.

And while Israel suffered, what of Elijah? We are told that no sooner had he condemned Israel to drought than he disappeared to Nahal Karit, a small spring near the Jordan Valley, where he was fed meat and bread twice a day by ravens. When the spring dried up due to the drought, he went of all places to Phoenicia, Jezebel's homeland, as though he were trading places with her. While she reigned in drought-ridden Israel, he would live in ease in her country of perennial rivers. While his own people suffered, starved, and died, he would find a welcoming widow in Sarepta, just north of Tyre, and she would take him in and care for him. In return, he would work miracles for her.

The legend of Elijah as the man of the people, the prophet who cares for the poor and the downtrodden, begins here, in Jezebel's territory. When all the impoverished widow has left to eat are just a single jar of meal and a little vial of oil, Elijah calls on Yahweh to multiply them, making it clear that if he so desired, he could do the same for all the people of Israel. And when her son takes ill and dies, Elijah stretches himself out on top of the boy and breathes life back into him, as he could also do, if he wanted, for Israel. "Now I know that you are a man of god," declares the newly converted widow, "and that when you speak the word of Yahweh it is the truth." The message is clear: if a simple Phoenician widow can accept the truth of Yahweh, why then can't a sophisticated Phoenician princess?

After three years, Yahweh finally relents. "Go show yourself to Ahab," he tells Elijah, "and I will send rain upon the land." In the mouth of the divine, that sounds straightforward enough, but actually bringing down the rain will be a complex and bloody business.

Elijah returns to Samaria as directed, doubtless expecting to be greeted as a savior. Ahab will surely fall down on his knees at the sight of the prophet, prostrate himself at his feet, and kiss them with a desperate "At last, you have come." There will be tears of gratitude, perhaps. At the least Elijah will be welcomed with honor and respect by a penitent king who has seen the error of his ways. But if this is indeed what he expects, he is severely disappointed. He arrives to a decidedly cool reception. "Is it you, you troubler of Israel?" Ahab says to him.

It is a famous phrase, that "troubler of Israel," but far too mild a one. The Hebrew uses the word *okar*, which means "someone who afflicts," and affliction is certainly more in line with a three-year drought than mere trouble. When he originally declared the drought, Elijah intended the blame to fall on Jezebel and Ahab, thinking that the people would rise up and unseat them. Instead the blame has fallen on him, the man who not only called down suffering on his people but then turned his back on them.

He lashes back at Ahab. "It is not I who have afflicted Israel," he says, "but you and your father's house, by forsaking the commandments of Yahweh and going after the Baals." In the heights of his self-righteousness, he cannot conceive of himself being in any way at fault. And besides, he holds the trump card. He knows that only he can stop the drought.

"Go gather all of Israel on Mount Carmel," he orders, as though the king were merely his servant, "together with the four hundred and fifty priests of Baal and the four hundred priests of Astarte who eat at Jezebel's table."

Ahab has no alternative but to obey. This is not emotional blackmail any longer, but blackmail clear and simple. He and his people are at the most untender mercy of this prophet. The drought will indeed end only at Elijah's word, and he will take his time about giving it. This will be his big moment, so he has every intention of drawing it out to the utmost. Thousands of Israelites will be gathered together, waiting for him to call down rain, and he will use every trick of stagecraft he can muster to create high drama, stretching their nerves to breaking point before giving the ultimate proof of Yahweh's power.

The great showdown between monotheism and polytheism, between Jezebel's priests of Baal and Elijah the prophet of Yahweh, is about to begin.

The place chosen for it is the highest point of Mount Carmel, the limestone ridge that rises dramatically out of the sea at the modern city of Haifa to stretch southeast in the shape of a giant longbow. In the ninth century B.C. this ridge marked the border between the Kingdom of Israel to the south and east, and Phoenicia to the north, and both peoples considered it a holy place. The Israelite name Carmel is a contraction of *kerem-el,* "the vineyard of God," and the name itself contained the essence of religious mystery since, then as now, no vines grew on the Carmel. Its steep sides could support only shrubs and scrub oak, so that humans never settled it, leaving it to the divine and to the work dedicated to the divine: the work of sacrifice, that is. This took place at the point still known as the Muhraka (pronounced *mookh-raka)*—Arabic for "the place of burning," as in burnt offering.

Elijah had chosen his stage shrewdly. The Carmel divided and united two kingdoms, and was sacred to both. There was no more perfect place for a confrontation between the priests of one people and the prophet of the other.

At 1,540 feet above sea level, the Muhraka is visible far away even at night, when a full moon silhouettes the monastery that now stands on the site. To reach it, you take a sharp right turn at the top of the road that snakes up the side of the Carmel from the west, and follow a narrow sun-dappled lane a few miles along the top of the ridge. To either side, through the pines and olives and scrub oak, you catch glimpses of the vast vistas beyond. It is a beautiful drive, and by the time the lane ends at the Carmelite monastery of Mar Elias—Master Elijah—you feel immensely peaceful. So you are not quite prepared for the first thing you see as you enter the courtyard, which is a ten-foot-high statue of Elijah standing in heroic warrior pose, sword aloft.

At first glance, there's something odd about this sword; it looks distinctly floppy. In fact it looks as though it had collapsed in on itself in time of need and completely failed its purpose. You examine the inscription on the statue's plinth, looking for an explanation. In Latin, Arabic, and Hebrew, it's a quote from the apocryphal biblical book of Ben-Sirah, also known as Ecclesiasticus: "Then the prophet Elijah arose like a fire, his word like a burning torch." And that's when you realize that the sword is supposed to be made of fire, not steel, and that the fire is not just the fire that came down from the skies and set ablaze Elijah's offering to Yahweh on this spot, but the fire of true faith, of zealous belief, and of wrath and vengeance on all who do not share this truth and this belief.

But there is something else disconcerting about this statue of Elijah with his sword of fire. The image is somehow familiar, but it takes time to make the connection because it's an ironic one, and you're not ready for the ironic quote in a place like this. The pose is exactly that of ancient statuettes of the Phoenician god Baal Shamem, who was shown just this way, one foot forward, lightning bolt aloft like a sword, ready to strike. Elijah in this pose can be seen as one more way of stealing Baal's thunder. And the floppy sword acts as a reminder, perhaps, that one should not try to carve metaphors in stone.

Jews and Muslims tend not to come here—it is a Christian monastery, after all—but every July 20, the feast day of Elijah, the place is filled with Arab Christians who come by truck and minibus, carrying blankets and barbecue grills, ice boxes and picnic hampers, and settle in the shade of the trees near the monastery walls, barbecuing and relaxing in the pine-scented air. The other Christians who come to the Muhraka do so by the air-conditioned busload: foreign evangelicals who waste no time relaxing under trees and give merely a passing glance to the statue in the courtyard. They're here not to remember Elijah, and certainly not Jezebel, but to see the view from the monastery's roof. For the point of a high place is not only that it is visible from miles away in every direction, but that you can see for miles in every direction from it.

Père Giorgio, the Italian monk in charge of the public sections of the monastery, accompanies me up to the roof. He's a gaunt but immensely affable man who delights in company to the extent that one wonders how he can stand the monastic life. When he realizes that I have read Kings and know the story of what happened here, his face brightens in anticipation of having a good conversation instead of giving the usual abbreviated Bible lesson.

We look out together over a large part of the land of the Bible. Just nine miles to the southeast is Megiddo, "the site of Armageddon," as the Israel Parks Authority has obligingly subtitled its official guidebook to the place, mindful of the number of evangelical tourists focused on the book of Revelation. Beyond Megiddo is Jezreel, built on a rocky spur commanding the whole of the valley named for it and thus the ideal place for Ahab's military command center, as well as the site of his and Jezebel's winter palace. Across the wide valley, Nazareth nestles into the first low ridge of the Galilee hills. A little farther along is Mount Tabor, site of the Transfiguration, where Jesus appeared to his disciples alongside Moses and Elijah. To the south you can see the hills of Samaria, with Jerusalem hidden in the higher Judean hills beyond, while far to the north gleams the unmistakable snow-covered peak of Mount Hermon, Jezebel's terrestrial Polaris.

From this high up, it all looks utterly peaceful. Unless your imagination rings with the doomsday forecasts of Revelation, it's hard to remember that this is perhaps the most blood-soaked valley in the world. Military historians have counted thirty-four major battles fought here from 2350 B.C. to A.D. 1967, and all for good strategic reasons, militarily speaking, because the Jezreel Valley was a major crossroad: not only the main east-west route from the Jordan to the Mediterranean, but also part of the main route from Egypt north to Phoenicia and Damascus—the route that the Romans would call the Via Maris, "the way of the sea," forced inland by the Carmel's abrupt rise from the sea at Haifa.

As Père Giorgio and I survey the scene, a tour group of American evangelicals stands behind us happily imagining the valley below running in blood. Two of the men try to calculate the precise number of gallons of blood it would take to fill the whole valley. I raise my eyebrows; Père Giorgio shrugs. He's heard it all before.

"What do you think?" I ask. "Did Elijah really defeat the priests of Baal on this spot?"

He shrugs amiably. "Let's put it like this," he says. "All the elements you need for the story are here. It's the highest place for miles, and yet there's a kind of natural platform just below the monastery where thousands of people could gather. You can see the sea from here, where the rain came from. Right down below us there's the Kishon River, where they massacred the priests of Baal. And it's close enough to Jezreel for Elijah to run there afterward in victory, ahead of King Ahab's chariot, as the Bible says he did." In other words, this place fits the bill, but as to whether it is historically the "right" place, who knows? Père Giorgio's eyes sparkle with amusement at the very idea of "proof" for matters of faith. "Yes," he says, "if you feel the need to fix a definite place, this will do very well."

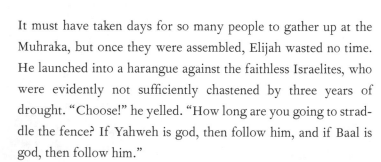

It must have taken days for so many people to gather up at the Muhraka, but once they were assembled, Elijah wasted no time. He launched into a harangue against the faithless Israelites, who were evidently not sufficiently chastened by three years of drought. "Choose!" he yelled. "How long are you going to straddle the fence? If Yahweh is god, then follow him, and if Baal is god, then follow him."

This is where it begins: the binary mind-set. Either/or. You're either with me or against me; either a believer or an infidel; either good or evil. There is no middle ground. The world separates into black and white, with not a shade of gray, let alone real color. Elijah issues the classic challenge, heard everywhere from Islamist madrasas and hardline yeshivas to evangelical seminaries: you're one of us, or one of them. Merely to tolerate the existence of other faiths is to be a dangerous weakling; it is tantamount to being an infidel yourself. Believe, or be damned.

It is hardly surprising that none of the assembled Israelites dares say a word in response. Why would they? After three years, the only thing they care about is that the drought stop and the rains come. Baal Shamem is a god of fertility, a bringer of rain. So too is Yahweh. Why tip their hand before the event? They'll declare their faith in whichever god is victorious, and watch silently until then.

Elijah is disgusted with them. He is the only one here of true faith, he declares. It is him alone against all the hundreds of Jezebel's priests. Never mind that this is supposed to be a contest of god against god, not human against human; Elijah instantly turns it into the classic story of one against many—a pattern that has figured large in the modern Israeli psyche, especially in the 1967 Six-Day War. And he states the terms of his challenge. The Baalite priests will prepare a bull for sacrifice; they will slaughter it, build an altar, and pile the altar high with wood. Elijah will do the same with a second bull. But neither side will be able to light the fire that will consume their offering. They must call on their respective gods to do that, and "whichever god answers by fire, he is the god."

Elijah has everyone wrapped around his little finger now. Who could resist such a showdown? A one-on-one, head-to-head competition, winner take all—it will be a wonderful nail-biter, and the best thing about it is that the finale is guaranteed: no matter which god accepts the sacrifice, the drought will end.

Jezebel's priests go first. They call again and again on Baal Shamem—"O Baal, answer us"—but "there was no voice, and none who answered." As the day wears on, they become more and more desperate. "They leaped around the altar they had made. And at noon, Elijah mocked them: 'Cry out as loud as you can, for he is a god; perhaps he's musing, or is answering a call of nature, or has gone wandering, or is sleeping and needs to be woken up.' And they cried out as loud as they could, and slashed at themselves with knives and spears, as was their custom, until they were covered in blood."

It is an intensely disturbing scene, written from a stance of assumed superiority. Like Elijah, the Kings authors saw the Baalite priests as maddened fools, an attitude that would be adopted centuries later by the Roman writer Apuleius, who used the strange-habits-of-the-natives style in his description of Syrian priests of the great goddess in *The Golden Ass*: "They began to howl all out of tune and hurl themselves hither and thither, as though they were mad. They made a thousand gestures with their feet and their heads; they would bend down their necks and spin around so that their hair flew out in a circle; they would bite their own flesh; finally, every one took his two-edged weapon and wounded his arms in diverse places . . . Meanwhile there was one more mad than the rest, that fetched many deep sighs from the bottom of his heart, as though he had been ravished in spirit or filled full of divine power; noisily prophesying and accusing and charging himself, he finally flagellated himself."

Ecstatic trance was clearly not within Apuleius' frame of religious reference. "Look how primitive these people are, compared to us sophisticates," he seems to be saying, helping pave the way for his successors, the Orientalists. But the details given in *The Golden Ass* and in Kings are essentially correct, as we know from accounts written within the Middle Eastern religions. As early as the twenty-third century B.C., Enheduanna, the Mesopotamian princess, priestess, and poet often referred to as the Shakespeare of Sumer, described the lamenting for the dead god of fertility, with priests and priestesses working themselves into a frenzy of self-laceration, tearing out their hair and clawing at their eyes and thighs and breasts. The flow of tears and blood is intended to imitate the flow of water from the heavens that will be provided by the resuscitated god. The priests are interceding between life—rain and its accompanying fertility—and death.

This is exactly what the Baalite priests try to do at the Muhraka. They do not pray directly for rain; instead, they mourn the lack of it. They act out the dramatic grief of the warrior goddess Anat when her brother, the rain god Baal, is taken into the underworld by Mot, the god whose name means "death":

> *She cut her skin with a stone,*
> *She cut herself with a knife,*
> *She raked her face and her cheeks.*
> *She plowed her chest like a garden,*
> *She harrowed her back like a valley . . .*
> *She sated herself with weeping.*
> *She drank tears like wine.*

The Baalite priests cannot call down the power of their god—that would be to assume that they themselves have godlike powers, which is precisely what Elijah assumes for himself, and what he will be criticized for later by rabbinical commentators. The priests can only re-create the conditions under which the god of rain can come back to life. They lament and grieve as did Anat. And Elijah mocks their grief. When he taunts them with the idea that Baal must be "answering a call of nature," the crude association with excrement and dung is deliberate—a theme, like harlotry, that surfaces repeatedly throughout this story.

For all their impassioned frenzy, Jezebel's priests fail. So, as the day draws to an end, it is Elijah's turn. With the flair of a consummate showman, he makes much of the preparations. He takes twelve stones, one for each of the tribes of Israel, and builds his altar. He slaughters his bull and places it on top of the wood he's piled on the altar. And in an extra fillip of showmanship, he orders four jars of water to be thrown three times over the wood— the twelve tribes again—so that it is thoroughly soaked. Then at last he prays, as briefly and succintly as possible so as to heighten the contrast with the drawn-out Baalite lamentations. "Yahweh, the god of Abraham, Isaac, and Israel," he intones, "let it be known this day that you are god in Israel, and that I am your servant, and have acted at your command."

The response is sudden, immediate, and literally striking. "And then Yahweh's fire fell and consumed the offering, and the wood and the stones and the dust, and licked up the water." Yahweh's fire: a lightning bolt out of the blue, with such magnificent force that it consumes not just the bull itself but the very stones of the altar on which it is laid out.

Lightning is one of the most sudden and terrifying natural manifestations, almost as rare as snow on the Carmel, and all the more terrifying when you have no idea of the physics involved and your only explanation for physical events is divine action. Baal's lightning bolt never strikes. He remains impotent. But Yahweh is in his prime: he is the virile, potent one. The sword of fire that is shown as Baal's and that will be immortalized as Elijah's is wielded with supreme power by Yahweh.

The response of the assembled Israelites is predictable: they fall flat on their faces crying out that Yahweh is god. But this isn't enough for Elijah. He has scored a great victory, and the defeated must now pay the price for their presumption. "Take hold of the priests of Baal," he orders. "Don't let a single one escape." And he has the people drag the pagan priests down the steep eastern side of the Carmel to the Kishon River, where every one of them is slaughtered.

Whether this means "only" the four hundred and fifty priests of Baal or also the four hundred priestesses of Astarte is unclear in the Kings account. Nor is there any sign of awareness that such a massacre might be literally overkill. Yahweh is the victor, and the losers fall under the law of *herem*. The defeated must be sacrificed, and their bodies will be expelled from the land of Israel, washed out to the Mediterranean from whence they came.

Scholars name Tel Qassis as the place where this massacre happened, but it is hard to find today, as though nobody in Israel has any desire to remember the event. There are no signs leading to the *tel*, nor any identifying it. It is only a small mound beside the shallow stream that is all that is left of the Kishon River, its waters diverted for irrigation in the early twentieth century. The Muhraka looks imposingly high from down here in the valley, and you can't quite see how hundreds of struggling Baalite priests could be dragged all the way down the dauntingly steep descent to be slaughtered at this spot. But as you sit on a stone by the side of the stream, staring up at the Muhraka, it occurs to you that Elijah was not so different from the Baalite priests after all; blood had to be spilled in imitation of rain, though where they shed their own blood, he shed the blood of "the others."

Now that the lightning had struck and the blood had flowed, it was time for the rain to appear. So Kings shows Elijah going back up to the Muhraka and bowing down, face to the ground, as a Muslim does in prayer. He sends his servant to look toward the sea seven times. Six times the servant comes back to report that nothing is happening, but the seventh time, he reports that a cloud "as small as a man's hand" has risen out of the sea. You know from that magical number seven what will happen next: the small cloud grows, "and in a little while, the sky grew black with clouds and wind, and there was a great rain."

Such "great rains" still fall in Israel. The first rain after a regular summer-long drought is a dramatic event. It begins with just a few heavy drops bouncing off the bone-dry ground like marbles, so loud that they startle you. Then more come, and more, until soon they're drumming at the earth, beating it with the rhythm of a tabla player. Only the first rain is ever so loud. Birds wake out of their torpor and join in like flutes to the drumbeat. Thunder starts to roll over the hills, adding in bass. Within minutes, sheets of rain slash across the landscape like giant white curtains, and the land is in flood. Roads become streams; dry wadis become torrents. Children shout in excitement, running out into the downpour to turn in circles with arms outstretched, dizzy with the freshness of it all, given over to the primeval human need for moisture.

And this is just after one normal dry summer. After three full years of drought, the first rain must have induced nothing less than ecstasy, and perhaps that ecstasy is what induced Elijah to do what we're told he did next. In celebration—in frenzy, you might say—he ran ahead of Ahab's chariot all the way from the Muhraka to Jezreel, through the rain and the mud and the suddenly swollen streams, to glory in his victory.

As Père Giorgio so gently indicated, there is really no point in asking if the story is literally true. If I can see no way that hundreds of struggling Baalite priests could be dragged down the steep side of the Carmel to be massacred in the Kishon River, that is not relevant. Neither is the fact that an aging man, even a prophet, is unlikely to be able to run nine miles ahead of a chariot, let alone the probability that after three years of drought, the Kishon was completely dry. The Elijah stories are legends woven into the biblical history of the kings of Israel, and they are powerful ones. Again and again, Elijah demonstrates superhuman powers—the kind of powers that he will hand on to his successor, Elisha, but that will never be seen in later Israelite prophets; from Isaiah on, they would have to content themselves with the written word.

Elijah was the great magus of Israel, the sorcerer, the man who could suddenly appear and just as suddenly disappear, who could call down lightning and rain, who could raise children from the dead, multiply grain and oil, and who, when he died, would leave no body, but would be carried up to heaven in a whirlwind. And if many of his actions seem familiar from other biblical legends, that was deliberate on the part of the Kings authors. They were establishing Elijah as the new Moses, the great liberator, which is why Elijah and Moses would appear together with a third great liberator, Jesus, at the Transfiguration on Mount Tabor. Just as Moses built an altar of twelve stones for the twelve tribes at Sinai, so did Elijah on the Carmel. Just as Moses said after the affair of the golden bull, "Whoever is on the side of Yahweh, to me," so too Elijah demands that the Israelites choose sides. Just as Moses led the Levites in the slaughter of the bull worshippers at Sinai, so Elijah leads the Israelites in the slaughter of the Baalite priests.

This is Elijah's high point, his great moment in Israelite history. And he has the spotlight entirely to himself. Jezebel, his prime antagonist, is strikingly missing from the account of the showdown at the Muhraka. The drought that has been so dramatically ended was called down because of her. The priests who were challenged were her priests, and their very public defeat was thus hers too. Ahab was there; thousands of Israelites were there; but Jezebel seems inexplicably absent. Unless, that is, you consider what she thought of a head-to-head competition between the gods.

To her, the very idea has to have been an affront. As a polytheist, to even conceive of seeing whose god was "better" or "the one" was breathtakingly absurd, an exercise in futility. To imagine that humans could challenge the gods to compete was an insult to all gods everywhere—an insult to the very existence of the divine, which was by definition on another level from that of humans. It was not merely distasteful and disrespectful, it was sacrilegious. No way would she dream of gracing such an occasion with her presence. She would boycott the event, wishing only that her priests and priestesses had displayed enough sense to do the same. Couldn't they see that this was merely the perfect opportunity for Elijah to grandstand? That the whole challenge was decided from the start, and he would never have issued it in the first place unless he was sure of winning?

In a way, Elijah understood their own faith better than they did. The gods of polytheism could be worshipped but not cajoled. They were independent agents whose actions merely happened to impinge on human life, so that while Baal Shamem could be celebrated, he could not be influenced. In Elijah's formative monotheism, however, Yahweh was open to human persuasion; he was a partner to humans, acting in concert with them. While no amount of prayer to Baal was guaranteed to produce a specific result, the right prayer to Yahweh could make him intervene. Jezebel's priests had been tricked into a situation in which they could not possibly prevail.

So while the god-on-god challenge takes place on the Muhraka,

Jezebel remains in the winter palace at Jezreel. If she is disgusted at the foolhardiness of her priesthood, she keeps her own counsel. The important thing, she reasons, is that the drought end— that the rains come and the resources of the kingdom, stretched to breaking point after three years, have a chance to recover. Let Elijah have his victory, let him declare Yahweh the only true god. The good of the kingdom is paramount.

Then Elijah comes running in through the main gate of Jezreel, soaked in rain, covered in mud, ahead of Ahab's chariot, and Jezebel hears the news: her priests slain, every one. Whatever terms of engagement she had thought existed between her and Elijah have been radically changed. To massacre hundreds of priests of another faith? She could hardly believe it if she had heard it of anyone other than Elijah. But as he stands panting below her balcony in the main courtyard of the palace, his sopping clothes running red with the blood of her priests, she can see the frenzy in his eyes. Did he give his order for massacre because he was so carried away with a sense of victory, or had he planned it all along? She has no way of knowing, and right now, overwhelmed as she is by a disgust so deep and so bitter she had no idea she was capable of it, she doesn't care.

She does not go into shock. She does not despair. She does not weep or mourn or waste time in recriminations against Ahab for not protecting her priests. Not Jezebel. She acts, and she does so with all the force of regal fury. She strides out onto her balcony, lifts her arms high to the heavens, and lets the rain stream down her face as she proclaims the following message to Elijah, loud and clear for all to hear:

"So may the gods do to me, and more also, if I do not take your life for theirs by this time tomorrow."

And then, in a magnificent coda included in the Septuagint, the third-century B.C. Greek translation of the Bible, she adds: "If *you* are Elijah, *I* am Jezebel."

This is great stuff: her life or his. Jezebel calls on all her gods as witnesses to her oath against the man who is now her arch-enemy. She gives him twenty-four hours. Either he flees the country by then, or he will die. And if he does not, she calls on her gods to kill her instead. This is her form of *herem*: she has dedicated Elijah's life to her gods, and pledged her own life as guarantee. "You think you are powerful?" she is saying. "Try this for real power."

There is no denying the force of such an oath, and Elijah does not. He knows what her gods are capable of. The Phoenician princess become queen of Israel is imbued with the spirit of Baal's sister Anat, the warrior goddess with her necklace of her enemies' skulls and her girdle of their hands—or, as some scholars have it, their penises. This is the Anat who exults in the slaughter as she fights to bring her brother back to life from the realm of Mot, the god of death:

> *Her liver swelled with laughter,*
> *Her heart filled with joy,*
> *The liver of Anat was exultant*
> *As she plunged knee-deep in the blood of the mighty,*
> *Up to her hips in the gore of warriors.*

She literally demolishes Mot himself:

> *She seized El's son Mot*
> *With a sword she cleaved him,*
> *With a sieve, she winnowed him,*

Carmel

With fire, she burned him,
With millstones, she ground him,
In the field, she sowed him.

Elijah has no intention of being cleaved, winnowed, burned, ground, and sown, even though he will soon declare that something horribly similar will happen to Jezebel. He is as terrified by her oath as she intends him to be. She has put her own life on the line—"so may the gods do to me"—and in so doing, she has placed him in thrall to her gods. If he stays, he will die. The man of Yahweh is now literally devoted—promised as a votive offering—to the Phoenician gods. For all his denial of them as false, if he acknowledges the force of her oath and flees, he will acknowledge their power and, by doing so, betray his own god Yahweh.

Or perhaps what he must really acknowledge is the sheer force of this woman, her terrifying courage and steely determination. She has placed her life on the line; now it is his turn. But Elijah doesn't have this kind of courage. He is not willing to pay the consequences of his absolutism, and Jezebel knows it. She has recognized this weakness in him. The grandstanding, the death-dealing rhetoric, the self-aggrandizement—none of these are the signs of a man willing to lay down his life for what he believes. The lives of others, yes, but not his own.

In the face of Jezebel's determination, Elijah withers and flees. "He ran for his life," Kings tells us, all the way down to Horeb, the ancient name for Mount Sinai. And in so doing, the warrior of Yahweh fails his god. He may be able to call down lightning, but he runs in terror from the word of Jezebel.

And yet why spare his life? Why does Jezebel give Elijah twenty-four hours, granting such leeway to an antagonist who seems bent on pushing her to the limits of ruthlessness? Surely the most efficient way of putting an end to his enmity would be to have him killed. There would be nothing easier for the powerful queen consort. A "heart attack," an "accident"—such a thing could be arranged at a moment's notice by loyal aides. Nobody would be any the wiser if the man were to keel over on the spot after a run such as his from the Muhraka.

But Jezebel's magnificent oath is clearly intended to bring about Elijah's exile, not his death. She wants to be rid of him, but not at the cost of killing him. She has a polytheist's respect for the divine—for all deities, both her own and those of others. To assassinate a prophet of another faith would run counter to everything she believes in, to the respect accorded all gods and their representatives. No matter what she may think of Elijah as a person, he represents Yahweh, and whatever she may think of Yahweh, he is a god, and so is to be honored on his own territory, here in the Kingdom of Israel.

Besides, Jezebel is a pragmatist, concerned with practical consequences. She knows there would be a heavy cost to having Elijah killed—not the risk of discovery, but that of creating a martyr, of elevating him from the stature of great prophet and rainmaker to that of the great prophet and rainmaker who died tragically at the peak of his powers. She can see how impractical revenge would be and how easily the cult of martyrdom could then take hold. The only thing more powerful than a vengeful prophet is a vengeful martyr. Let Elijah be the one consumed with vengeance; she has no intention of allowing the desire for revenge to trick her into making a martyr out of him.

And there is one still more cogent reason for what has to be seen, under the circumstances, as Jezebel's magnanimity. She has read Elijah well enough to know that exile will be a crueler fate for him than death. By choosing exile, the prophet will bend not only to her power but also to that of her gods. For a man like Elijah, death would perhaps be a mercy by comparison.

When she swears by her gods and Elijah flees, he proves himself the weaker of the two. She lays her life on the line; he runs for his. Instead of the unwavering courage Yahweh demands from his prophet, he displays cowardice. Jezebel has called Elijah's bluff and emerged the victor.

But only for now, because no matter how long the odds, Elijah has yet to make one final appearance. Jezebel may have spared his life; he will not spare hers.

5.

The Vineyard

in which Jezebel is accused of murder

The city that gave the whole of the Jezreel Valley its name is long gone. Even Tel Jezreel, the mound that accumulated over its rubble, has reverted to thorny wilderness since it was last excavated. In late spring, wildflowers bloom among the chest-high weeds and thistles: anemones and cyclamens and red Flanders poppies, like those still handed out every Remembrance Day in England, where soldiers' lore has it that their color comes from growing in the blood-drenched battlefields of World War I. Here and there you can make out the remains of an ancient wall or the collapsed opening of a cistern, now a nesting place for doves.

This was the winter palace, the place where the whole royal court moved in the fall, when the cold winds began to blow in the highlands of Samaria. Its ruins were uncovered only in the late 1980s, when heavy machinery was sent in by the nearby kibbutz to clear ground for a military memorial, and a bulldozer rammed straight into what were clearly ancient fortifications. Exit the bulldozers, enter the archaeologists. A series of excavations led by Tel Aviv University's David Ussishkin revealed the remnants of a rectangular walled city surrounded by a deep dry moat handhewn into the bedrock on all but the north side, which falls steeply to the valley floor and the Jezreel spring. Inside the moat, huge ramparts were topped by casemate walls—inner and outer walls with chambers between them. At each corner was a massive round guard tower, thirty feet in diameter, and on the south side an imposing triple gatehouse served as the main entrance. This thorny mound of rubble had once been an impressive fortified city, and for good reason.

Omri and Ahab had built the Israelite military into a major force with strong cavalry and chariot units. But Samaria, the capital, was up in the hills, not a good place for chariots. As Ussishkin put it, "A large fortified military center had to be built, to serve first and foremost as a central base for the enlarged army, and also as a strong fort for the newly established ruling dynasty." Where Samaria was the capital, the ceremonial center, and the locus of power, Jezreel was built as the locus of force. Jezreel was to Samaria, perhaps, as the Tower of London once was to Windsor Castle: one was for affairs of state, the other, for security.

The fortress city was perfectly sited on a spur of rock three hundred feet above the wide flat floor of the valley—a natural vantage point with clear views of the Galilee and Mount Hermon to the north, the Samarian highlands to the south, Gilead across the Jordan River to the east, and the longbow shape of the Carmel to the west. But despite its massive fortifications and control position, Jezreel did not last long. Ussishkin's most striking find was that the city existed for only some forty years. His team definitively established that it had been built by Omri and expanded by his son Ahab, and had then been completely destroyed, to be the home thereafter of only an occasional small village. Jezreel means "God will sow" in Hebrew, but it was clear that all that had been sown in this city was strife.

"Once there was a vineyard belonging to Naboth in Jezreel, close to the palace of King Ahab." This is how the Kings account opens its chapter on the episode that will definitively indict Jezebel, but it seems at first an odd way to go about it. We know nothing about Naboth except that he owns this vineyard. From the great doings of gods and nations, the account turns abruptly to a dispute over landownership. Ahab wants to buy the vineyard, Naboth refuses to sell, and Jezebel intervenes with fatal consequences. It sounds like the tale of a real estate deal gone horribly wrong, yet it is central to Jezebel's story, for her involvement in the matter will lead to one final grand appearance by Elijah. In the same city where she so recently declaimed her magnificent oath against him, the prophet will now reappear to declaim a still more chilling sentence on her.

"Give me your vineyard so that I can turn it into an herb garden, because it is close to my palace," Ahab says to Naboth, "and I will give you a better vineyard in return, or if you prefer, I will give you its worth in money."

This may seem a reasonable proposition to the modern reader, but in fact it is a very strange one. Why would anyone want to make a vineyard into an herb garden? Uproot all those vines, which had taken years to train and make productive? Give up fruit and wine, shade and coolness, for a garden that could be planted anywhere? It is even more puzzling when you consider that the Hebrew *gan yarok*, literally "green garden," today means a vegetable garden; it is hard to imagine any king giving a moment's thought to something as lowly and commonplace as a vegetable garden.

Ahab might, however, have had a different kind of garden in mind: a show garden, to be filled with exotic plants and animals such as monkeys, peacocks, and leopards, the showier the better. Such gardens were status symbols favored by powerful kings throughout the region, like Nebuchadnezzar's famed Hanging Gardens of Babylon, one of the ancient seven wonders of the world. Similar gardens existed in Egypt and in Persia, while an important part of the later cult of Adonis, the Greek adaptation of Phoenicia's Baal Shamem (the Semitic word *adon*, like *baal*, meaning "lord"), was to plant ornamental gardens in his honor.

Not that the idea of an herb garden hasn't its own intriguing possibilities. Herbs were not merely means of flavoring food; they were primarily used for healing. Medical knowledge was herbal knowledge. Healers and midwives—the "wise women"—did the everyday work of collecting and preparing herbs and administering them, but the public healing of a miracle worker like Elijah was seen as a manifestation of the divine. Which left open the question of which divinity was at work. Elijah healed in the name of Yahweh, but the best-known healing divinity throughout the Middle East was the Mesopotamian goddess Gula, she of the giant mastiffs guarding the doors between life and death. The herb garden may well have been a euphemistic scribal shorthand for a temple to Gula, to be built by Ahab as another gift to Jezebel.

Whether garden or temple, however, one thing can be said for sure about Naboth's vineyard: it was not actually a vineyard. The Jezreel Valley is no place for vines, not now and not then. Vines were grown on the higher land of the hillsides. They would only rot in the humid summers and marshy subsoil of Jezreel.

But this is the logic of reality, and stories do not necessarily reflect reality. Whatever the facts of the matter, the Kings story demands that the *gan yarok* be a vineyard. This is its point. As all who first heard the story knew, the vine is the biblical symbol of beneficence and well-being, as in the swollen bunch of grapes carried back by Moses' spies from the land of Canaan in Numbers—an image now used as the logo of Israel's Ministry of Tourism. Grain was a lot more important to everyday survival, as was olive oil; the vine was a luxury by comparison, and that was the whole beauty of it. The sweetness of the syrup made from its fruit, the delicacies wrapped and baked in its leaves, the canopy of shade from the blinding glare of the summer sun—all these were a bounty, a delicious gift. And of course the vineyard's wine was the source of intoxication. It took you out of the daily struggle for existence and into the ecstatic realm of the divine, which is what the vineyard really represents.

This is no mere plot of land with vines on it. The vineyard is Israel itself, in fidelity to Yahweh. It is land that belongs to Yahweh; he has not given it to Israel but merely granted the use of it. It remains his land in eternity: *kerem-el,* as in Carmel, God's vineyard. We're not talking physical land here, but metaphysical land.

In biblical metaphor, when Ahab says that he wants to uproot the vineyard, what he really wants is to uproot Israel, to pull it out of its covenant with Yahweh. Blind to his duty to Yahweh—or blinded by Jezebel, as the Kings authors would have it—he sees the vineyard simply as real estate. The "real" of real estate is an adaptation of the old French for "royal," since in feudal times all land was considered the property of the king; but Yahweh is the feudal lord here, not Ahab, and though the king may wish to ignore this fact, Naboth does not. Hence his answer to Ahab's offer: "Yahweh forbids me to give the inheritance of my fathers to you."

The word Naboth uses for his vineyard is *nahala,* which implies not only human but also divine inheritance. Since the land is ultimately not his but Yahweh's, his refusal to sell is a matter of faith. As biblical scholar Walter Brueggemann writes, "Land is a central, if not *the* central theme of biblical faith. Israel's involvement is always with land and with Yahweh, never only with Yahweh as though to live only in intense obedience, never only with land as though simply to possess and manage . . . Land and covenant, inheritance and fidelity, belong together." There is no separating them; they form a kind of holy trinity of Yahwism— this god, this people, this land.

The covenant made with Abraham and renewed with Moses on Mount Sinai promised the land of Israel to the Hebrews, the people whose name came from the Canaanite word *habiru,* "wanderers." It was a magical gift to a wandering people—an end to wandering; a home. The story of that covenant can be seen in many lights: as the foundation story of the shift from nomadism to agriculture; as the respect for land as a divine gift; but more commonly and more enduringly as the claim to ownership of the land, a claim for which blood is still being shed in the Middle East.

If the Israelites are loyal to the covenant, they will keep the land and it will be fruitful. But only on that condition. In a sense, the covenant is a long-term lease, cancelable at the discretion of the owner. Due warning will be given, but the lessees should never imagine that they have an absolute right to the land. Absolute ownership is Yahweh's; the people only hold it in trust. And this means that they cannot give up the land. It is non-negotiable.

This attitude to the land of Israel is directly mirrored in the modern Islamist one to Palestine, the same land by a different name. The charter of the ruling Hamas party—its covenant—describes the land as a *waqf*, a religious trust or endowment, and declares that "the land of Palestine has been an Islamic *waqf* throughout the generations and until the Day of Resurrection. No one can renounce it or any part of it, or abandon it or any part of it."

Both sides to the Israel-Palestine conflict see this literally as holy land. In fact not just the land but the very soil is holy. Later in Kings, when a military commander goes to Damascus, he takes two mule-loads of Israelite soil with him so that he can worship Yahweh on foreign soil. You can still see the same thinking at work on the television news, when returning exiles or captives step down from an airplane, fall to their knees, and kiss the ground of their home country. It is an ancient concept of land common enough in the Middle East but deeply antithetical to the Western mind-set, which may help explain why the best minds, most sincere efforts, and longest all-nighters by negotiators at Camp David still falter in the face of emotional, historical, and religious complexity.

This is why Naboth says no. He invokes the covenant: the land does not belong to him as much as he belongs to the land. The *na-*

hala is his not merely by human inheritance but by inheritance from the divine. No mere king can insist otherwise.

Ahab does not react well to being treated as a mere king. He is shown behaving with astonishing gracelessness, especially for so highly reputed a statesman. He returns to the Jezreel palace "sullen and displeased," then lies down, turns his face to the wall, and refuses to eat.

This is not the first time Ahab is described as "sullen and displeased." Exactly the same words were used for his reaction when the unnamed Yahwist prophet castigated him for sparing the life of King Ben-Hadad of Damascus. In fact the phrase might be better translated as "displeased and angry." The choice of "sullen," with its implication of a teenage sulk—a spoiled child's protest at not getting what he wants—is a product of translators' preconceptions. In modern psychiatric terms, however, Ahab's turning his face to the wall seems a clear sign that he is depressed, as any king used to the exercise of power might be when he discovers that his power is not absolute.

Jezebel is naturally disturbed at her husband's state of mind. "Why are you so displeased that you will not eat?" she asks. And when he tells her about Naboth, she assures him that all will be fine. "Are you not the ruler of Israel?" she says. "Get up, eat, and feel better. I will give you the vineyard of Naboth."

How strange that Jezebel, the slut and the harlot of legend, here looks the picture of a loyal wife. Her concern for her husband's mood and health make her more of a Yiddish mama than a fount of evil, to the extent that you can almost imagine her saying *"Ess, mein kind!"* She sounds anything but the harlot. In fact scholars like famed Talmudist Adin Steinsaltz argue that she can be seen as too devoted a wife, too eager to please and to put her husband's interests and desires above all else. The argument is somewhat tongue in cheek, of course; Steinsaltz, like Père Giorgio at the Muhraka, is poking mild fun at fundamentalist preconceptions, all too aware of the dangers of literal interpretation of a story that may or may not have happened as told.

Few commentators are this open-minded, however. Elie Wiesel, for instance, accepted the classic line of later rabbinical literature, which assumed that Jezebel used sex to wrap her husband around her little finger. "Clearly," he wrote, "Ahab was so addicted to her that he allowed her to run the business of government. Jezebel charted the nation's domestic policy, its foreign policy, and its theology—with Ahab's permission. We are told that he was a great commander, but only when she was not around; he was a weakling, but only when she was around."

"A weakling"—the greatest insult for a man, the ultimate challenge to his masculinity. Wiesel gives neither Ahab nor Jezebel any credit, merely taking the very modern notion of sexual addiction and reading it back, Orientalist style, onto Jezebel's presumed harlotry. It's the language of machismo, of "he wasn't man enough," the kind of locker-room thinking that fears female sexuality to the degree that it assigns it omnipotent power—the power, that is, to sap men of will and strength and reason, making crew-cut Samsons of them all.

By this reasoning, when Jezebel says, "Are you not the ruler of Israel?" she is taunting Ahab, as though she were saying "Are you a man or a mouse?" She is seen not as reassuring her husband but as challenging his masculinity. She becomes the prototype of another "fiendlike queen," Shakespeare's Lady Macbeth, who challenges her husband's masculinity in order to spur him to murder. Does Macbeth want to be "a coward in thine own esteem"? his wife asks. She calls him "infirm of purpose" and "unmanned in folly," and urges him on with "When you durst do it, then you were a man." And to top it all, she usurps the male role; since he will not act like a man, she will. "Come you spirits, unsex me here," she cries out, calling on them to give her the presumably masculine resolution to act where Macbeth is paralyzed by indecision—by being, as she jeers, "too full o' the milk of human kindness."

The two women, Jezebel and Lady Macbeth, are almost twin images; indeed it is quite likely that Shakespeare took his cue for *Macbeth* from Kings. Like Jezebel, Lady Macbeth is the one with the determination to do what needs to be done to consolidate her husband's power. Like Jezebel, Lady Macbeth is turned into a castrating witch. But even she pales by comparison. She is shown urging her husband to murder; Jezebel is shown doing the job herself.

While Ahab pouts, Jezebel acts. "She wrote letters in Ahab's name, and sealed them with his seal, and sent them to the elders and the nobles of the city." These letters read: "Proclaim a fast, and give Naboth a seat at the head of the council, and set two base fellows there who will bear witness against him and say that he cursed God and the king. Then take him out and stone him to death."

Naboth is to be framed and then killed in an act of judicially sanctioned murder. In what biblical scholar Alexander Rofé describes as "a kind of lynch law of ancient times," the law of the kingdom states that whoever curses God and the king is to be stoned to death for blasphemy and treason, with the traitor's possessions then forfeit to the crown. The moment Naboth is killed, then, his vineyard will be Ahab's. And it all seems easy enough for Jezebel to arrange. As Ahab's regent, the one who rules in his name while he is away on military campaigns, she uses his seal as a matter of course. Declaring a fast is a perfect ruse: a fast can be proclaimed in times of national crisis, along with a search for the sinners who have caused the crisis—a custom that will persist through to Talmudic times. Exactly what national crisis Jezebel uses as an excuse remains unclear, but Naboth is clearly to be the designated sinner.

The plot contains just enough plausible detail to mask its basic implausibility. It is, in many ways, an Iron Age version of the Whitewater affair of the 1990s, another real estate scandal blown up out of all proportion for political purposes. In the end, the Naboth story is as hard to swallow as the Whitewater one. As Rofé notes, "Jezebel reveals the whole plot in her letters to the notables, instead of secretly hiring false witnesses." His succinct comment: "Too overt a game!" Too overt by far, especially for someone as sophisticated in the ways of power as Jezebel. To expect all those nobles and elders, let alone the two perjurers, not to expose the plan—indeed to expect all of them to go along with it—stretches credulity, to say the least. In a small walled city like Jezreel, word would have been out instantly; there is no way the queen could have hoped to get away with it.

The real Jezebel would have scorned the whole clumsy scheme laid out by the Kings writers. Even if she was guilty as charged, she would have gone about the matter more skillfully. In fact she'd have been regally insulted at the very idea of such an absurd plot being attributed to her. You can all but hear her scoffing that this was the sort of thing only storytellers would imagine, and second-rate ones at that, fabulists who wanted to work their audience into a frenzy of booing and hissing the villain. Did they think she was an idiot, these scribes who wrote this story? Did they think she didn't know how to arrange matters with nobody any the wiser? Only a rank amateur in the exercise of power would go about things so transparently. There were so many better ways to get her hands on that piece of land, if that was indeed what she had in mind—if, that is, the very existence of this particular vineyard was not itself an invention. Violence was the least of the options. It would have been easier and far more elegant to produce forged papers, for instance, in which Naboth could be shown agreeing to sell the vineyard to Ahab, then reneging on his commitment and thus forfeiting the property in question. Why go so far as murder when a simple letter would do the trick? A queen as resourceful and sophisticated as Jezebel would know that the real exercise of power is never to overplay your hand.

But this kind of chicanery? This laborious and transparent pretense of legality with its involvement of "base fellows" and elders, nobles and judges? Jezebel would have been infuriated at the very idea that such ridiculous overplotting could be attributed to her. This was the woman who had called the bluff of the great prophet Elijah, who had declared, "If *you* are Elijah, *I* am Jezebel," and with her oath sent him running for his life, his fire and brimstone squelched, his faith in his own god shaken. Jezebel would certainly have been proud to be called ruthless, and expected nothing other than to be called arrogant. But never, ever foolish. And this plot as it was written was simply foolish. She would have seen instantly that the whole creaky mechanism of the episode of Naboth's vineyard was written as a means of setting her up for her eventual fall.

Foolish or not, the story served its purpose. The Kings authors had at last firmly established Jezebel as a murderer. They had dropped hints of her murderous nature before, but those hints were oddly ambiguous. During the account of the drought, we are told that she had "cut off" the priests of Yahweh, though it is unclear exactly when or how. The Hebrew word is *karat*, which is generally used as an antithesis to *yarash*, "possess," so that we still speak in English of someone being cut out of a will, or dispossessed. The same word, *karat*, is also used when a covenant or treaty is made, so that you would "cut" a treaty. In ancient Greek, Homer used the phrase *horkia tamnein*, literally "to cut oaths," and in modern English we still talk of "cutting a deal."

Originally, the cut was literal. The sign of the covenant between Yahweh and Israel was the cut of circumcision, with the solemnity of blood sealing the pact. You can see a faint echo of this in the way kids cut one another's fingers to make a blood pact, or draw a finger across the throat in a solemn oath as they intone, "Slit my throat, cross my heart, and hope to die." Such childhood rituals are pale reflections of an ancient practice referred to in Jeremiah, in which a treaty was sealed by having both parties walk between the two halves of a slaughtered animal. One immediately thinks of sculptor Damien Hirst's installations of divided animals—pigs and cows cut up into sections and then displayed in separate showcases so that viewers can literally walk between them. Hirst, the personification of the hypermodern, may be working in one of the most ancient traditions known.

In the ninth century B.C., then, you could both cut a treaty and cut someone out of one, which would seem to indicate that what Jezebel did when she "cut off" the priests of Yahweh who had criticized her was cut them off from official support. They'd have been cut off from the palace, from the city, from their jobs—cut off, that is, from the body politic. Yet just seven verses later, when the charge is repeated, the word *karat* is abruptly changed to *harag*, "killed," and we are suddenly asked to believe that Jezebel "killed the priests of Yahweh"—all but a hundred who had hidden away in caves.

The change of word seems to indicate a later editor, and a careless one, especially when you consider the strange paucity of detail. If Jezebel had indeed ordered all the Yahwist priests to be killed, it is hardly likely that such antagonistic chroniclers as the Kings authors would have passed up the opportunity to detail the massacre. They went to such trouble to show her murdering one man, Naboth; they would surely have expended far more ink on the murder of hundreds of priests, with the fullest possible detail of such sacrilegious horror. We would have been told of the blood and the screams, the public mourning and the national outrage. But though we are shown exactly when and where the Baalite priests are massacred, Jezebel's assumed massacre of the Yahwist priests is mentioned only in passing, and long after the presumed deed.

Most scholars conclude that even if she wanted to, Jezebel could not have ordered a massacre of the Yahwist priests and survived as queen—or survived at all, come to that. Besides, she was too expert in the exercise of power to allow herself so rash an in-

dulgence in vengeance. The primitive desire for blood and retribution had to be subordinated to the national interest, to a
pragmatic acknowledgment of reality. What was emotionally desirable was not necessarily—in fact was very rarely—politically
desirable.

Could she have given the order for all the priests of Yahweh to
be murdered? Most certainly. Did she? Almost certainly not.
Such an act would have been both self-defeating and out of character. The onetime insertion of that word *harag*, "killed," has to
be seen as an editorial afterthought, to prepare us for the judicial
murder of Naboth. But this time, every detail would be labori-
ously put in place. This time, the Kings authors would use bold
colors to paint Jezebel as the villain.

Improbably, the whole ornate vineyard scheme works. The elders
and nobles do precisely as they are told, and the "base fellows"
give their false testimony; Naboth is convicted of cursing God
and king, and is dragged out and stoned to death. In triumph,
Jezebel tells Ahab, "Get up and take possession of the vineyard of
Naboth."

The king is now fully implicated in Naboth's murder. Jezebel
may have been the one to take the initiative, but when Ahab goes
down to the vineyard to claim it, we realize that he has to have
known what his queen did. He has become an accessory after the
fact and is now a partner in evil—a silent partner, but nonetheless
guilty for that. So too are his subjects, not one of whom has dared
stand up to denounce what has happened, if indeed they know
about it at all. But the ultimate owner of the land does know about

it. How not? Naboth had invoked Yahweh as his reason for not selling the land, and so Yahweh himself now intervenes, instructing Elijah to go to Jezreel and confront Ahab.

So what if Elijah has already fled to Mount Sinai? Emotional logic rules this story, not rational logic. The prophet is still the man who defeated the priests of Baal, who brought down rain and demonstrated the power of his god. He is still the magus who can perform the impossible. No Yahwist will begrudge him this one last chance to prove his mettle, to redeem himself after his ignominious flight from Jezebel. So despite everything, we see him appearing one last time in Israel, splendid and terrifying in his resuscitated wrath.

The moment Elijah enters the vineyard, Ahab knows the game is up. The very appearance of the prophet is proof that the king's guilt is out. Elijah is no longer merely a "troubler of Israel" but something far more direct and far more personal.

"Have you found me, my enemy?" Ahab says. The Hebrew word he uses is *matza*, and it rings strong with double meaning: not just "to discover" but also "to uncover." What he is really saying is: "Have you found me out?"

Elijah brushes off the question with one of his own: "Have you murdered, and also taken possession?"

The phrase is just three words in Hebrew—*ha-ratzachta v-gam yarashta*—but these three words reverberate through the millennia to haunt Israel to this day. They are the words that came at the end of a letter written in 2005 to Prime Minister Ariel Sharon by a woman from one of the Gaza settlements he had ordered dismantled: "I want to ask you whether you are able to look me straight in the eye and tell me to leave my home, the same home where my son grew up until the age of eighteen, and give it as a gift to the murderers of my son. *Ha-ratʒachta v-gam yarashta*—have you murdered and also taken possession?"

As the writer intended, these ancient words would haunt Sharon to the extent that he kept the letter for weeks in his personal briefcase. They accused him of being another Ahab, of betraying the covenental bond between people, god, and land. Never mind that the logic did not quite hold up; the choice of the phrase was a kind of emotional blackmail, made possible only because the writer knew that Sharon was open to it. Inevitably, when Sharon suffered a massive stroke and went into a deep coma just a few months later, his fundamentalist critics—Christian as well as Jewish—would call it divine punishment for giving up land in Gaza.

Ahab, "incited by his wife Jezebel," had forgotten that all land was held in trust only by the grace of Yahweh. He had assumed the prerogative of real estate, or royal estate. This is why Jezebel is still remembered in modern Israel less for her supposed harlotry than as the foreign queen who murdered in order to steal land. This is the moral of every Israeli portrayal of the story, from Mattitiyahu Shoham's 1930 play *Tyre and Jerusalem*, which had a grand revival at the Jerusalem Theater in late 2004, to an anniversary pageant put on at Kibbutz Jezreel a couple of years earlier: be loyal to the land, never give it up, never let it go. The Naboth story is not merely religious; it is also nationalist. And in this it speaks directly to modern Israeli fears and insecurities. The land can never be taken for granted. It must always be defended.

The message reverberates on even the most mundane everyday level. In a country whose borders have been in dispute since its inception in 1948, it sometimes seems as if every Israeli homeowner is in some kind of dispute over real estate. It may be something as minor as objecting to neighbors closing in their balcony, or as sad as a grand old house standing empty, going to ruin as the heirs to the estate squabble over what to do with it and how to divide the eventual proceeds. It may be an argument over the exact location of a property line, or the right to pick lemons from a neighbor's tree overhanging a wall. But however small, it rankles. Real estate issues, even the most minor, are among the touchiest of subjects, reflecting the deep-rooted existential anxiety of the nation as a whole. The episode of Naboth's vineyard is an almost perfect expression of this.

Under the influence of Ahab and Jezebel, the ancient Israelites had begun to take the land for granted. The experience of Israel as a normal kingdom in peaceful, prosperous relations with surrounding kingdoms had lured them into forgetting the conditionality of the covenant. Prophet after prophet warned that they were being seduced by the physical solidity of the land into ignoring the precariousness of their claim to it. "Woe to those who are at ease in Zion, and to those who feel secure on the mountains of Samaria," Amos would write, and in clear reference to Ahab and Jezebel: "Woe to those who lie upon beds of ivory." You can never allow yourself the luxury of feeling at ease on the land. Be unfaithful to your god and his covenant, and the land will be forfeit. The ultimate landlessness—exile—awaits.

This is the real story of Kings: the anticipation, the experience, and eventually the memory of exile. In the words of Walter Brueggemann: "Kings is the history of landed Israel in the process of losing the land."

Jezebel and Ahab have been found out, their crime revealed. It is only biblically fitting that judgment now be passed in the very place they so coveted. In the vineyard that is the symbol of divine beneficence, among the vines laden with huge bunches of swollen grapes—fruit the same color as the spilled blood of Naboth— Elijah now speaks as the great defender of the Israelite trinity of people, god, and land. In the voice of Yahweh, he proclaims sentence.

"I will bring evil upon you, and destroy you," he tells Ahab. "In the place where the dogs lapped up the blood of Naboth, they will lap up Ahab's blood too."

But the king's death will not be enough to avenge the insult to Yahweh. Nor will the unpleasant idea of his blood shed in such abandon that dogs will crowd around to lap it up. Elijah's mission is to call down the end of the whole dynasty founded by Ahab's father, Omri, and to this end he reverts to the crude, vivid language of curse: "And I will cut off from Ahab every one that pisses against a wall."

The anatomical precision of that phrase "every one that pisses against a wall" is deliberate. It brings attention to the male genitals in order to emphasize that there will be no Omride "seed" left on the face of the earth. Every one of Ahab's male family members—sons, nephews, grandsons, any male related to him however remotely—will be killed, and the dynasty definitively wiped out of existence.

Even this mass death is not enough, however. There will be a second death after the first one, equally terrifying if not more so.

"Ahab's people who die in the city, the dogs will eat," Elijah continues, "and those that die in the fields, the fowls of the air shall eat."

Simple death is too good for them; they will not only die but become carrion. Their corpses are to suffer the further ignominy of being torn apart by predators, by the clasping talons of vultures and the sharp fangs of wolf-dogs. Worse still, they are condemned to the ancient horror of remaining unburied, their souls left to wander in restless pain for eternity. Even after death, they will suffer for Ahab's sins.

Within the framework of the Kings narrative, there is no doubt as to the power of this curse. The same fate has been proclaimed before against the descendants of two of Ahab's predecessors on the Israelite throne—King Jeroboam and King Baasha—and though both rulers died in their sleep, their descendants were indeed eventually massacred, and their corpses left as carrion. But this time, the feral wolf-dogs of the Kingdom of Israel are to feast more royally than ever before.

Elijah has been saving his full fury for last. His mission will be fulfilled only with the death of the woman whose presence in Israel brought him into being: his raison d'être, Jezebel. So now he draws himself up to his full height, splendid in his wrath, to unleash the utmost of his curses. This one is without precedent in the Bible; it is a death reserved especially for her. It is to be the prophet's revenge, his payback for Jezebel's having made him waver in his loyalty to Yahweh when he fled her wrath after the murder of her priests on Mount Carmel. He intends his awesome and terrifying judgment to strike abject fear into his enemy's heart. In his mind, it will haunt her days until the very moment it will be fulfilled, so that she will die the death he prophesies not just once but a thousand times and more in her imagination. In the ultimate horror, she may even be relieved when it finally comes to pass.

And so in the name of his god, Elijah passes sentence on his nemesis. In his final words before he disappears forever from Samaria, he proclaims the infamous *fatwa*: "And the dogs shall eat Jezebel by the walls of Jezreel."

Now he can leave, his work done.

6.

Sinai

in which Elijah rides a whirlwind

Mount Sinai is an imposing mass of jagged red granite in the southern Sinai desert, set off from the surrounding mountains not only by its height but by deep ravines. At the very top, a bolt of black volcanic rock thrusts up through the granite to form the peak of the mountain, known as Jebel Musa, Arabic for Moses' Peak. Stand here at sunrise, and it's as though you are at the highest point of a massive altar. With majestic slowness, the universe seems to reveal itself at your feet, range after range of mountains, until you have the entrancing illusion of being truly on top of the world.

Strange things happen in these high desert mountains. Strange tricks of the light, as when you walk along a narrow shaded defile and suddenly emerge into a deep red light that seems to infuse you with unearthly beauty. Strange tricks of the wind too. At times you swear you can hear the mountain breathing, even moaning. In the dry desert heat and the thin air of altitude, it's hard to tell what's real and what's in your mind. The slightest things—a sudden flight of three birds, a single ray of light shining through a gap in the rock—seem like omens. The mountain's reputation suffuses every moment you spend on it. It becomes, as Nikos Kazantzakis called it, "the God-trodden mountain."

From the third century A.D. on, Christian hermits seeking mystic revelation made their way here, each finding his own cave near the high mountain hollow just below the peak. The local Bedouin call it Farsh Elias, Elijah's Hollow, and it is the mountain's secret. You have no idea it's there until you suddenly emerge into it from a narrow track between towering rock faces. If Jebel Musa acts as the eyes of Mount Sinai, this cave-ridden hollow is its hidden heart.

Eventually there would be so many hermits here that the solitary life became impossible, and the hermits had no choice but to form a community at the foot of the mountain, known today as the monastery of Santa Katerina. But it's safe to assume that twelve centuries earlier, when Elijah fled here from Jezebel's fury, there was nobody else on the mountain.

The details of his flight are the stuff of legend. It took him forty days and forty nights to get here from Jezreel, echoing the forty days and nights Moses was said to have spent on the mountain. He was fed by angels as he had formerly been fed by ravens. He found shelter in one of the caves surrounding Farsh Elias, then climbed up to the summit, where Yahweh appeared in one of the most beautiful and mysterious passages in the whole of the Hebrew bible. In the unmatched musicality of the King James translation, it reads:

And behold the Lord passed by,
And a great and strong wind rent the mountains,
And broke the rocks into pieces,
But the Lord was not in the wind.
And after the wind an earthquake,
But the Lord was not in the earthquake.
And after the earthquake, a fire,
But the Lord was not in the fire.
And after the fire,
A still small voice.

It is the most extraordinary manifestation of the divine. Wind, earthquake, fire: all the manifestations of great natural power, and yet Yahweh chooses that "still, small voice." This moment of pure poetry—the essence, surely, of religious experience—calls up a sense of power so awesome that it supersedes the forces of nature, making them irrelevant by comparison. Even the literal translation evokes awe: that still, small voice is "a sound of thin silence"—the silence you find only in the remote heights of mountains, where the air is so pure that if you stand very still, it seems to ring in a high, numinous note that you know cannot possibly exist even as you hear it.

And then the still small voice speaks, and what it says is equally extraordinary, only not for its transcendental beauty. Quite the contrary. What makes it so extraordinary is its sheer colloquial familiarity.

Ma lecha po, Eliahu?—"What are you doing here, Elijah?"

It's an abrupt, no-nonsense tone of voice, the sort of thing a busy parent might say to a child who suddenly turns up at home when she should be in school. And indeed Elijah responds like a whining child who's been beaten up by schoolyard bullies, telling his father how unfair it all is because he's been so good and yet everyone has been picking on him:

"I have been very zealous for Yahweh the lord of hosts," he says, "for the children of Israel have forsaken your covenant and destroyed your altars and put your priests to the sword, and I, only I, am left, and they seek to take my life."

It is a patently exaggerated tale of woe, absurd with self-pity and its correlate, self-aggrandizement. No wonder Yahweh has little patience with his prophet. Elijah is not supposed to be here in the Sinai desert pouring out his heart in a one-to-one with God. He's supposed to be fighting the good fight up north in Israel. Instead, he's abandoned his post. He's gone AWOL—fled for his life in fear and panic, and left Jezebel triumphant. His fear is testimony to the power of her gods, the very gods he denounced and ridiculed on Mount Carmel. And it is testimony to her power too. Elijah has been unmanned by Jezebel. He is a failed prophet, and he knows it.

So does Yahweh. Like a corporate boss, he has no time for self-pity or failure. If you expect him to be understanding, to encourage Elijah and renew his confidence, to be a sentimental god who acts like a nurturing parent—you have the wrong god. Elijah may want a heartfelt tête-à-tête with Yahweh, but that's not what he gets. Yahweh is icy cold, all divine ruthlessness as he gives Elijah his orders:

"Go back by way of Damascus, and anoint Hazael as king of Aram. And anoint Jehu the son of Nimshi as king of Israel. And anoint Elisha the son of Shaphat of Abel Mehola as prophet instead of you. And whoever escapes the sword of Hazael will be slain by Jehu; and whoever escapes Jehu shall be slain by Elisha. And I will leave seven thousand alive in Israel—all those whose knees have not knelt to Baal, and all those whose mouths have not kissed him."

A bloodbath is clearly in the offing, but Elijah is too miserable to raise even a word of protest. He hears only one thing: "Anoint Elisha as prophet instead of you." His time is done, and he's being put out to pasture. Decommissioned. Recalled. Fired. He is of no use any longer to Yahweh. All he can do is pass on his prophetic mantle and die.

The whole scene, from the setting to the words used, is wonderfully high drama. There is just one rather major problem with it: the chronology is all wrong. In the sequence of the Kings account, this scene takes place *before* Elijah appears in Naboth's vineyard. Which means that he has already been fired by Yahweh when he pronounces his *fatwa* on Jezebel and Ahab. One moment he's done for; the next he's in full fighting form. How could this be?

The problem goes far beyond suspension of disbelief; the timeline just doesn't make sense. Not, that is, if we insist on being logical. But chronological sense is not necessarily emotional sense, as anyone knows who has ever told a well-practiced anecdote only to have someone who was there say, "No, that's not the way it happened, you've got it all wrong." Stories create their own dynamic. Details get rearranged; time, place, even the precise words said get subtly and sometimes not so subtly altered. We are not necessarily lying when we tell stories this way; rather, our memories have adapted to the demands of narrative. And the way they adapt is a function not only of the story itself but of the motives and circumstances of whoever is telling the story. We need to pause a moment here, then, and look at how the narrative we now know as Kings came into being.

To the modern reader, a book is a cohesive work written within a limited time frame by a single person, unless other authors are specifically named. When we think of the biblical books, we imagine either divine authorship or a single human author, presumably writing at the time of the events narrated. Yet decades of modern scholarship have shown that Kings was begun only in the early sixth century B.C., shortly before the Babylonian exile, and was finished at least some fifty years later, in exile, since that is where the narrative ends. To assume that it was entirely written earlier is rather like assuming that a first-person narrative by someone who gets killed at the end is true. You know it has to be a fiction, or the author couldn't have written the book. Not that author, in any case.

But this was only the first draft. Further drafts were made after the return from exile. They had to be, and the reason why was entirely practical. The texts of what would become the Bible were written on papyrus scrolls, and these scrolls deteriorated rapidly unless they were sealed and buried. The only way to preserve their contents was for scribes to copy them onto fresh papyrus, over and over, through the centuries. These copyist scribes were what scholars now refer to as the biblical editors.

Say the word "editor" today, and we think of someone concerned with bringing a manuscript together, editing it for style and consistency, accuracy and reliability. The phrase "biblical editors" seems to indicate a kind of ancient equivalent of the famed fact-checking department of *The New Yorker*. But the conditions under which they were working were very different. In fact they were any modern editor's nightmare. The physical problems alone were immense, since the papyrus scrolls were so unwieldy that it was difficult to unscroll them and check back for what had been said a few chapters or even a few verses before. The closest modern comparison to the way in which the biblical writers and editors worked might be that of someone writing a computer document consisting entirely of a single run-on paragraph, with no ability to either print out hard copy or scroll back and check what had already been written. The writer would have no option but to keep on going, relying on memory (influenced, as always, by imagination and emotion) and on reason (influenced, as so often, by politics and theology) to fill in the gaps. And thus, inevitably, ever larger gaps would be created.

To complicate matters, the scribes were working with a language still only partially developed for reading. All the things we take for granted as part of what makes writing readable, like paragraphs and quotation marks, did not exist in ancient Hebrew. Inevitably, each copyist had to exercise some degree of interpretation. And that degree of interpretation was widened by the fact that the author-editors lived in a different time and place from the one they were writing about. They were working not in the Kingdom of Israel, where most of the action of Kings takes place, but in the southern kingdom of Judea, hundreds of years later. None of them had ever been to the Kingdom of Israel. They couldn't have gone there even if they wanted to, since by the time they first committed ink to papyrus, the northern kingdom no longer existed; it had been swallowed up by the Assyrians, and most of its population had been transferred to other parts of the Assyrian empire to become the legendary "ten lost tribes of Israel." The fall of the northern kingdom was the object lesson for the southern Judeans who developed the Kings account. Exile—the nightmare of what could happen and indeed was about to happen in Judea—had already happened up north. Neglect Yahweh's word, and this was what lay in store. Allow the Jezebels of the world to influence you, and you would lose all identity. You would disappear into the proverbial mists of time.

Like most storytellers, then, the Kings scribes had an agenda. They were not independent historians but employees of the Jerusalem temple, consciously working on sacred texts that were central to the identity of the Judean nation. And these were indeed texts, not books, because books didn't exist then in the way they do now. These narratives were not something that could be picked up and read. Hardly anyone could read, let alone write, which is why a special class of professional scribes existed. The books of the Bible were originally written not to be read the way we read today, but to be recited out loud on ceremonial occasions, as the Torah still is in synagogues worldwide. Since the oral traditions they were based on were so strong, they didn't need to be consulted for information; their unwieldiness made them all but useless for that purpose anyway. The written word was not a means of communication but a sacred object in and of itself, intended to preserve, sanctify, and enshrine traditions of nation and identity. So with each consecutive copy, the scribes "improved" the text to bring it into line with their purposes.

The basis of Kings, often referred to in the text, is "the chronicles of the Kings of Israel," though no copy of this has ever been found. Assuming that it did indeed exist, it is only one of the multiple strands within Kings. Over the centuries, the scribal copiers expanded the narrative, dropping in whole sections such as the miracle tales about Elijah and his successor, Elisha, which bear the distinct signs of folk legend. They added in stand-alone chapters like the one on Ahab sparing the life of the king of Damascus, or the story of Naboth's vineyard, and because it was so difficult to scroll back to check the chronological flow of the narrative, they dropped them in where it seemed to them appropriate. They worked, that is, by intuition rather than by logic. Or rather, they used emotional logic.

None of this created any problem so far as the scribes were concerned. They weren't after consistency. That's a modern hobgoblin, one that constantly taunts the modern reader, especially when the most famed inconsistency in the Hebrew bible occurs right at the beginning, with the first two chapters of Genesis offering entirely different and mutually exclusive accounts of the creation of Adam and Eve: in the first chapter, at the same time on the sixth day of creation, and in the second, Eve out of Adam's rib in the Garden of Eden.

Kings reached the form we now know only in the third century B.C., when the Hebrew bible was translated into Greek and began to be canonized—set in stone, as it were. By then, it had taken on a kind of dream logic. Time is condensed or spaced out or even reversed. Geography expands or contracts at whim. What we know to be impossible takes place with the nonchalant certainty of fact. But none of this mattered. This was a narrative history of the relationship of the human to the divine, a testament to the trinity of god, people, and land. And it made its own demands.

The narrative demanded that Elijah not be defeated by Jezebel. It demanded that he have the last word, that he redeem his cowardice and fear, and that he impose the judgment of Yahweh on her. So the vineyard story was dropped in where it was by a later editor because this is where it made emotional sense. Elijah needed to emerge anew as the champion of justice and the defender of the covenant. Naboth's vineyard was his last chance, and thanks to the Kings authors, he used it splendidly. Now that he had earned his place in legend, he could pass on his prophetic mantle to Elisha, and die.

Elisha's name means "God saves." He is a man of some wealth, it would seem, since when Elijah finds him, he's plowing the fields of Abel Mehola with no fewer than twelve pair of oxen. We need to remember the tribal symbolism of that number twelve, however, because one look at Abel Mehola today and it's clear that no peasant farmer in this place could ever have become wealthy enough to own that many oxen.

My map showed the place just inside Palestinian territory, some twenty-five miles south of the Sea of Galilee in the heat-scorched Jordan Valley. But when I reached what I thought was the right spot, I could see nothing to indicate the birthplace of the second of Israel's two great militant prophets. I stopped at a roadside stand with little produce other than onions and browned bananas, but the Palestinians there merely shrugged when I asked about Abel Mehola. I understood their silence just a few miles farther on, when I saw a new road leading up to a massive yeshiva on a promontory overlooking the valley. The signpost read Mehola, and it was clearly a religious Israeli settlement—not a place local Palestinians were in any hurry to acknowledge.

The soldier assigned to guard the electronic metal gate to the settlement had no idea if it was built on the site of the ancient Abel Mehola. I suggested that maybe one of the settlers would know. He shrugged and opened the gate. "Good luck with them," he said, implying that I'd need it.

I drove past the yeshiva, which was still under construction. It was hard to imagine black-garbed yeshiva students here in the oppressive afternoon heat. The stark desert landscape felt hostile, as did my welcome at the settlement's grocery store, where I stopped to get a bottle of water and inquire again about Abel Mehola. "Why would you want to go there?" asked the proprietor, as though I had asked the way to a secret military installation.

"Isn't it the birthplace of the prophet Elisha? Where he was plowing with twelve pair of oxen when the prophet Elijah came and anointed him?"

He allowed himself to relax just a little. "Which way did you come from?" he asked.

"From the north."

He gave a slight sneer: "You passed it."

"Where?"

"North of here."

I finally managed to drag out enough information to pinpoint the spot, paid for my water, and left. As I drove off, the rearview mirror showed the proprietor standing outside the store, staring at the back of the car. I realized he was memorizing the license plate number.

When I finally saw the *tel*—easier to identify from the south than from the north, which is how I'd missed it—I could understand his suspicion a little better. Why indeed would anyone want to come here? It was a small, almost conical mound with just a bit of exploratory archaeological digging on the south side—enough to know that no luxurious palaces lay undiscovered here, and so no glory was to be gained from pursuing the dig. A few meager plantings of wheat and a half dozen fruit trees below the *tel* indicated fresh water, which turned out to be a small spring, barely more than a puddle, hard by a couple of ruined mud buildings. A hundred yards off was a Bedouin encampment with two long black tents but, oddly, not a soul to be seen. Everything to do with this place seemed to be shrouded in silence and suspicion.

Any farming here could only ever have been a marginal, hardscrabble business. There was hardly any arable land aside from the small patch where the Bedouin had pitched their tents. Yet the biblical writers' decision to make this Elisha's birthplace served their purpose well. A background as "a man of the people" was as useful to a prophet in biblical times as it is to a politician today, if just as questionable. As the Kings narrative continues, it becomes clear that Elisha could not have come from an impoverished village far from the centers of power; his contacts, his access, and his attitude all indicate someone of high social rank, born to influence. But image was as important in the first millennium B.C. as it is now, and the image of Elisha at the plow instantly establishes his role in the central covenantal unity of god, land, and people.

The account of what happened at Abel Mehola is almost abrupt. Elijah simply walks up to Elisha and throws his mantle over him—his cloak, that is, the one made from untanned animal skins, which serves as the symbol of his prophetic powers. We are left to assume that Elisha recognizes Elijah, that he is somehow prepared for this and knows that having a reeking animal hide thrown over his head is an honor that cannot be refused. He promptly bids his family farewell and sets out with Elijah on the prophetic road.

Sinai

One expects more of an anointing ritual, somehow: the use of scented oil, special prayers and invocations, a sense of occasion. This one seems oddly perfunctory, as though Elijah's heart isn't in it. But then you can hardly blame him. To be fired is bad enough, but to then have to anoint your own successor throws a whole handful of salt on the wound. In the event, this will be the only one of the three tasks assigned him on Mount Sinai that Elijah will actually carry out. The other two will be left to Elisha, since it's clear by now that the older man is no longer up to the job. He lacks the absolute ruthlessness that Elisha will display. There'll be no more prophetic breast-beating and whining. Yahweh wants a man of action, and Elisha fits the bill.

The first mission of the newly anointed prophet is to act as witness to the death of his predecessor and, by so doing, to inherit his powers. The two men travel together down the Jordan Valley to Jericho. At three stages of their journey, Elijah tells Elisha to let him go on alone to meet his death, and three times Elisha replies: "As Yahweh lives and as your soul lives, I will not leave you."

It is a profession of loyalty and devotion, to be sure, and yet one can't help thinking that Elisha protests too much. Could he be sticking so close to Elijah's side because he wants to make absolutely sure that the older man does indeed die, leaving the field clear for him?

In Jericho, they meet up with fifty "sons of the prophets"—antiroyalist priests who have found refuge in the cliffs above the town—and go on down to the River Jordan. There, Elijah strikes the surface with his mantle and the water parts, just as it had for Moses at the Red Sea. He and Elisha then leave the sons of the prophets behind and walk across to the other side on dry land.

In fact the use of the mantle to part the waters is purely demonstrative, since there were plenty of fordable places across the Jordan. Moreover, there was no compelling reason for the two men to cross the river; in fact there was every reason not to, since the far side of the Jordan at Jericho was as barren then as it is now. But this is the classic stuff of master and disciple crossing to "the other side" so that divine mysteries can be imparted. The gift of the magus is being transferred from one man to another, and in that same mystical tradition, the older man has one last bequest for the younger. "What can I do for you before I am taken from you?" he says.

Elisha replies with none of the modesty one might expect in such circumstances. He expresses no desire to die instead of Elijah, makes no declaration that simply having been in Elijah's presence has been gift enough. On the contrary, he is all ambition. "May your spirit be doubled in me," he replies.

This could be his way of asking Elijah to regard him as his son, since, under traditional rights of inheritance, a double portion is given to the firstborn son. But it could also be pure ambition: Elisha wants to be twice as powerful as his predecessor, and Elijah clearly understands him this way. "What you ask is difficult," he says, "but if you see me when I am taken from you, it will be so, and if not, it will not be."

But of course the whole point of the story is that Elisha does indeed see what takes place next. He is the privileged observer, the only one to witness what happens as a chariot of fire appears out of nowhere, drawn by horses of fire. Without another word, Elijah steps up into the chariot, and a whirlwind descends from the sky and envelops him, carrying prophet, chariot, horses, and fire up into heaven.

Elisha cries out in awe at the sight: "My father, my father—the chariot of Israel and its horses!" We don't know if "father" refers to Yahweh or to Elijah, but the rest of the exclamation was most likely familiar to Israelites as a charioteer's war cry. Elisha now becomes the new warrior of Yahweh. Having witnessed Elijah at the moment he is "taken," he takes over his role as the great defender of the faith. He picks up Elijah's mantle, which the whirlwind has conveniently dropped to the ground, returns to the river, and in full view of the fifty sons of the prophets waiting on the other side, strikes the water with the mantle as Elijah had done. The water parts as it had for Elijah, proving that the prophetic mantle is now Elisha's to command. Fifty witnesses hasten to testify to this. "The spirit of Elijah rests on Elisha," they say, and bow down at his feet. The transfer of power has been accomplished.

The story bears all the signs of mystical legend. Elisha's thrice-repeated oath of devotion to Elijah, the Moses-like parting of the waters, the crossing to "the other side," the chariot of fire, the whirlwind carrying Elijah upward—all these indicate a mystic transformation. Elijah is borne upward into the realm of spirit, leaving no body behind. His ascendance is transcendence, and his chariot of fire is so powerful in the imagination that it will eventually inspire the whole school of kabbalah known as *merkaba* (chariot) mysticism. He has been transformed from prophet into eternal hero, and his story is now fully in the universal tradition traced by Joseph Campbell in *The Hero with a Thousand Faces*. Uncertain origins, trials and wanderings, victory, despair, transformation into spirit—all are the phases in his struggle against Jezebel and her gods.

To ask what really happened at the Jordan River, then, is rather like asking what really happened in the Garden of Eden. The rational mind concludes that Elijah died on Mount Sinai, when he was decommissioned. A more devious rational mind might even suspect that if he did survive Sinai and meet up with Elisha, the younger man killed the older one and buried him on the far side of the Jordan in order to usurp his prophetic mantle. But the story has nothing to do with reason or logic. Elijah's death firmly establishes him as the second great hero of the covenant, standing squarely in the footsteps of Moses. Both men died within sight of their goal, but neither would see it accomplished. The hero is, after all, a tragic figure: he has to die on the brink of success.

Moses died on Mount Nebo, fifteen miles south of the spot where Elijah would ascend in the whirlwind. He died within sight of the promised land of Canaan, but was never to set foot there. Why so near and yet so far? Rabbinical tradition has it that he could not be allowed to tread on Canaanite soil because he had known what it was to live in slavery in Egypt, and so was disqualified from entering the land as a free man. By the same reasoning, the Israelites had no choice but to wander in the wilderness for forty years; the generations that had known slavery had to die off so that only those untainted by it could enter the new land promised under the covenant. And now Elijah was similarly tainted— not by slavery but by his contact with his arch-enemy Jezebel. The very fact that he had experienced awe and trembling when she swore by her gods meant that he was compromised. By fleeing from Jezebel's oath, he had succumbed to her power. Though he was allowed to declare the *fatwa* on her, he would not be allowed to live to see it carried out.

Elisha, on the other hand, is untainted. He has never laid eyes on Jezebel. He has never encountered her, and he never will. Even though he will devote himself to her destruction as surely as if he himself were the one to throw her to the dogs, he will never even utter her name, as though the very fact of its passing his lips could compromise him. Only absolute purity—ruthless absolutism—can fulfill the *fatwa*.

Elisha thus becomes a new, improved version of Elijah: younger, more virile, not "unmanned" by Jezebel or by any contact with her. If he can control twelve yoke of oxen, he can control their symbolic counterpart, Israel. In fact one could think of him not as a separate person at all, but as a second manifestation of Elijah, transformed by the encounter with Yahweh on Mount Sinai and reincarnated in the form of a younger man to serve as an effective instrument of divine vengeance.

The Kings authors waste no time making it very clear just how effective Elisha can be. The moment he crosses back over the Jordan River and is hailed as the inheritor of the spirit of Elijah, he performs two miracles designed to illustrate his power. The first is a classic miracle story. The spring of Jericho has become tainted, and the town will be uninhabitable unless the water can be purified. The townspeople appeal to Elisha to "heal the water," and he does so, giving life back to the town. The spring is still known as Elisha's Spring and is still the main source of the city's water supply—a vaulted stone-lined holding basin, newly enclosed and roofed, close by the remains of ancient Jericho. Inside, the air is cool and sweet-smelling. You can lean over the railing and watch the water bubbling up between the rocks at the bottom of the basin; it seems to have a life of its own, making real the ancient Hebrew phrase *mayim haim*, "living water."

But what Elisha does next is not quite so classic a miracle story. In fact it is downright disturbing. It is not a gift of life but a punishment of death. And for the most trivial of reasons: vanity.

The new prophet, it turns out, is bald. We tend to imagine Hebrew prophets in the mold of Elijah, with a leonine mane of hair, especially since long hair was the sign of the warrior. The very idea of a bald prophet seems incongruous, and it evidently seemed as incongruous in ancient times as it does now, because once he's restored Jericho's drinking water and set out on the road, Elisha encounters a group of boys who, being boys, can't resist taunting him for his lack of a prophetic mane.

"Rise up thou bald one, rise up thou bald one," they shout, or at least so most translations have it. What they really say—*aleh kareach*—is "Up, baldhead," which is as close as you can come in ancient Hebrew to a sneering "Yah, baldy!"

One might think that a newly confirmed prophet would have the confidence, let alone the love of his people, to smile indulgently at a gaggle of unruly kids. Not so. Elisha's sense of prophetic dignity will not tolerate the slightest deviation from all-out reverence, let alone such flagrant disrespect. He curses the boys in the name of Yahweh, and calls into being two bears to attack and tear them to pieces, all forty-two of them.

The whole thing happens almost casually, in just a couple of verses, followed by: "And he went from there to Mount Carmel, and then on to Samaria." It's as though killing forty-two children—Israelite children, his own people—is merely a minor incident on the road, hardly worth mentioning if it weren't proof of his magical powers. The coldest, most horrifying proof.

Yet the story is chillingly effective. If Elisha is capable of casually punishing childish teasing this way, there can be no doubt what he will be capable of when it comes to people he really detests. We are at a new level of ruthlessness. Elijah may have issued *fatwas*; Elisha will execute them.

7.

Damascus

in which Ahab fights his last battle

Iranian imams did not invent the religious ruling known in Arabic as the *fatwa*, made infamous by the one placed on novelist Salman Rushdie by Ayatollah Khomeini on St. Valentine's Day 1989. It existed in ancient Israel too, and as in modern Islam, once such a religious ruling was pronounced, it became infused with the aura of divine inevitability.

Jezebel was fully aware of this. But if Elijah had hoped for nothing but nightmares for her, he would have been badly disappointed. Anyone else might have been dogged by visions of wolves ripping their body limb from limb, of their blood pouring on the ground as feral creatures snarled and drooled and fought one another for the choicest morsels of flesh, so it would have been inconceivable to Elijah that Jezebel not quake at the idea of being singled out for annihilation in this ghastly way. Some part of her, in spite of herself, would be sure to fear the wrath of Yahweh. But the tragedy of these two great antagonists is that they were fated to consistently underestimate each other. Just as Jezebel's conviction and arrogance had not allowed her to take the full measure of Elijah's power, so his own conviction and arrogance prevented him from taking the full measure of hers. So clear an attempt to intimidate her—to bully her into cowering submission—could only fail.

Jezebel must have read Elijah's threat as crude rather than terrifying—and as such, downright pitiful. To be eaten by dogs when she was under the protection of Gula, who guarded the portals of death in the form of a giant mastiff? The very idea was so absurd that it was barely worth a second thought. It was merely another blast of rhetoric from an unruly prophet so carried away with his own words that they ceased to have any meaning.

That Elijah wished for her death, let alone by such grisly means, could have come as no surprise. As queen, Jezebel may have expected adoration, but she knew that hatred came with the territory. It was part of the equation of power, something to be handled and dealt with expediently, not to be taken personally. If she even deigned to register Elijah's words as a threat to her life, she'd have shrugged it off. So far as she was concerned, he was merely a troublemaker, and no match for her.

Was this arrogance on her part? Undoubtedly. There was no way to be a ruler in the ancient Middle East—or at any time and in any place, in fact—without at least a solid streak of arrogance. Then as now, humility was not part of the conceptual language of power. Nor, by the evidence of the Kings accounts of Elijah and his successor Elisha, was it part of the job description of an Israelite prophet. If arrogance was to be held against Jezebel and not against her opponents, then one can only conclude that she alone should be singled out for condemnation because she had three counts against her: as a powerful woman, a foreigner, and a polytheist, she was an all but irresistible target for the Yahwist scribes who would write her story.

Yet the fatal judgment most certainly did register with Jezebel, and affected her deeply: she did not fear for her own life, but for her husband. We are told that when Ahab heard those terrible words pronounced by Elijah in the vineyard, "he rent his clothes, and put on sackcloth, and fasted." And this time, there was nothing Jezebel could do to help. It may have been easy enough for her to shrug off the *fatwa*—Elijah's god was not hers, and so she could not conceive of his having any power over her—but Ahab had no such psychological immunity.

The shadow of Elijah's words darkened every moment of Ahab's life. How not, when his death had been wished for by his own god? Ahab tolerated other faiths for pragmatic reasons, but only his faith in Yahweh could have sent him into such remorse. This did not mean, however, that he renounced what the Yahwists saw as the error of his ways. A less brave man would certainly have knuckled under to the divine threat to his life, but Ahab had lived his whole life with the constant awareness of death. And he was, despite the Kings portrayal of him, a man of principle. Even as he renewed his commitment to Yahweh through sackcloth and fasting, he held firm to his pragmatic policies of tolerance and alliance. As a consequence, he became a divided man, torn more than ever between Yahwist purism on the one hand and rational leadership on the other, and the rift between the two sent him spiraling down into despair. For this reason alone, Elijah's words weighed heavy on Jezebel, and all the heavier when, inevitably, Ahab did indeed die.

It was to be a hero's death, in the heat of battle. And though the arrow that would deliver the fatal wound was fired far from home, it was unnervingly close, in retrospect, to Elijah's birthplace.

What was once the fortress of Ramot Gilead—the Heights of Gilead—is now a low mound to the east of the northern Jordanian city of Irbid, fifteen miles from Listib. Its wide, raised-earth ramparts now host nothing more than a herd of black goats, and behind them only a jumble of half-buried stones remain in testimony to all the blood shed here. But as soon as you stand on top of the mound, you see why this place was so strategically important: it is at the center of a high plain stretching for miles around, and when you're at the center of a plain, even the smallest rise creates a major strategic advantage, especially when you are right on the King's Highway, the main trade route south from Damascus to the Red Sea.

When Ahab spared the life of the Damascus king Ben-Hadad, the treaty he concluded assured continued Israelite control of Ramot Gilead. But this was to be only one phase of a hundred-year war between the two states for the stronghold. No treaty could last long in this time and this place, and this one would end with the death of the aging Ben-Hadad. His son succeeded him, taking the title of Ben-Hadad II, and immediately abrogated his father's treaty with Ahab. Seething with resentment at his father's agreement to cede such a vital fortress, the new king attacked Ramot Gilead. Damascus and Israel were at war once again.

It has to have been a severe blow for Ahab. The treaty with the elder Ben-Hadad had been a cornerstone of his foreign policy. He had taken immeasurable grief from Elijah and his supporters because of it, flouting the law of *herem* by honoring Ben-Hadad instead of sacrificing him, and insisting on cordial relations with Damascus for the sake of his kingdom's long-term well-being. With that treaty in place, he had even taken steps to heal the rift with the southern kingdom of Judea, moving toward a reunited kingdom by arranging the marriage of Athaliah, his daughter by Jezebel, to the heir to the Judean throne. Just as Jezebel's own marriage had sealed an alliance, so too would her daughter's; and just as Jezebel's son would soon become king of Israel, so her daughter's son would soon become king of Judea. The marriage was both a brilliant political move and a strategic military one, since the new alliance of the two kingdoms included a mutual defense pact. Now Ahab invoked that pact, and called on the Judean king Jehoshaphat to help him retake Ramot Gilead.

As the joint force prepared for action, the two kings called on their priests to give Yahweh's blessing for battle. Ahab's court priests consulted their oracles—the intestines of sacrificed animals, the positions of the stars, the colors of the sunrise—and assured him that all the omens were in place for victory. "Go up to Ramot Gilead and prosper," they said, "for Yahweh will deliver it into your hand." But when it came to the Judean priests, Ahab was dismayed to see that they were led by Micaiah, one of the "sons of the prophets" who supported Elijah and Elisha. "He will not prophesy good for me, only evil," Ahab exclaimed. And he was right.

At first, Micaiah repeated what Ahab's priests had said: "Go up to Ramot Gilead and prosper." But Ahab could tell when someone was merely feeding him what they thought he wanted to hear. "How many times do I have to make you swear that you will tell me only the truth in the name of Yahweh?" he said in exasperation.

So now came the truth. "Yahweh has put a lying spirit in the mouths of all your priests," said Micaiah. "Yahweh has spoken evil of you."

Such a strong prophecy against battle would normally have deterred any king. But national security was at stake here, and besides, this warning came from a man Ahab knew wanted nothing more than to subvert his rule. He tried calling Micaiah's bluff, threatening to have him thrown into prison on a diet of bread and water as a hostage against ill fortune "until I return in peace," but Micaiah stood firm: "If you return at all in peace, Yahweh has not spoken through me."

Trapped between the rock of his fear of Yahweh and the hard place of his kingdom's security, Ahab chose as any great warrior would, and gave the signal to attack. Yet Micaiah's words had clearly unsettled him, because instead of going into battle with the royal banner flying high over his chariot, he went without his usual insignia, disguised as a regular charioteer. So when that arrow struck him "between the lower armor and the breastplate," it could not have been intended specifically for him. It was a stray arrow strung and fired by an enemy archer "in innocence," as Kings puts it—without knowing if anyone at all would be hit by it, let alone who.

You could call this inevitable. A man can fight only so many battles until sooner or later—and in Ahab's case later, after a nineteen-year reign—an arrow finds its way home, slipping under the armpit or into the waist at the moment when an arm is raised, and penetrating the vulnerable inch or two of suddenly unprotected flesh. But so far as Ahab's Yahwist enemies were concerned, it was the fulfillment of Elijah's curse on him. As they would tell it, there was nothing chance about this arrow's flight. A rationalist might call it a random act of war; someone who believes that every bullet has a number on it would call it the fickle finger of fate; but a believer would call it the harsh hand of Yahweh, imposing retribution.

There is no doubt that Ahab knew his injury was fatal. A lesser man would have collapsed and had himself taken away from the battlefield, but the king insisted on staying. He bundled a robe against his side to hide the arrow and stanch the flow of blood, then ordered his aides to prop him upright in his chariot so that his men could see him and not be discouraged. He remained this way until the battle was won, and only then, as darkness fell and his troops retook control of Ramot Gilead, did he allow himself to give in to death. "And the blood ran out of the wound into the bottom of the chariot." Ahab died as he had lived, displaying courage, fortitude, and leadership.

It must have been a long journey back to Samaria for his aides, bearing the body of a commander and ruler they loved and respected. Yet the Kings authors give no details of how the kingdom reacted to Ahab's death, let alone of his funeral. Instead, they focus on the blood-soaked chariot. We are told that it was "washed by the pool, and the dogs lapped up Ahab's blood, and the harlots bathed in the water as Yahweh had said."

The choice of details is careful and deliberate. The bloody chariot stands in striking contrast to the chariot of fire that carried Elijah up to heaven. The dogs lapping up Ahab's blood are forerunners of the dogs that will tear Jezebel apart. And those harlots? The Kings authors were clearly improving on their god, since Yahweh had never said a word about harlots bathing in Ahab's blood; instead, what we have here is another outrageous instance of biblical wordplay.

The Hebrew for "prostitutes" is *zonot*, and as John Gray points out in his commentary on Kings, it is most probably a deliberate contraction of the original word *ziyunut*, meaning "weapons" or "armor." Indeed, the Hebrew phrasing makes far better grammatical sense when read not as "the harlots bathed" but as "his weapons were washed." It makes far better historical sense too, since Ahab's servants would have cleaned his swords to be buried alongside him. In all probability, the weapons were transformed into prostitutes not by the original authors but by a later editor offended at having to record the heroic death of this "most evil of all the kings of Israel" and thus seizing the opportunity to take one last dig at Ahab. Since the Yahwist view was that Ahab had prostituted himself to false gods by marrying Jezebel and tolerating Baalite worship, so in death his companions would be dogs and harlots—the very figures that will play such pivotal roles in the impending account of Jezebel's own death.

As she stood at the main gate of Samaria to receive the body of her slain husband, her face set in the regal mask of ceremony, Jezebel surely cursed this land. Her marriage had been a rare thing by the lights of her time—a true partnership, despite the antagonism of Elijah and his supporters. She knew they had to be rejoicing at Ahab's death, and the very thought of their joy served to increase her bitterness.

She was in her mid-thirties now. Even more striking, perhaps, than when she was a teenager. Her features had become aquiline, no longer softened by youth. Her nose was sharper and more aristocratic, her lips thinner, her kohl-rimmed eyes heavier and deeper set. From one moment to the next those eyes could still flash with anger or go black with brooding, but now there was a hardness in them that hadn't been there before. You might almost call it defiance if that hadn't implied a recognition of some other authority to defy. It was the hardness of the place, perhaps, of the stone and dust of this landlocked kingdom far from the mild Phoenician coast, as though the stone had found its way into her soul just as it had found its way into the souls of the militant prophets.

You'd have to be able to look past the regal mask to see the pain in her eyes, the buried longing for what was once home and was no longer. There was no going back for her, not now. Her father, King Ithbaal, had died six years before, and her stepbrother had taken over the throne of Tyre. She no longer had any place there—only here, in the place that had finally claimed her husband's life.

"A land that devours its inhabitants" is how Moses' scouts would describe this country in Numbers. But Jezebel was not to be devoured. Not yet.

As she began the process of shepherding Ahab's body into the next life, she could feel the power of Gula watching over her, protecting her in this no-man's-land of bereavement, where life and death meet. She ordered a full week of public mourning, and as the ritual wailing and keening began, she supervised the priests as they washed the body and oiled it, covered it with myrrh and balsam and spices, then wrapped it tightly in shrouds. She walked before the bier as Ahab was carried in ceremony to the deep-cut rock tomb of the kings of Samaria, and stood unflinching as he was laid beside the remains of his father, Omri. She watched as jars of wine and grains were placed beside him to feed his spirit on the long journey into the next world, and bent her head in acknowledgment as one by one, his arms—his exquisitely decorated Phoenician swords and daggers with their gem-studded hilts—were interred along with him, each one ritually bent and "killed" before being laid on his chest. She stood tall and stone-faced as the chants of the funerary ritual rang out inside the tomb:

You have been called, O Ahab,
You have been summoned.
O throne of Ahab, be wept for,
Shed tears over his footstool.
Into the earth descend,
Into dust be lowered.
Desolation, and desolation of desolations!

And then, when the heavy stone door to the tomb was sealed again and not even Ahab's body remained with her, she gave herself over to the self-abasement of mourning.

When Baal was killed by his half-brother Mot in the epic *Baal Cycle* of poems, his sister Anat "drank tears like wine." And to help the flow of tears, she raked her face and arms and breasts with a knife until blood flowed alongside the tears—the ritual of mourning that was acted out by the Baalite priests on Mount Carmel as they called on their god to stop the drought and bring rain. Men usually performed this ritual, not women, but what did a great goddess care for such distinctions? Anat purposely overstepped the bounds, and so now did Jezebel. Like the warrior goddess, she slashed herself with a knife till the blood ran down her face and her neck, over her breasts and her arms. She gave voice to the pain inside her with pain on the surface. Blood for blood, her life's blood for Ahab's.

For the full week of mourning, she went without her face powders and rouges and kohl and eye shadows. She put aside her silks and fine linens, her embroidered robes and heavy jewelry, and wore instead a coarse-woven hemp shift—the sackcloth of mourning. She forbade her servants to dress her hair, and heaped dust on her head until it was a Medusa's nest of grayed tangles. She wailed and keened in grief, allowing the heavy pain inside her to move up through her body and into her throat, to emerge in the long, piercing, spine-chilling moan that humans make if they allow themselves to, the sound of a creature in mortal pain, utterly eerie and terrifying.

If these sounds that came out of her were unrecognizable, so be it. If for the duration of this one week she forewent the calm, regal, impassive mask of the queen, so be it. The mask would be all the more impressive once she resumed it. There was important work to be done first. Nearly three millennia later, Sigmund Freud would call it "the work of mourning," and work it is—exhausting, draining, all-consuming, as though not just the heart but the whole body is dissolving into grief. Jezebel expected no less from herself. Nor did her court or the Israelite people. This was the ritual, and if it seems to lack dignity to the modern eye, that was precisely the point. It was a deliberate accession to grief, a willed surrender of self-control so that the pain could be fully experienced until the mourner, bereft even of tears, was ready to stand and again assume the responsibilities of everyday life.

And so Jezebel mourned, and the whole court mourned with

her. For seven full days and nights, mourning was the only business of the royal palace of Samaria.

Outside the acropolis, life was subdued. If anyone in the city believed that Ahab's death was the fulfillment of Elijah's *fatwa,* none dared say so. At least not in public. But mourning was not the only reason for the pall that fell over everyday life. Ahab had ruled for nineteen years, and those were years in which the kingdom was at the height of its power and prosperity. He had decisively defeated Damascus not once, but twice. But when a strong king dies suddenly, the future becomes uncertain for his subjects. There was fear mixed in with the grief—fear of a coup d'état that would send the whole kingdom into a tailspin of insecurity and turmoil, even anarchy. Fear too that at the least whiff of weakness, Damascus would attack again, and this time, without the strong leadership of Ahab, do so successfully.

But as Jezebel saw it, to succumb to this fear was to ignore the whole point of the *Baal Cycle.* Out of death would come renewal. In the great fertility paradigm, Anat revenged herself on the murderous Mot by cutting him into pieces, then winnowing and grinding him, and finally sowing him in the ground in order to bring Baal back to life. Just as Jezebel had mourned like Anat, so she would now move into action like the goddess and ensure that the cycle continue. Mourning the deceased king went hand in hand with crowning his living successor. Jezebel's task was to ensure that her elder son take the throne in an orderly succession of power, and so on the eighth day, the chant rang loud and clear throughout the palace:

Well-being for Ahab,
Well-being for his house.

Well-being for Israel,
Well-being for her gates.

The king was dead—long live the king! Jezebel's son was crowned, and the order given to the whole city to rejoice in acclamation.

Jezebel was no longer the queen consort, but that did not mean she was diminished in status. On the contrary, she took on a still more powerful role. She was now the queen mother, with the title of Great Lady or *gevira*—the feminine form of *gevir*, meaning "master," from which comes *gevirut*, "manhood." Her sexual role as mother of the heirs to the throne was now formally behind her; in her new postsexual role, as the title of *gevira* suggests, she abandoned her femaleness and took on maleness to become the protector of the throne, the one who ensured the continuation and well-being of the dynasty.

The position of queen mother was nothing like the merely decorative one still recognized in the British monarchy. In fact it was a feared and respected institution throughout the Middle East. In fifteenth-century B.C. Egypt, for instance, the cult of Hatshepsut, the best-known female pharaoh, was nearly as great as that of her husband Thutmose II. After his death, she reigned as regent for her stepson Thutmose III, who was still a minor, but even when he came of age, she dominated him and ruled as "co-regent" for twenty-one years—years in which she gradually abandoned the titles and insignia of a queen and adopted those of a king, which is why sculptures of the time show her bearded and dressed like a man, and why her titles included "Son of Re," "Lord of the Two Lands," and "King of Upper and Lower Egypt."

To the north, several Phoenician clay tablets show that queen mothers wielded great economic power from at least the fourteenth century through the eighth century B.C. Unlike ordinary women, they could own, buy, and sell real estate—a fact that may well have provided the basis for the story of Jezebel's alleged murderous dealings over Naboth's vineyard. Where everyone else bowed down to the king, the king bowed down to the queen mother, addressing her as *adat,* the feminine form of *adon* or "lord." If her son was still a minor, she acted as the regent, ruling in his stead, but even when the king was adult, she took precedence. And not only in Phoenicia. When King David ruled in Jerusalem and Bathsheba was the queen consort, Kings shows her visiting her husband and bowing down to him, but with the death of David and her elevation to the role of queen mother, the balance of power shifts: her son, King Solomon, bows down to her, and seats her at his right hand.

To the east, the queen mothers of the powerful Assyrian empire were legendary. Semiramis, for instance, would later be portrayed as a warrior queen who killed her paramours after one night of love so that they would have no sway over her. But once more, a powerful woman's supposedly voracious sexuality is a distortion of historical reality. The real Semiramis was the late-ninth-century B.C. queen Samur-Amat, who became regent after her husband Shamsi-Hadad's death and ruled firmly but wisely for five years until her son came of age to assume the throne. A century later, Naqia-Zakutu would become still more influential as queen mother. After the death of her husband King Sennacherib, she would seize the throne for her son despite the fact that he was not the firstborn son nor she the senior wife, and when he died, she again intervened to secure the throne for the last great Assyrian king, Ashurbanipal, whose library in Nineveh was to become the main source for texts of the Epic of Gilgamesh.

This was the tradition into which Jezebel now stepped. As queen mother, she would be the guardian of Ahab's legacy—of his policies as well as his sons. But she can have had no illusions about just how hard this task would be. With Ahab's death, his enemies—and hers—had been empowered, and her two sons had neither the wisdom nor the courage of their father. When Ahab came to the throne, he had not only inherited his father's power but also built on it; now that it was his sons' turn, they would whittle it away. And in the one place that would matter most, the battlefield, Jezebel was powerless to help. The spirit of the warrior Anat may have been strong in her, but even she was bound by the conventions of her time.

Just a year after being crowned, Jezebel's elder son fell from a second-story balcony—the kind of fall that one suspects was aided by a strong push—and died of his injuries. Though the queen mother quickly had her younger son Joram proclaimed king, the scent of weakness was out, and the first to exploit it was the Kingdom of Moab. Conquered by Omri and kept strictly in line by Ahab, the desert kingdom across the Dead Sea from Judea now surged up in full-scale rebellion against Israel.

One version of this rebellion is told on the Mesha Stele, the densely inscribed basalt stone from the former Moabite capital of Dhiban that is the longest ninth-century B.C. text found so far. It records the exploits of Moab's King Mesha, focusing on the role of his god Chemosh in expelling the Israelites from his land. "I am Mesha, son of Chemosh-Yat king of Moab, the Dibhanite," it reads. "My father was king over Moab for thirty years, and I became king after my father . . . Omri King of Israel oppressed Moab many days, for Chemosh was angry with his land. His successor said, I will oppress Moab. In my days he said it . . .

"Chemosh said to me, Go take Nebo from Israel. So I went by night, and fought from break of dawn till noon, and took it and slew all in it, seven thousand men and women, natives and aliens and female slaves, for I had dedicated it to Ishtar-Chemosh. I took from there the vessels of Yahweh and dragged them before Chemosh . . . I saw my desire upon the House of Omri, and Israel perished utterly for ever."

Well, not quite. Like modern rulers, ancient ones tended to exaggerate their accomplishments, especially when they were being chiseled for eternity onto stone tablets. The Kingdom of Israel did not "perish forever" due to Mesha's rebellion; that would happen more than a hundred years later, and the agents of absolute destruction would be the Assyrians. But Mesha did indeed drive Israel out of Moab. Even the Kings authors ceded the point, but as they would have it, this was only because Mesha cheated.

The Kings account of what happened starts when King Joram follows his father's example by calling on Judea to form a joint military campaign, this time against Moab. Judea's elderly King Jehoshaphat agrees, not the least because Moab is right on his doorstep, as it were, just across the Dead Sea. But when the time arrives for the priestly blessing before battle, Jehoshaphat insists on calling on no less a figure than the prophet Elisha, who makes no secret of his antagonism toward Joram.

"What have I to do with you?" Elisha tells the Israelite king. "Go to your father's priests and your mother's priests"—to Jezebel's priests of Baal, that is, and the Yahwist priests of the Samarian court—"for as Yahweh lives, before whom I stand, I would neither look at you nor see you if it were not for the presence of the king of Judea."

The insult is immense. What Elisha is basically saying is "Go run to your mommy and daddy." It is a measure of the awe in which prophets were held that Elisha could speak this way to King Joram and not be killed on the spot. Or more likely, it's a measure of Joram's weakness. Yet despite his palpable loathing of the new king, Elisha gives the all-important prophetic thumbs-up. "Yahweh will deliver the Moabites into your hands," he says. "And you will smite every fortified city, and fell every good tree, and stop up all the springs, and spoil every good piece of land."

If Ahab had heard this from Elisha, he would have been as suspicious as he was when he heard Micaiah's optimistic prophecy before the fatal battle of Ramot Gilead. But King Joram has none of his father's wisdom. He hears what he wants to hear, and gives the order to march into Moab, where indeed all seems to go as Elisha had said. Cities fall, trees are cut down, springs are stopped up. Victory seems inevitable. But then comes Mesha's masterstroke, at least according to Kings. On the point of absolute defeat, the Moabite king "took his eldest son, the heir to his throne, and sacrificed him as a burnt offering on the wall of his city. And a great dismay came over the Israelite forces, and they ceased their attack and returned home."

The retreat in "great dismay" is presented as a matter of ceding to the inevitable—in this case, the dominant power of the Moabite god Chemosh on his own territory. When Chemosh accepts such a terrible sacrifice, the Israelites recognize that he will ensure their defeat, and they acknowledge this by pulling out. By doing so, they are not being unfaithful to Yahweh; they merely accept the divine realpolitik of the time. This was not yet the age of full-fledged monotheism; it was still the age of its forerunner, monolatry, where each people worshipped one god above all. Monotheism—the insistence on one universal god—would come later. In the meantime, monolatry was still a matter of physical territory. On Yahweh's own soil, he was all-powerful, but on alien soil, so radical a sacrifice to the local god Chemosh outranked Yahweh in the divine scheme of things.

All this would seem to make sense until you realize that if King Mesha had indeed made such a drastic sacrifice, he would surely have mentioned it on his victory stele, if only as a measure of his devotion to his god and to his kingdom. "And I offered up my oldest and most beloved son to the fire and wrath of Chemosh," he would have written, "for the sake of my people and my kingdom, to expel the invaders from the land of my father and of my forefathers." No such language appears on the stele for the excellent reason that such a sacrifice most likely never took place.

Child sacrifice is part of the Western legend of ancient times. For instance, when archaeological excavations unearthed jars full of ashes and burned bones of infants at Carthage, the Phoenician colony established on the coast of what is now Tunisia, they were taken as proof that the Phoenicians practiced child sacrifice. But such an argument favors fantasy over a far more persuasive reality. The extraordinarily high infant mortality rate of the time—as many as three out of five—meant that newborns were not even named until the fortieth day of life; those who died unnamed either in childbirth or shortly after were cremated and their ashes stored separately in testament to their special status in a kind of limbo, much as an unbaptized infant's death was once regarded in the Christian West. The assumption that their remains are proof of child sacrifice is based on ancient Greek and Roman writings accusing other cultures of precisely this practice, but to accept such accounts as historical fact is risky business. As with the supposed practice of ritual prostitution, the rumor of child sacrifice was a means of labeling others as unbelievably primitive and barbaric, and thus ripe for the civilizing influence of colonization. Despite Edward Said's famed analysis, Orientalism was not a nineteenth-century invention; it was an ancient tradition of empire.

If Moab's King Mesha did in fact make a sacrifice to Chemosh when on the verge of defeat, an animal would almost certainly have been substituted for the child, as in the Abraham and Isaac story. The child would then become the guarantee of his father's oath, so that if the father broke his vow to the divine, his child would be forfeit. In this, Israelite culture was no different than its neighbors. "Consecrate unto me each firstborn. Breach of each womb among the Israelites in man and in beast, is mine," says the first verse of Exodus 13. The Hebrew makes it clear that the intention is sacrifice, but the context implies a permanent redemption of each firstborn in the form of either an animal sacrifice or a payment to the temple priests. The idea is that all new life is by the grace of Yahweh and so belongs to Yahweh, but to imagine that this means that every firstborn son was killed is to be literal to the point of absurdity. Unless, of course, it is imagined about an enemy culture.

The Kings authors called up the old saw of child sacrifice to rationalize the Israelite defeat despite Elisha's prophecy of victory.

"What else could civilized people do in the face of such barbaric behavior?" they imply. We are given to believe that having witnessed such religious extremism, the Israelites had no option but to retreat in shock and horror. In fact, the retreat speaks of weak leadership. King Mesha's victory was a clear sign to all Israel's neighbors, and first and foremost to its long-term enemy Damascus, that the era of Omri and Ahab was over. King Joram was neither the warrior nor the leader his father and grandfather had been, and Israel was vulnerable. From here on in, events would conspire rapidly against the Israelite king and the queen mother. Or rather, Elisha would.

No matter what happened, it seemed that Elisha could do no wrong—or at least not be held accountable for it. His prediction of success in Moab had been demonstrably false, but if questions were raised about why so powerful a prophet could not have foreseen the rout, we know nothing of them. One can't help but wonder if the "lying spirit" that led Ahab to his death at Ramot Gilead could have been in Elisha's mouth too. Did he deliberately mislead Joram and send him off to defeat in Moab, thus weakening the Kingdom of Israel and furthering the plan for the destruction of the Omride dynasty and the final defeat of Jezebel? Exactly how ruthless a manipulator could he be?

With his reputation firmly established by such drastic means as killing the boys who teased him for being bald, and apparently undamaged by the events in Moab, Elisha now turned to more classical forms of miracle. Over the next few years, he multiplied loaves of barley to feed hundreds; he made a single jar of oil fill endless other jars; he raised a dead child back to life. He was everywhere: sometimes on Mount Carmel, sometimes in Samaria, sometimes down in the Jordan Valley. Word of his ability as a miracle worker spread far and wide, gaining him renown not only among Israelites and Judeans but also abroad—and most particularly in Damascus, Israel's constant rival.

Elisha's involvement with the court of Damascus is astonishing. In the whole of the Hebrew bible, it is the only instance in which an Israelite prophet prophesies at the service of a foreign country, let alone an enemy one. It begins when a senior Damascus general is stricken with leprosy and, in desperation, turns to Elisha for help. In the name of Yahweh, the prophet tells him to bathe seven times in the Jordan River. The general emerges not only cured but an ardent convert to Yahwism, even taking two mule-loads of Israelite soil back to Damascus with him so that he can worship Yahweh on his own soil. Elisha now has a powerful ally at the right hand of King Ben-Hadad II of Damascus, and so begins his role as a kind of double agent—a triple agent, in fact, since his ultimate loyalty is only to Yahweh. In a strategy that will make a Machiavelli seem amateur by comparison, he will manipulate Israel's chief enemy into doing much of his work for him.

The prophet becomes a regular visitor to Damascus, assiduously courting the king's chief advisers until he is known in the city as "the man of God." So when the king himself falls seriously ill, he orders his chief of staff, Hazael, to ply Elisha with gifts in the hope of a cure. Such cures evidently come at a high price, since Hazael deploys "every good thing of Damascus, forty camel loads," when he goes to visit Elisha at his lodgings in the city.

"Your son Ben-Hadad, king of Damascus, has sent me to ask 'Shall I recover from this illness?' " Hazael says. His attitude is one of pure deference in the presence of this foreign prophet, his choice of the words "your son" expressing his humility.

Elisha replies with a carefully phrased double message. "Go tell the king that he will certainly recover," he says, then adds sotto voce: "But Yahweh has shown me that he will certainly die." Ben-Hadad will recover from his illness, that is, but will die nonetheless. And then, without warning, Elisha breaks into tears.

"Why do you weep, my lord?" asks Hazael, and again the choice of words—"my lord"—indicates how highly regarded the prophet is here in Damascus.

The answer, coming as it does from an Israelite prophet in the capital of his country's chief enemy, is enough to make your jaw drop in disbelief. "Because I know the evil that you will do to the Israelites," Elisha tells Hazael. "You will set their fortresses on fire, and you will kill their young men by the sword, and you will tear their little ones to pieces and rip the bellies of their pregnant wives."

In the ear of the Damascus chief of staff, this has to sound less like a prophecy than like detailed instructions as to exactly what he should do.

Elisha's outburst can certainly be seen as the despair of a man helpless to prevent the wrath of Yahweh against his own people for tolerating the evil Omride dynasty, his tears as those of a man in submission to the force of the inevitable. This is presumably how the Kings authors intended them to be understood. But to a less devoted reader, they seem more like crocodile tears. From the man so ruthless as to casually kill children out of vanity, they look suspiciously staged, as though produced on demand to give extra emphasis to his instructions to Hazael. What he did to those boys, Elisha is now planning to do to the whole Kingdom of Israel, using Damascus as the agent of his vengeance. The bald-headed prophet has the long-haired warriors of Israel at his mercy, and those of Damascus at his command. He has demonstrated the power of brain over brawn, of manipulation over muscle and might.

Hazael, as you might expect, is stunned. "But who am I, your servant, a mere dog, to do such a great thing?" he says.

And now it comes, the fulfillment of the second part of Yahweh's instructions to Elijah on Mount Sinai, the instructions that Elijah was not ruthless enough to carry out, which is why he was fired and told to anoint Elisha in his place. "Yahweh has shown me that you will be king of Damascus," Elisha tells Hazael.

The manipulation is perfect. Elisha does not have to say any more. He knows exactly how his words will combine with Hazael's ambition and greed to fatal effect. If Ben-Hadad is to recover from his illness and yet die, there is only one way this can happen, and Hazael is the man to make it happen. Elisha has issued a blatant invitation to high treason in the court of Damascus. He has elegantly engineered an assassination and a coup d'état, and now has only to sit back and watch the machinery roll into motion.

Sure enough, Hazael goes back to Ben-Hadad with the good news that the king will recover. "Then the next day, he took a cloth and soaked it in water, and spread it over Ben-Hadad's face until he suffocated and died." It is a perfect act of assassination, bloodless and undetectable. "And Hazael became king of Damascus instead of Ben-Hadad," the narrative continues. King of Damascus, with his marching orders from Elisha.

Only one more element has yet to be put into play, and then the Omride era of pragmatic statesmanship will meet its violent end. Yahweh's final order to Elijah on Mount Sinai was to "anoint Jehu son of Nimshi as king of Israel," and the task now falls to Elisha, who picks the perfect time and place: renewed hostilities for control of the stronghold of Ramot Gilead.

Emboldened by Elisha's vision of the future, the newly crowned Hazael launches a surprise attack on the fortress, aiming to use it as a base for a full-scale invasion of Israel. King Joram rushes to the defense but is wounded in the battle—lightly, as we will soon realize—and leaves the field. Even as his men fight on, he heads back across the River Jordan to recuperate in Jezreel, where Jezebel is in residence. This is the moment Elisha has been waiting for.

"Gird up your loins," he tells one of his disciples—a phrase usually reserved for battle—"and take this vial of oil to Ramot Gilead. Look for Jehu the son of Nimshi and take him aside. Then pour the oil on his head and say: 'Thus says Yahweh: I have anointed you king of Israel.' Then leave, and come back quickly."

If Joram were still at Ramot Gilead, Elisha could never have made such a move. But Joram is no Ahab. Where Ahab stayed on the battlefield despite a fatal wound, stemming the blood pouring out of his side with a bunched-up robe, Joram has taken advantage of a flesh wound to extricate himself from the fight, leaving command in the hands of his chief of staff—none other than Jehu the son of Nimshi. Neither his father nor his grandfather would have made such a mistake. As a matter of good leadership, they led their troops into battle themselves; as a matter of survival, they never left their forces under the command of anyone else, since they knew all too well that senior military officers in this region had a long record of seizing power. Omri himself had been a chariot commander before seizing the throne; in Damascus, Hazael had been the chief of staff. And Jehu was as ambitious a chief of staff as any, a fact Elisha now uses to his own ends.

The disciple does as instructed, taking Jehu aside and anointing him with oil. But his speech to the chief of staff develops into a full tirade as he repeats not just Elisha's words but also Elijah's *fatwa*, along with a repetition of the charge that Jezebel had killed Yahwist priests: "Thus says Yahweh the god of Israel: I have anointed you king over Yahweh's people, Israel. Go strike down the house of your lord Ahab, so that I can avenge the blood of my servants the priests of Yahweh at the hands of Jezebel. The whole House of Ahab shall perish. I will cut down every one that pisses against a wall, wherever he may be in Israel . . . And the dogs will eat Jezebel by the walls of Jezreel, and no one will bury her." The stern editorial hand of the Kings scribes is clearly at work, dotting the *i*'s and crossing the *t*'s. Now Jehu has his marching orders.

The other generals acclaim Elisha's choice. With Joram's absence from the battlefield and his poor record as commander in chief, they are ready for rebellion. Given the chance to rally to one of their own, "they blew the horn, saying, Jehu is king." The whole of the Israelite high command is now in a conspiracy to seize power. And as they prepare to ride from Ramot Gilead to Jezreel to dispatch the king and the queen mother, you realize that all this has to have been done with at least the tacit acquiescence of Damascus, since it would be impossible for Jehu and the other generals to leave Ramot Gilead unless Hazael had called off his troops. Jehu thus becomes the puppet of the king of Damascus, and both in turn are the puppets of Elisha, who has stayed firmly behind the scenes, pulling every string with masterful precision.

The howling for blood has begun, and the *fatwa* on Jezebel can finally be executed.

8.

Jezreel

in which the dogs feast

There were once literally such creatures as dogs of war. Spe-
cially bred mastiffs trained by both the Egyptians and the
Assyrians for use in battle, they were tightly tethered to make
them more aggressive, then taken into battle on long chains to
lunge and tear on command at any exposed body parts. The very
idea of them was terrifying, let alone the reality. American soldiers in Iraq were working in a far more ancient tradition than
they knew when they used attack dogs to terrorize and torture
prisoners in Abu Ghraib.

This is a region where dogs still take advantage of human
bloodthirstiness to assuage their own. "The wild dogs of Najaf
ate well this week," began a *New York Times* front-page story on
the aftermath of a three-week battle between Americans and
Iraqis in August 2004. "One house at the edge of the city held

four blasted corpses, their stench heavy in the midday sun. Dogs had been at the bodies overnight. Indeed a dog skulked nearby as Iraqi medics carried the remains to an ambulance."

Westerners have the luxury of thinking of dogs as their best friends, but in the Middle East they have inspired a complex mix of fear and awe since the earliest times on record. In the cycle of poems called *The Exaltation of Inanna,* written by the high priestess Enheduanna in the twenty-third century B.C., the fierceness of the Sumerian warrior goddess is compared in awe and trembling to that of dogs:

> *That you roar at the land—be it known!*
> *That you kill—be it known!*
> *That like a dog you eat the corpses—be it known!*

Certainly dogs could be trained for use in the hunt, on the battlefield, or as guards, but their obedience was always sensed as conditional. You were never allowed to forget how easily they could turn against you, or how horrifying that return to the feral state could be. In Homer's *Iliad,* the aging Priam foresees what will happen when the Greeks take Troy: "When someone's javelin or sword has laid me dead, I shall be torn to pieces by ravening dogs at my own door. The very dogs I have fed at table and trained to watch my gate will loll about in front of it, maddened by their master's blood."

Dogs were seen as the guardians not just of a building's threshold but also of the threshold between life and death, a role that would be adopted and expanded in later European legend, where terrifying images of legendary canines reflected the terror of death itself. In Greek mythology, the gates of Hades were guarded by the monstrous watchdog Cerberus, while the beast of

Hecate, the goddess of ghosts, darkness, and sorcery, was shown as a giant mastiff. The wolf-dog Garm of Norse legend guarded the entrance to the underworld, and the hellhounds of Celtic folklore flew through the air on the howling wind, their baying the omen of death—a legend famously adopted by Arthur Conan Doyle in *The Hound of the Baskervilles.* All these dogs are beyond human control; they are of another world, an unpredictable world of spirits and mysterious forces. They remind us that the line between fear and awe is a blurred one—indeed, that awe may be our ritual way of accommodating fear.

The awe in which dogs were held was all the stronger given the idea that they could heal as well as kill—a contradiction that could belong only to the realm of the divine. The threshold between life and death was the domain of illness, which is why the Mesopotamian Gula and her Egyptian counterpart Anubis, the jackal-headed god who guided dead souls to resurrection, were both revered as healing deities. The belief in canine healing properties continued in the temples of the Greek healing god Asculepius, where dogs were encouraged to lick the wounds of the sick and injured. This practice may sound like mere superstition, if not downright revolting, yet modern chemical analysis of canine saliva does indeed show it to have mild antibacterial properties, and experiments have demonstrated that dogs are as effective as high-tech medical testing, and sometimes more so, in detecting the presence of cancer in humans. No such scientific support has been found for another ancient healing practice: a fourteenth-century B.C. clay tablet discovered at the northern Phoenician city of Ugarit recommends the hair of a dog placed on the forehead as a cure for hangovers—the earliest known source for the stiff drink at breakfast referred to by heavy drinkers as "the hair of the dog that bit you."

Archaeologists have uncovered ancient dog cemeteries in which the animals had clearly been ritually slaughtered and then mummified in an apparent attempt to immortalize their healing powers. Such remains have been found in both Mesopotamia and Israel, where a huge canine necropolis in a fifth-century B.C. temple near the coastal city of Ashkelon raised the possibility that the legend of Asculepius was born here, not in Greece. Outside the temples, however, the existence of most dogs as scavengers meant that contempt for them was more the order of the day. On several inscribed clay tablets sent from field commanders to their kings, the writers refer to themselves as "your servant, a mere dog," making it clear that they do not just bow down to their lords but grovel at their feet. In the same way, Hazael's response to Elisha when prompted to attack Israel was "But who am I, your servant, a mere dog, to do such a great thing."

Dogs were the lowest of the low, which is why the biblical scribes regularly referred to Baalite priests as dogs. All infidels were dogs in the eyes of those who considered themselves the possessors of the true faith, and this tradition has continued through the ages and across cultures. Today's radical Islamists use the word "dog" interchangeably with "infidel," while to call someone a dog is still an insult in most Western languages. And of course one of the first words to be hurled at any woman considered too competitive or ambitious is "bitch."

Given this contempt, it is hardly surprising that the threat of being eaten by dogs was a standard curse in the ancient Middle East. Not only would there be no burial—a fate as terrible then as it would become in Jewish and Christian tradition, where "a soul that knows no rest" is condemned to wander in agony for eternity—but insult would be added to injury by the very idea of being devoured as carrion, of one's own flesh becoming nothing more than dog food. In a treaty dictated by the seventh-century B.C. Assyrian king Esarhaddon, one penalty for abrogating the treaty read: "May the valley be filled with their bodies and the dogs eat them." Another, dictated by his son Ashurbanipal, threatens: "Their corpses will be eaten by dogs." The identical threat was issued by Yahwist prophets against two Israelite kings who preceded Omri and Ahab, though in the event, both would die a natural death and be buried to "sleep with their fathers." The one and only time the threat is actually carried out against a specific person is with the *fatwa* on Jezebel. And it is carried out with gusto. Nowhere in the whole of the Hebrew bible is any death reported in such grisly and precise detail, down to the last body part.

The final scene in Jezebel's life starts with the newly anointed Jehu riding as fast as he can down from Ramot Gilead and across the Jordan to the fortress city of Jezreel, where King Joram is recuperating from his battle wound. Jehu needs to move quickly lest word get to Joram of what has happened. He doesn't want to give the king a chance to muster a defense, so he rides, as the Hebrew puts it, *be'shigaon*, literally "in madness." In his eagerness to possess the throne, that is, he rides like a man possessed.

He has apparently not foreseen that Joram is not the only king in residence in Jezreel. Judea's newly crowned King Ahaziah—Jezebel's teenage grandson, the son of her daughter Athaliah—

has arrived with a large entourage to offer support to his uncle in the war with Damascus. The two rulers are in consultation with the queen mother as Jehu and his men race up the valley toward the city. When the guards on the towers recognize Jehu's pennants, they send word that the chief of staff is on his way. Assuming that Jehu is coming with good news from the battlefront, Joram eagerly calls for his chariot so that he can ride out to meet him. Ahaziah orders his own chariot readied so that he can ride out alongside his uncle, and both kings, suspecting nothing, set out unarmed.

That Joram rides out at all is a sure indication that his wound was only a slight one, and that he should never have left the field of battle. And while the lack of weaponry may be a touching sign of trust in his chief of staff, it also displays a startling lack of awareness of the resentment that has been brewing within his own military. The fact that such an ineffective ruler lasted a full decade on the throne of Israel has to be seen as testimony not to his own abilities as king but to Jezebel's as the queen mother.

The two kings and Jehu meet, we are told, at the precise spot of what had formerly been Naboth's vineyard. It is too obvious a coincidence, of course, but one the Kings writers could not resist. True, the vineyard was first described as alongside Ahab and Jezebel's palace, and is now suddenly a chariot ride away, but poetic justice demands that it be the place where Ahab and Jezebel's son will die. Stories of vengeance have their own dynamic, and are rarely subtle.

"Is it peace, Jehu?" Joram asks. The irony is so strong that one almost pities a man who can ask such a stunningly naïve question under the circumstances. Joram's hope that the battle for Ramot

Gilead has been won and Damascus defeated overtakes all sense of reality. The answer to his blithe optimism must come like a bolt from the blue.

"What peace, when your mother Jezebel's harlotries and sorceries are so many?" retorts Jehu.

And there it is, for the first time in the whole Kings account of Jezebel's life—the direct accusation that she is a harlot and a sorcerer to boot, using wicked charms and spells to impose her evil ways on Ahab, on Joram, on the whole of Israel.

There is no avoiding reality now. Joram realizes he's walked into a trap. "Treachery, Ahaziah!" he cries out, and turns his chariot around to race back to Jezreel. Too late. In the classic act of cowardice and deceit, Jehu shoots the unarmed king in the back. "He drew his bow with his full strength and hit Joram between the shoulders, and the arrow came out through his heart, and he sank down in his chariot." Just as his father Ahab had sunk down in his chariot before him.

Ahaziah doesn't wait for the next arrow. With the advantage of that moment's warning from his uncle, he flees south toward Ein-Gannim, the modern Palestinian city of Jenin on the road to Samaria, but Jehu gives chase. "Cut him down too," he orders, and his archers obey. Jehu has now killed both the king of Israel and the king of Judea. He is a double regicide, and his day's work has only begun.

When Joram's aides rush back to Jezreel to report that the king is dead, Jezebel sees clearly what will come next. There can be no doubt. The usurper who has just murdered her son will be her assassin too. As she receives the news, he and his men are still in pursuit of Ahaziah, but it is only a matter of time until they get to Jezreel, and very little of it: a few hours at most. Yet what happens in that time is stunning. If we can only imagine the wailing and panic in the palace as the royal attendants realize what is in store, we do not have to imagine Jezebel's reaction. That is spelled out for us: "She painted her eyes, and dressed her hair, and looked out the window."

Her son dead, her grandson as good as dead, her own death imminent, and all she can do is put on makeup and do her hair? At first glance, Jezebel looks like a woman in severe denial, even shock. But to see her in such a way is only to underestimate her once more. The eyes, the hair, the window—all mean far more than a modern reader might first suspect.

"Putting on the war paint" is how many American women used to describe applying heavy makeup, and this is how Jezebel's painted eyes have to be seen—literally as war paint. They are a proud and defiant adoption of her role as public enemy number one. The queen mother has no illusions about what is to happen; her exit is inevitable, and so she will face it with dignity. She will not quaver, will not buckle at the knees, will never dream of pleading for her life. She will meet her death with the composure fitting her rank. She will exit boldly, every inch a queen.

Shakespeare surely had Jezebel in mind when he wrote the final scene of *Antony and Cleopatra* in which the Egyptian queen—another woman ruler whose power has been diminished by legend to little more than a sexual frisson—prepares for her death. "Show me, my women, like a queen," she orders her servants. "Go fetch my best attires . . . Give me my robe, put on my crown;

I have immortal longings in me." Like Jezebel, Shakespeare's Cleopatra knows that the more dramatic her death—the more beautiful and regal she is—the greater the impression it will make. Like Jezebel, she will die in a way that will be remembered forever.

So under Jezebel's direction, her attendants prepare her. Just as they had done for her wedding thirty-one years before, so now they do for her imminent death. They part her long hennaed hair into strands and then artfully pile them one by one high on her head, creating a massive wreath of braids and ringlets looped through gold chains and a gem-studded diadem. They fasten a high choker at her throat, raising her chin and making her long neck seem longer still. They hang heavy loop earrings from her lobes; slide ornate bands over her wrists and elbows and ankles; lade her fingers and toes with rings.

They drape the most sumptuous of all her robes over her shoulders—a deep purple brocaded silk lavishly embroidered with gold and silver—and then they turn to their cosmetics. They use freshly ground henna paste to draw lotus flowers on her forehead—the flowers of the great goddess Astarte—and trace delicate tendrils stretching from her palms to her fingers, circling her ankles, twining around each toe. They apply white lead powder to her face, and the black antimony powder known as kohl in long strokes around her eyes, and gold eye shadow from her eyelids up to her elegantly arched brows. And last of all, they outline her mouth in deep scarlet, and fill out her lips with a startling, shining red.

Hair, makeup, robes—the mask is in place. If Jezebel feels the slightest hint of fear, her enemies will never see it. But the mask is not merely a means of concealment. It is the way the queen now steps into another persona. As her assassin rides toward Jezreel to perform his final murder of the day, Jezebel orders her throne to be placed on the balcony, in the window. Seated there in full regalia, she will not merely represent the great goddess; she will become her.

To understand Jezebel at this moment, we have only to look at the numerous intricately carved ivory bas-reliefs known as the "woman at the window" plaques, found by archaeologists in the acropolis of the Israelite capital of Samaria. No more than three or four inches high and two or three inches across, they show a woman's head. Her eyes are heavily outlined with kohl, her hair elaborately arranged in a mass of long ringlets, her ears weighed down with ornate earrings. An inscrutable kind of Mona Lisa smile plays on her lips, making her seem utterly mysterious and other-worldly. She is framed by a triply recessed window of the kind found in ancient temples, and the windowsill is supported by ornate columns whose capitals echo the arrangement of her hair. The style and the craftsmanship of the plaques are unmistakably Phoenician, not Israelite—clear testimony to Jezebel's presence and influence.

Today, the image of a woman in the window, especially in the context of Jezebel's corrupted reputation, brings to mind prostitutes displaying their wares in the windows of the red-light district in Amsterdam. We have been so conditioned to think of Jezebel as a harlot that the association is practically inevitable. But as you gaze at these exquisite ivory plaques, even through the glass of museum showcases, it becomes quite clear that they are not merely decorative but ritual objects. The woman at the window is the representation of the great mother goddess Astarte, and this image of her was as accepted and beloved in its time as is the modern one of the Virgin Mary in her blue mantle with arms outstretched in blessing.

Astarte's ivory image is what Jezebel has firmly in mind when she has her hair dressed, her face painted, and her throne brought out to the balcony, there to await her overthrow in the mask of inscrutable divinity. Like Astarte, she is framed in the window. She becomes literally a woman framed.

What went through her mind as she sat in splendor waiting for her assassin? Did she regret her life? Curse the memory of her father for ever having sent her to this kingdom? Acknowledge the power of the Israelite prophets? The biblical writers may have wanted us to think so, but in fact if she regretted anything at all, it was surely having allowed Elijah to go into exile instead of ordering him killed. It is doubtful, though, that she even thought that; regret may have haunted Ahab, but it was not part of Jezebel's vocabulary. Instead, she chose defiance. She knew her death was inevitable, but that does not mean she acceded to it. If anything, she rose above it. Instead of raging helplessly at the cowardly murder of her son and grandson, she adopted a steely, ice-cold disdain for the murderer; instead of tears, the ivory mask of divine superiority.

In an unusually sympathetic portrayal of Jezebel, Israeli poet Shulamit Kalugai slipped beneath that mask, finding a deep sense of loss and vulnerability as she adopted the voice of the queen in those last hours of her life:

My life begins to dissolve like mist,
I lose all sense of when and where.

Jezreel

Baal and Astarte seem far away,
And my kingdom too, and my enemies.

Surrounded, framed, I see no future,
No one will come to save me now,
Not even a raven from Nahal Karit
With an olive branch held in his mouth.

A dream my father's realm of Tyre,
A dream my coming to Samaria's walls,
A dream my priests, and Yahweh's prophets,
Wild bitter men full of righteous wrath.

Sons and allies, power and love,
The memory of Ahab, of my whole life
As proud resplendent glorious queen—
All vanished, ruined, mere pillars of smoke . . .

Dark as the grave this summer night,
Only a few stars in the heavens above,
Then a watchman's call, a rustle of leaves,
And the short sharp bark of dogs,
Of dogs.

Kalugai is right: Jezebel can have had no fantasies of rescue, no dreams of a white knight riding up to save her at the last moment. She was far too much the realist for that. But the pity the poem arouses is precisely what Jezebel would have rejected. She would have scorned a poet's sympathy. She would never stoop to appeal to anyone's understanding, let alone their pity. That would be beneath a queen's dignity. Her pride—her arrogance—would not have allowed it. Neither would her anger.

And never, ever would she have dreamed of letting Baal and Astarte slip away from her. On the contrary, she would die in the fullest awareness of Astarte, as the human embodiment of the goddess.

Jehu arrives in Jezreel, his chariot thundering through the gates of the silent city where everyone except Jezebel is hunkered down indoors, waiting for the worst to pass. He rides up to the walls of the palace, drawing to a halt right below the balcony where Jezebel sits framed by the arch of the window behind her. His horses snort and steam at the sudden halt, shifting in their traces, but Jehu ignores them. For a moment he is as still as Jezebel, as though in freeze-frame, and in that moment the scene looks shockingly familiar: it is almost a perverse inversion of the famed balcony scene in *Romeo and Juliet*. Love would bring Romeo to Juliet's balcony, while hate has brought Jehu to Jezebel's. Yet here they are, he looking up, she looking down, each the focus of the other's most intense emotion.

Perhaps influenced by Shakespeare, some commentators have added insult to the coming injury to Jezebel with the peculiar idea that this is in fact a seduction scene. The argument is that Jezebel has made herself up and presented herself in the window in a desperate last attempt to seduce Jehu and thus save her life. There is no hint of this in Kings, however; even the ancient authors had more respect for her. And how could anyone seriously mistake the scene for an attempt at seduction? Such commentators are so in thrall to Jezebel's degraded reputation as slut and hussy that they retroactively impose it back onto the historical queen. They cannot see that the makeup is a mask, and the mask a means of establishing control.

As she looks down on Jehu, Jezebel calls on all her reserves of pride and defiance. She will not ask for mercy, not from anyone and especially not from the man who has assassinated both her son and her grandson. She takes refuge in contempt. Another mask? Most certainly, but one that will allow her to die like a queen and defy the indignity of dogs—both the dogs waiting for her body and the dog who is about to give the order to kill her. She has no control over what is to happen, and yet she acts as though she does. In fact she all but spits in the face of her assassin.

Her voice rings out clearly, without a tremor: "Is it peace, Zimri, your master's murderer?" And the sarcasm is sharp as a swordpoint. It was Zimri who killed the Israelite king Elah just forty-five years earlier and ruled for a grand total of seven days before Ahab's father Omri unseated him. Zimri who burned to death in his palace, and whose name became the byword for falsehood and treason. Now Jehu is another Zimri, another murderer and usurper, beneath Jezebel both morally and physically as she taunts him from the balcony. She knows he does not know the meaning of peace; let him kill her if he dares.

Yet Zimri's name reverberates even deeper in this story, precisely as the Kings authors intended it to. It derives from the Hebrew for "pruning a vine," so that Naboth's vineyard comes instantly to mind. Divine retribution is at work here. As Yale biblical scholar Saul Olyan points out, Jehu takes on the role of the pruner, given the task of cutting down what the Kings writers see as the rotten branches—the House of Ahab. But he will not sully his hands by touching Jezebel himself. Others will do his work for him.

"Who is with me? Who?" he cries out. And when three of Jezebel's eunuchs come to the window in response, he barks out his order: "Throw her down."

It is just one word in Hebrew: *shimtuha*. Short, sharp, and dismissive. And with that one word, we realize that what is to be thrown down—overthrown—is not only Jezebel herself but everything she represents: pragmatism, pluralism, and, above all, polytheism. Jezebel has assumed the image of Astarte, and the goddess herself is to be overthrown. The queen's death is not merely a personal defeat; in the minds of the biblical authors and those who first heard them, it represents the ultimate victory of Yahwism over polytheism, the critical turning point in the centuries-long evolution toward monotheism.

And of course it has to be eunuchs who throw Jezebel down. She has emasculated the warrior ethos of the kingdom, so that only men who are already unmanned could possibly attend her. In fact they may or may not have been literally castrated, since the Hebrew *srisim* may be used here as a play on the older Semitic word *sarisi*, meaning "he who is at the head of the king," or a senior royal counselor. If so, the pun is effective: Jezebel is to be thrown down by her senior counselors, who have been unmanned by being in her service, so much so that they have neither principle nor loyalty. Seeing that the locus of power has shifted to Jehu, they shift their allegiances accordingly:

"And they threw her down. And some of her blood spattered on the wall, and some on the horses, and the horses trampled her underfoot."

His day's work done, Jehu leaves the bloodied corpse crumpled by the palace walls, enters the throne room in triumph, and orders a celebratory feast. Only when his stomach is full does he give a second thought to Jezebel. "Go see to this cursed woman, and bury her," he tells his aides, "for she is a king's daughter." Not a queen, mind you, nor a queen mother, but only her original status before she ever came to Israel: daughter of the king of Tyre. So far as Jehu is concerned, the House of Ahab has already been wiped out of history. Jezebel's corpse is a mere afterthought.

Still, the order to bury her is strange. Jehu is surely aware of Elijah's *fatwa,* and there is no way the dogs can eat her if she is buried. Perhaps the assumption of power has sobered him enough to realize that since he has just killed a princess of Tyre in the most ignominious manner, the least he can do is bury the evidence if he is to have any hope of salvaging relations with her home state. Or perhaps—and more likely—a later editor was trying to rescue Jehu's reputation by according him enough of a sense of honor to give his enemy a decent burial, though in fact Jehu's reputation would turn out to be irredeemable.

Burial was indeed a basic decency. To kill someone was one thing; to leave them unburied, quite another. "Men feared death itself less than deprivation of burial," says historian Herbert Chanan Brichto. This was "the most terrible punishment, reserved for those guilty of great crimes." The threat of nonburial was a standard curse not only in the Hebrew bible but throughout the Middle East. Egyptian pharaohs had it inscribed on the doors of their tombs as part of their imprecations against grave robbers, as did the fifth-century B.C. Phoenician king Ithmunazar, whose sarcophagus included a dire warning for those who might disturb it: "May they have no resting place among the shades; may they not be buried in a grave." In both Greece and Rome, suicides and criminals would be deliberately left unburied, to be eaten as carrion, and later still, in medieval England, the bodies of executed traitors would be drawn and quartered, and the pieces strung up to rot.

When Jehu's aides go to carry out his order, however, the horror ramps up. They come to the spot by the palace walls where Jezebel was trampled by Jehu's chariot horses only to find that there is no body left. While the usurper has been feasting inside the palace, feral dogs have been feasting outside. All that is left of Jezebel is "no more of her than her head and her feet and the palms of her hands."

Dogs, the animals that in Phoenician tradition heal the sick and lead the dead safely into the afterlife, have instead turned on Jezebel. The very creatures she believed would protect her have devoured her.

The horror is now compounded, the revulsion extreme. If human corpses are disturbing, fragmented ones are all the more so. In Jewish tradition, the body has to be whole for burial, which adds distress on distress when body parts are picked up off the street after a terrorist bombing in Israel. People hearing the story of Jezebel's death for the first time will often say, "No, that can't be. The Bible can't really say she was eaten by dogs." And indeed I might agree that the dogs were a fictional elaboration by the Kings authors if it were not for that particular detail of their leaving behind Jezebel's head, hands, and feet. The rest they gorged on, but those parts they left untouched. And when we ask why, the answer is a compelling indication that the grisly account is true.

When Jezebel ordered her attendants to prepare her to meet her assassin, they painted her with henna as the sign of rank used regularly at the time by high-status women, especially for ritual events such as temple festivals and royal celebrations. In the Phoenician epics, henna was the war paint of the warrior goddess Anat, who applied it before she went to do battle with Mot, and it must have been in that spirit that Jezebel had it applied on her forehead, her hands, and her feet for the ritual of her own coming death. Today, henna is still used in many parts of Asia and the Middle East, especially for brides; but it is never used around the mouth since its active agent—a tannin dye—is intensely bitter to the taste, so strong that some people claim they can tell when food has been prepared by someone with hennaed hands. Used in moderation, the herb is safe, but applied too lavishly, it can be poisonous; there have even been cases of children dying from cutaneous absorption of the paste. Dogs, with their highly developed sense of smell and taste, would certainly never touch anything with henna on it, which is why the wolf-dogs of Jezreel left precisely what they did.

We still have no idea what happened to Jezebel's head, hands, and feet. Were they left where they were to rot? Were they gathered up and buried? Were they thrown outside the city walls as trash? The Kings account never tells us. They float dreamlike in history, uneaten and unaccounted for. The ancients were right: unburied, they haunt us still. But not Jehu. When his aides come back to tell him what has happened, he pronounces what the Kings authors clearly intend to be the final judgment: "This is the word of Yahweh when he spoke to his servant Elijah and said that the dogs will eat the flesh of Jezebel by the walls of Jezreel, and that the carcass of Jezebel will be as dung spread upon the fields, so that they shall not say, This was Jezebel."

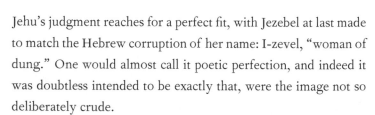

Jehu's judgment reaches for a perfect fit, with Jezebel at last made to match the Hebrew corruption of her name: I-zevel, "woman of dung." One would almost call it poetic perfection, and indeed it was doubtless intended to be exactly that, were the image not so deliberately crude.

Like the idea of carrion-eating dogs, so too the theme of dung runs throughout the Hebrew bible. "You shall bake barley cakes with human dung," says Yahweh in the book of Ezekiel, calling these cakes "defiled bread." Psalm 83 tells how Israel's enemies "became as dung for the earth." In Jeremiah, the prophet returns obsessively to the image: "They shall be dung upon the face of the earth," he has Yahweh saying of those who have betrayed him, and shows him threatening not once, but three times, that "the carcasses of men shall fall as dung upon the open field." In Malachi, Yahweh says: "Behold I will corrupt your seed and spread dung upon your faces" so that "you will be contemptible and base before all the people." And in Daniel, the Assyrian king Nebuchadnezzar twice threatens that "your houses shall be made into a dunghill"—an omen of what the Romans would do to the Jerusalem temple when they destroyed it in A.D. 70 and turned the site into a cesspool. Defeat is not enough; the defeated must be taken to the utmost depths of degradation.

The body automatically protects itself from contact with

dung, as French philosopher and psychoanalyst Julia Kristeva notes in an essay on abjection. "The repugnance, the retching, thrusts me to the side and turns me away from defilement, sewage, and muck . . . I do not assimilate it, I expel it. Dung signifies the other side of the border, the place where I am not, and which permits me to be." Fecal matter, she theorizes, "is the price the body must pay if it is to become clean and proper." The filth must be ejected. And execrated.

To be execrated is to be accursed, and that is exactly how the threat of dung—of eating it, of being turned into it—is used in the Bible. It is the punishment for defiling the purity of the Yahwist ideal by worshipping other gods and thus entering a state of abject impurity. And if this seems primitive, consider the fact that the idea has stayed with us in the concept of "foul" or "dirty" language—language that is impure or out of bounds, even when not as explicit as calling someone "a piece of shit." To give oneself over to the world of dung and excretion is to go over to "the other side of the border," as Kristeva puts it. It is to cross the line between human and bestial. It is truly to go to the dogs.

Jezebel has been submitted to abjection not once but three times: she has been thrown to the dogs, then eaten by them, then excreted by them. The degradation has finally reached its limits. What the individual body rejects is rejected by the body politic; Jezebel is beyond the pale. Now the dogs' dung will dry in the sun, to be eroded by the wind into dust, invisible to the human eye. There will be nothing left of Jezebel—no tomb, no monument, no shrine. In the minds of the biblical authors, the gods she represents have been overthrown and trampled, devoured and ejected, to be erased from human memory.

Yet memory persists. Once we know the details of how Jezebel died, they remain engraved in our minds. In a perfect twist of irony, Jehu's insistence that she be forgotten makes her death—and thus her life—unforgettable. When he says, "They shall not say, This was Jezebel," he assumes that along with her body, her name will be dispersed over the face of the earth into nothingness.

How wrong he would be.

9.

Babylon

in which Yahweh is reborn in exile

Walk into Room 6 of the British Museum—the long ground-floor gallery that is the Assyrian room—and you can almost feel Jezebel standing beside you, a half-smile hovering at the corners of her mouth. It is not a smile of satisfaction or of triumph, but one of pure scorn. "See," you can almost hear her saying, "you do not kill Jezebel with impunity. There are consequences. And they are swift, dire, and incontrovertible."

Before you is the six-foot-high pillar known as the Black Obelisk. Discovered in the ancient Assyrian bastion of Nimrud in 1846, it offers dramatic proof of the price paid for Jehu's overthrow of the Omride dynasty. Dense cuneiform inscriptions and graphic bas-relief panels carved into the polished black stone record the military conquests of Assyria's Shalmanezer III, "king of multitudes of men, marcher over the whole world." In one of the most prominent panels, Shalmanezer is shown shaded by an attendant bearing a parasol; his face is strong and sensual, his hair a Pre-Raphaelite flow of rippling tresses bound by a gem-studded headband, his beard curled and braided. He looks straight out over a man bowed low in submission at his feet, as one would someone who was beneath notice, let alone contempt. The man is on his knees, his head on the ground and his rump raised high in the air in the posture of a fawning dog. "Jehu of the House of Omri," reads the inscription.

The usurper who ordered Jezebel thrown to the dogs is now depicted as a dog himself, groveling to his new master. Shalmanezer evidently shared Jezebel's scorn. The inscription accompanying this panel identifies the new Israelite ruler not as "Jehu King of Israel" but as "Jehu of the House of Omri," since even if he had eradicated the Omrides, he still existed only in the shadow of their greatness. And only by virtue of their wealth. The inscription makes it clear that the price for Israel's entry into the Assyrian empire was heavy: the tribute paid by Jehu included gold, silver, arms, and regal insignia, all the usual payments in what was essentially a kind of imperial protection racket. But the most striking detail is the date given for this tribute: the eighteenth year of Shalmanezer's reign. That is 841 B.C.—just one year after Jehu seized the throne.

Rarely does history reveal political folly so quickly and so dramatically. One moment, Jehu seems to be riding high; the next, he is literally brought low. Yet from the moment he set out to seize the crown, spurred on by the prophet Elisha, his humiliation—and that of his kingdom—was inevitable.

The story of how it happened is told in Kings with righteous, blood-drenched fervor. The morning after his triple regicide, Jehu set about consolidating his power with a brutal purge of the kingdom. He sent instructions to all the elders and local governors: "If you are with me, cut off the heads of your lord's sons, and come to me in Jezreel at this time tomorrow." Every male in any way related to the House of Omri, that is, was to be seized and beheaded. The meaning was clear: "You are either with me or against me; prove your loyalty to the new regime."

Fearful for their own lives, the elders and governors followed orders. Seventy heads were duly sent to Jezreel, where they were heaped in two piles by the main gate as a suitably ghastly backdrop for Jehu's first speech to the Jezreelites. "You are righteous," he declared. "I conspired against my lord and slew him, and whoever has slain all these, know that this is the word of Yahweh against the House of Ahab, and that Yahweh has done what he declared by his servant Elijah."

It is a classic example of how to institute a totalitarian regime. Manipulate the public into doing your work for you, so that the blood is on everyone's hands; all are thus thoroughly compromised, and resistance will be minimal. The elders and governors had been co-opted into Jehu's reign of terror, and now he reassured them with the self-justifying cliché that is as potent today as it was three thousand years ago: they were doing the will of God. "See my zealousness for Yahweh," he declared, wrapping himself in the flag of Yahwism to present his personal ambition as the highest principle. It was the first time we know of that faith was so cynically manipulated. But not, of course, the last.

The law of *herem* was now invoked against "the enemy within." The kingdom had to be purified of Omride contamination, the last stain wiped out. Massacre built on massacre. Next to die were all the slain King Joram's counselors and priests, followed in short order by the entourage that had accompanied the Judean king Ahaziah to Jezreel, caught as they were trying to flee back home. And last but most definitely not least, "the priests and worshippers of Baal" in Samaria, who were summoned into the temple built for Jezebel and systematically put to the sword. The temple itself was demolished and turned into a cesspool, an act that would be mirrored nine centuries later, when the Romans would take Jerusalem, burn the second Yahwist temple to the ground, and put the site to the same use.

In just a few days, Jehu had undone all that decades of Omride rule had achieved. Tyre, outraged at the savage death meted its former princess royal, cut off all relations with Israel. So too did Judea, where Jezebel's daughter Athaliah was now the reigning queen mother. Outrage would be a mild term for her reaction to her son being murdered in the most cowardly fashion and her mother in the most ghastly one; she lashed out in absolute fury, seizing the Judean throne for herself and instituting her own massacre of all who might be inspired by Jehu's "Yahwist" rebellion to rise up against her. The split with the northern kingdom was now irrevocable.

Israel had never been more isolated. In its newly cleansed state, it was easy prey for its traditional enemy, Damascus, where King Hazael set about fulfilling Elisha's prophecy that he would wreak havoc on Israel. "I killed Joram the son of Ahab king of Israel, and I killed Ahaziah son of the House of David, and I set their towns into ruins and turned their land into desolation," he boasted on the remains of a victory monument found by archaeologists at Dan, the northernmost Israelite outpost.

He did? It seems at first to be a flat-out contradiction of the Kings account, which places the lethal arrows solidly in Jehu's hands. But it makes sense if Jehu was indeed operating under the aegis of Hazael and thus, in effect, as his agent. And in fact Jehu's coup d'état could only have happened if Hazael had agreed to a cessation of hostilities at Ramot Gilead, leaving the usurper free to go about his bloody work on the home front. Essentially, Jehu acted as Hazael's pawn, blinded by ambition to the obvious: the agenda of the king of Damascus was not his own.

His eyes were opened soon enough. The moment the Omrides and all their supporters had been slaughtered and Israel's alliances irrevocably broken, Damascus renewed its attack, leaving Jehu with only one desperate option: turn for protection to Assyria, the powerful empire to the east of Damascus. So the self-declared zealot for Yahweh pledged his loyalty to Assyria, fawned at Shalmanezer's feet, and thus betrayed his god.

Even Jezebel would have been rendered speechless at Jehu's folly. Any vengeful satisfaction she might have felt in seeing him abase himself this way would have been far outweighed by the fact that she'd have seen instantly what Jehu could not: you invited the Assyrians in only at the expense first of your independence, and then of your very existence. Jehu had not only killed the whole of the Omride dynasty; he had in effect killed the whole Kingdom of Israel. Though it would take more than a century to come to pass, he had signed Israel's death warrant as surely as he had carried out the one on Jezebel.

When the Kings writers told Israel's story, they stuck close to a highly parochial point of view, obscuring the larger political reality, which was that Israel's dramas were enacted entirely in the shadow of the Assyrian empire, administered from its capital of Nineveh on the Tigris River—a magnificent city of canals and aqueducts, ornate palaces and colossal bas-reliefs, reduced today to the battle-scarred misery of the Iraqi city of Mosul. So far as the Assyrians were concerned, the conflicts between Israel and its neighbors were as squabbles between ants on the back of an elephant. Their interest in the area focused on gaining access to the Mediterranean and control of the trade routes; to this end they required peace, so Shalmanezer and his successors imposed a kind of Pax Assyriana, reducing all the Near East kingdoms to vassaldom. Israel was now entirely dependent on the good grace of the Assyrians. And they were not known for good grace.

Jehu's totalitarian regime lasted twenty-eight years, but the kingdom was so badly weakened that it would never recover. The eighth-century prophets Amos and Hosea both saw what was coming. "They multiply falsehood and violence. They make a bargain with Assyria, but Assyria will not save us," said Hosea. As violence built on violence, Yahweh would "avenge the blood of Jezreel on the House of Jehu." The kingdom soon became so anarchic that four rulers were assassinated in the space of fifteen years, one of them after only six months on the throne. And since the Assyrians, like all imperial powers, liked their vassal states quiet and docile, they moved in to "pacify" the kingdom they still called "the land of the House of Omri."

Pacification Assyrian style was a brutal business. There was no mercy. A mere beheading was almost an act of kindness. A cuneiform inscription in the name of Sargon, the Assyrian king who took and destroyed Samaria in 722 B.C., gives the grisly details: "I built a pillar by the city gate and I flayed all the chief men, and I covered the pillar with their skins . . . Some I impaled. And I cut off the limbs of the officers . . . Many captives from among them I burned with fire . . . From some I cut off their noses, their ears, and their fingers. I put out the eyes of many."

The flaying, impaling, burning, and mutilating done, Sargon then implemented the standard Assyrian strategy of population transfer. All elements capable of resistance—scribes and priests, officials and craftsmen, and of course soldiers—were deported, to be replaced by settlers from other parts of the Assyrian empire. The strategy was horribly effective. Only the peasants were left in place to keep the land productive, and they had been thoroughly terrorized into submission.

By one estimate, more than four million people were displaced in various population transfers during the three hundred years of the Assyrian empire. Even if you move the decimal point one place to the left, as is often wise with ancient numerical tallies, the number is close to half a million. The Israelites were just a small portion of this vast population transfer; Sargon listed 27,290 deportees from the city of Samaria, presumably all those who had survived the initial onslaught and been unable to flee. They were chained together using rings punched through their noses and then force-marched hundreds of miles east; those who did not die on the way were then dispersed to various corners of the vast Assyrian empire. The ten tribes that by legend had made up the northern kingdom would never be heard of again, becoming the legendary "ten lost tribes of Israel."

Exactly 120 years had passed since the day Jezebel was thrown to the dogs—the ideal biblical lifetime. Now the whole kingdom had suffered the equivalent fate. It was literally wiped off the map. In an emphatic twist of historical irony, Jehu's declaration on Jezebel's fate could as well have been "They shall not say, This was Israel."

But if there was a horrible kind of poetic justice in Israel's destruction—or as Kings would have it, divine justice—Jezebel would have been the first to reject it. Retribution was for the militant Yahwists, not for her. "Who do you think I am to take satisfaction in such suffering and misery?" she would have said, her voice heavy with insult and heavier still with the knowledge that her policies had been proved right by their negation. Not only had the pride and power and independence of the Israel of her time been utterly undone; the most bitter pill of all was the fact that this downfall had essentially been willed into being by the kingdom's own prophets. In a stunning example of self-fulfilling prophecy, Elijah and Elisha had helped bring about exactly what they most feared. Ideology had replaced pragmatism; faith had ridden roughshod over a sense of reality. As it still is today, the result could only be disaster.

Refugees poured from the north into the southern kingdom of Judea, bringing with them the terrible knowledge of irretrievable loss. A new generation of prophets warned that only the most exclusive adherence to Yahwism could save Judea from the same fate. But that was not to be. Even though the throne was back in Yahwist hands—Athaliah had held power for only six years until she too was assassinated—the Judeans ignored every "woe unto you" from their prophets. They worshipped Asherah "the queen of heaven" just as the Israelites had done in the north; they "played the harlot," as the prophets put it, refusing to believe that they too could be thrown to the dogs. And for more than a century, it looked as though they might be right. Assyria was distracted both by internal power struggles and by a fight for regional dominance against the rising power of Babylon to its south. But early in the sixth century, when Babylon conquered Assyria and Judea made an ill-judged attempt to take advantage of the situation and throw off the yoke of vassaldom, the prophetic warnings came true. Babylon's King Nabu-Kaduri-Usur II, better known today by the Hebrew version of his name, Nebuchadnezzar, may have been devoted to culture—he commissioned the famed Hanging Gardens of Babylon—but he was equally devoted to establishing firm control of his new empire.

In 586 B.C. Babylonian forces took Jerusalem. The temple was set alight until its stones cracked and crumbled into rubble. The Judean king was blinded after being forced to watch his sons killed, and once again a terrible forced exodus took place. The aristocracy, regional governors, generals, soldiers, elders, traders, craftsmen, priests, and scribes, all were force-marched east across the desert, leaving only a cowed peasant population behind. As with the northern kingdom, so now with the south.

It could have been—should have been, by any rational analysis—the end of the Israelites as a people, certainly the end of Yahweh as a god. His people uprooted, his center of worship destroyed—what hope could there be? And yet against all likelihood, the Judeans did not disappear into the mists of ancient history. Quite the contrary: they would write it.

Jezebel

By the rivers of Babylon,
There we sat down and there we wept,
When we remembered Zion.

As the psalmist wrote, memory was all that was left. The trinity of the covenant was broken: the land gone, the people dislocated. And the god? How could he exist distant from his own soil, his own territory? How could he possibly prevail in Babylon, the city whose name, Bab el-Ili, meant "gate of the gods"—all the "other" gods? Surely Yahweh had utterly failed his people?

But as Edward Said pointed out, "Exiles cross borders, break barriers of thought and experience." The break with the land brought about an extraordinary innovation. Yahweh could no longer be seen as a fertility god bringing rain to his land; with the land gone, the very idea of a territorial god had become untenable. If Yahweh was to exist at all, then, he would have to be beyond all that. A dislocated people needed a dislocated god—a god whose power was no longer limited to the soil of his own land. An abstract, universal god, that is. And so the Babylonian exile became the tipping point for monotheism. It forced the monotheistic idea, which paradoxically could take root only in the absence of soil.

Here, in the very "gate of the gods," the Judean scribes and priests staged one of the most stunning acts of defiance of all time: seemingly abandoned by their god, they re-created him. The "no other gods before me" of the Ten Commandments, with its implicit recognition of the existence of other gods in other territories, would now become Isaiah's "there is no god but me"—the first definitive assertion of monotheism. It was the beginning, essentially, of God with a capital *G*. And by re-creating their god—by creating God—the Judeans also re-created themselves.

Much of the Hebrew bible was first written in Babylon by a people determined to preserve their identity. Before the exile, their identity had been determined by their geography; now, in the absence of that geography, their identity could lie only in their history, so that is what they wrote—the story of how they came into the land and, in Kings, of how they then lost it. As biblical scholar Mark Smith put it, "The text was substituted for the land."

But as in all ancient storytelling, there was also a magical aspect to the process. A story well told could not only explain why things had happened the way they did; it could also have the power to alter what happened next. In the fervor of this story's longing for the land—a longing palpable throughout the Hebrew bible—lay the hope for a return to it, and hope was sustenance. By writing, an uprooted people gained not just a past but also a future.

The Yahweh they wrote into being determined his people's history according to whether or not he was pleased with them, and this was oddly reassuring. It meant that they were not subject to the vagaries of fate or the whims of many gods but were part of a systematic pattern of cause and effect, human guilt and divine consequence. It meant there was a reason for what had happened to them. They had been punished for following "false gods" and "playing the harlot," but the punishment had been deserved. Divine goodwill was not free; it came with conditions. Yahweh would not tolerate disloyalty.

This new sense of conditionality reflected the anxiety of exile. But it also had a plus side: if Yahweh acted according to what humans did, he could then also be controlled by what humans did. For all its radical punitiveness, the monotheistic idea empowered the dispossessed Judeans in a way that only kings had been empowered before. It placed them in control of their destiny; what they did, how they acted, mattered in the world. In exile, a people without control found a way to regain it.

The scribes and priests and prophets carried one god into exile, and quite another out of it a hundred and fifty years later. By the time Persia conquered Babylon and the Judean elite acted on Cyrus the Great's permission to return to their land, the territorial national god had been written into the abstract universal God, his power all the more awesome and terrifying precisely in the invisibility of its source. Prophets would no longer speak directly with him. There would be no more manifestations in burning bushes or lightning bolts, in voices loud with thunder or even still and small. There would be no more kings and queens to rail against either. Power would now be held by temple priests, and sacred texts would be the focus of allegiance. Religion as we know it today begins here.

That Jezebel should have been accorded the role of the prime villain in the biblical story is hardly surprising. An outspoken foreigner, a faithful polytheist, and a powerful woman—she was the perfect outsider so far as the Judean scribes were concerned, all the more suited to the role of "fall guy" since she had been safely dead for three centuries. Yet they may well have written something of themselves into their portrait of their most treasured enemy, for perhaps no one would have admired the sheer daring of what they did in exile more than Jezebel herself. In what seemed to be a hopeless situation, they displayed defiance and pride, the very qualities that exile was designed to undermine. They did indeed break barriers of thought, challenging their fate and taking control of it. And though Jezebel would have found the result abhorrent, she would surely have applauded the process. She could afford to do so, after all, because though the scribes intended that her polytheistic faith be trampled into the earth as surely as she was, their vengeful ardor contained the seeds of its own failure. Polytheism would not disappear. As Jezebel could have told them, even to imagine so was an overweening act of hubris. The victory they proclaimed was never complete. In fact it still is not.

If the idea of a sole universal god was stunning, it was also inhuman. That, of course, was precisely the point. But mere humans need humanity, which is why, despite all the zealotry and fanaticism rationalized in the name of the one god, there has never been such a thing as pure monotheism. The abstract god is too stark for the human mind, the lone god too lonely.

There appears to be a basic human need for a multiple sense of divinity—a need for intercessors, for messengers, spirits, saints, and prophets, a whole world of divine and semidivine beings who can intercede between us and the sole, unapproachable deity. Like the polytheists of old who believed in what historian Keith Hopkins called "a world full of gods" ruled by one supreme and remote father god, we have developed a richly populated layer of protection from the awe and terrible power of the sole universal god, a kind of safety zone that we can approach without fear of being consumed or of having our humanity burned out by the sheer heat of the encounter, as surely happened when Elijah called down drought on his own people, or when Elisha killed young boys out of mere vanity, or when murders and massacres are committed in the name of Yahweh or Allah or Jesus Christ.

We need softness and gentleness, and the sheer ineffable mystery of the Catholic Holy Ghost or the Kabbalistic Shekhina or the mystical Islamic figure of El-Khadr, "the green one." But we need clear images too. Anthropomorphism still informs our concept of the divine, as is clear when we talk of God as "he," and despite that insistently singular maleness, we have found ways to incorporate the feminine as well as the masculine, the mother as well as the father, the daughter as well as the son. The appeal of early Christianity in the Roman world, for instance, was due not only to the persuasiveness of Paul, but to the fact that it was familiar. Here was a monotheistic religion that included the benefits of a rich polytheistic world. The Holy Trinity—the idea of three in one—was a brilliant incorporation of a polytheistic concept into a monotheistic system, with the Holy Ghost filling the space of the Great Mother. Only the daughter was missing—an absence that may account for the modern fascination with the figure of Mary Magdalene. Whether in scholarly analyses of the Gnostic gospels or in popular fiction like *The Da Vinci Code*, the central role accorded the Magdalene seems to express an unacknowledged longing to complete the holy family with the daughter figure, the one who resurrects the dead son through her love and her grief.

There appears to be no suppressing the infinite human desire for a world rich in divinities. You can find a reflection of ancient pantheism in even the most insistent agnostic, who will acknowledge the transcendental quality of a sunset viewed from a mountaintop, or stand in awe as thunder and lightning sweep in across the plains. In such natural phenomena, we apprehend, if not the one god with a capital *G*, then at least a real sense of the divine, of something that transcends the scale of the human. Throughout the world, springs and grottoes, mountaintops and trees still take on sacred, numinous qualities. The divine is read into the landscape by Australia's aboriginal peoples, glimpsed in the water at the French shrine of Lourdes, and expressed in the glowing needles of the golden spruce that was revered by the Haida nation of Canada's Queen Charlotte Islands until it was cut down. The fundamentalist disdain for nature—the certainty of messianic extremists that all natural resources can be exhausted without care since the coming of the Messiah or the Mahdi and the "end of days" is imminent—looks not just destructive by contrast but downright heretical.

Monotheism survived and thrived not because it negated all other divine beings but because it incorporated them. It was a new form of religious expression that came into being in a time of crisis, when the old one was unable to meet the needs of a people exiled from their land. But no religion arises perfectly formed like Aphrodite on her half shell; faiths cross-breed and interconnect. In the words of Harvard theologian Harvey Cox, "Every religion is like Peer Gynt's famous onion. If you tried to peel away all they have absorbed from other faiths, which are in turn already conglomerates, you would find only more and more layers underneath . . . The genius of a faith is found more in its characteristic ways of combining things than in some induplicable inner essence."

Those who wrote into being the first great monotheistic religion did so indeed in an act of genius, but the stark purity they created in exile would prove too much for their descendants, who would need humanizing divine figures as much as anyone else. And in the ultimate irony, one of these figures would be none other than Elijah.

10.

Carthage

in which the spirit of Jezebel lives on

When you die and leave no body behind, you do not, as Jezebel's assassin so fondly imagined, disappear. Without the irrefutable proof of death, the human mind tends to reject nonbeing and to insist that life continues in another dimension, which is why throughout the history of religion, the absence of a body leads to a long and healthy afterlife, one lived in the minds and souls of others. Resurrection is not a matter of physics but of metaphysics—literally, beyond the physical. So when the Kings writers showed Elijah carried up to heaven in a whirlwind, leaving no body behind, they ensured that his spirit would live on. But by the same token, when they showed Jezebel devoured by dogs, they unwittingly ensured that her spirit too would endure. And they would have been horrified at the form the two afterlives would take.

Elijah is celebrated throughout the Middle East, from Egypt to Syria and as far afield as Kurdistan, where an astounding number of grottoes, caves, shrines, trees, churches, and monasteries are named after him. They are particularly numerous in his traditional stomping grounds of Israel, Palestine, and Jordan, where he is venerated by Jews, Christians, and Muslims alike in what to Jezebel would seem the perfect blending of religions, and to Elijah himself the purest anathema. You can almost hear Jezebel's laughter rippling through the centuries as she taunts her arch-enemy: the fierce guardian of the one true faith was destined to become the folk hero of no less than three true faiths. He has become literally a polytheistic saint.

In Judaism, rabbinic lore spins a dense mesh of legend and ritual around the prophet. Since circumcision is the mark of the covenant, a special chair is reserved for Elijah, the guardian of the covenant, at every *brit milah*—a tradition Hebrew University religion scholar Melila Helner calls a kind of educational punishment for the great Yahwist; with every newborn Jewish male, the man who claimed on Mount Sinai that he and only he was loyal to his god is now forced to witness the lie to his self-pitying plaint. But the prophet is invoked not only on special occasions such as circumcision or the Passover freedom feast, when a goblet of wine is set aside for him, but every week, when Elijah songs are sung for the end of the Sabbath, and every day in the Hebrew grace after meals, which includes the incantation: "May Yahweh in his mercy send us the prophet Elijah, may his memory be blessed, and may he bring us good tidings, help, and comfort."

Good tidings, help, and comfort are not exactly what one

might expect from the biblical Elijah, but afterlives are lived by very different rules than physical ones. They are the products of those who believe in them, images molded to desire. The stark absolutist has been transformed into a tender, caring presence always available in time of need. In a series of unintended ironies, Elijah's afterlife is the antithesis of his biblical one.

The apocryphal book of Ben-Sirah, also known as Ecclesiasticus, predicts that Elijah will "restore the tribes of Israel"—the very tribes in whose destruction he played such a pivotal role. Rabbinic literature has him directing the souls of the pious to their place in paradise—the same task accorded the giant mastiffs of the goddess Gula. He appears in various guises, as a beggar or a horseman or a soldier, or even, irresistibly given his battle against Jezebel, a harlot. He brings rain, rewards the pious, comforts the afflicted, feeds the hungry, heals the sick, protects the persecuted—a life-giver instead of a death-dealer. And instead of making brief appearances in which he metes out terrible judgment, he sits down with great rabbis for long sessions of counsel and guidance, which is why medieval kabbalists referred to mystical experiences as *giluai Eliahu*, "revelations of Elijah."

Yet the biblical Elijah still endures in what for many is his main role: the precursor of the messiah. In Malachi, which is positioned as the last book of the Old Testament in Christian Bibles, we are promised that "I will send you Elijah the prophet before the coming of the great and dreadful day of the Lord." Just as the last book of the New Testament, Revelation, inspires end-of-days fantasies for fundamentalist Christians, so Malachi serves the same purpose for fundamentalist Jews. As a result, Elijah has become the patron saint of the messianic Jewish settler movement in the Palestinian territories, where he almost exactly duplicates his biblical role, since the settlements originally allowed by the Israeli government in the name of security have instead created the kind of radical insecurity that was Elijah's legacy to the ancient Kingdom of Israel. This is why fundamentalist Christians eager for "the rapture" are so peculiarly supportive of the Jewish settler movement; while zealous settlers think the messiah will come when Israel regains all its ancient territories, their Christian supporters see them as a means of hastening the final war of Armageddon—those rivers of blood filling the Jezreel Valley at the foot of Megiddo—and the second coming of Christ.

Elijah's role as herald of the messiah is written into the New Testament as well as the Hebrew bible, but in a new manifestation: in Matthew he takes the form of John the Baptist. The precursor of Christ wears the same pelts as Elijah, feeds off the same carobs—the fruit of the honey-locust tree—and is clearly identified as Elijah by Jesus himself when he appears at the Transfiguration on Mount Tabor, which is just across the Jezreel Valley from Megiddo. Using the Greek form of Elijah's name, Jesus tells his disciples that "Elias truly shall come first and restore all things. But I say unto you Elias is come already, and they knew him not." The disciples then "understood that he spoke unto them of John the Baptist."

In Islam, Elijah lives on as Ilyis, the Arabic form of his name. "We also sent forth Ilyis, who said to his people, 'Have you no fear of Allah? Would you invoke Baal and forsake the Most Glorious Creator?' " reads Sura 37 of the Koran, which makes Elijah one of the great forefathers of Islam. "We bestowed on him the praise of later generations. Peace on Ilyis! Thus we reward the righteous. He was one of our believing servants." As Islamic lore developed, so Elijah's role expanded to fulfill the same functions as in Jewish lore: counselor, healer, comforter, protector, guide to the afterlife. And as in both Judaism and Christianity, so too in Islam, he will usher in the end of days, when the words of the Koran will return to heaven. Taking the form of the mysterious El Khadr, "the green one," he will herald the coming of the Islamic messiah, the Mahdi.

Jezebel's afterlife seems doomed to be the polar opposite of her antagonist's. As biblical scholar Phyllis Trible puts it: "A whirlwind sweeps him up, eunuchs throw her down. Horses transport him, horses trample her. He ascends into heaven, she descends into earth. The numinous clothes him, excrement clothes her. His image lives on exalted, hers lives on debased." But despite the best—or worst—intentions of the Kings writers, Jezebel would undergo a transformation as stunning as Elijah's, if not more so.

True, there are no places named for her—no shrines, groves, or sacred places. And if she were to see Tyre today, she would weep. Or perhaps not: no tears for Jezebel, or at least none she'd let you see. Instead she'd laugh—a cold, mocking laugh that would send chills down your back even in the Mediterranean heat—and give you a look of such withering scorn that you'd wish the sand and stones beneath your feet could open up and swallow you.

You are delusional, she'd insist. This is not the place. Cannot be the place. Not this backwater of a town, this provincial sprawl punctuated with the bombed-out rubble of war. And she'd turn on her heel and leave you wondering if you were indeed delusional, if all the geographers and archaeologists weren't wrong, and the name of Tyre had merely been appropriated by this place in a hopeless bid for lost grandeur.

The city that was once the master of geopolitics is now the victim of it. Just twelve miles north of the border with Israel, in the most politically unstable part of Lebanon, it is, to all intents and purposes, the end of the road. Even the island itself no longer exists. The viaduct from the mainland was destroyed when the city was besieged by Alexander the Great in the fourth century B.C., and the crude berm that Alexander built to replace it stayed in place, sand and silt accumulating on either side of it until what had once been an island became a mere promontory. The gleaming marble walls, the glorious temples, the luxurious palaces, all have been razed and built over so many times—by Greeks and Romans, Byzantines and Saracens, Ottomans and Arabs—that there is barely a sign of what once was.

But though even the greatest cities can be razed, the greatest spirits are another matter. Jezebel's magnificent pride and courage did not know the meaning of the word "defeat," even in death. In trying to "disappear" her body by having it excreted "as dung upon the face of the earth," the biblical scribes defeated their own purpose. Though they intended to write her out of history, they wrote her into it; they wrote so vividly that they helped ensure not that she would be forgotten, but that she would be remembered.

In fact, Jezebel would have endured even without biblical help.

Long before the Kings authors ever sat down to write their indictment of her, her name was destined to live through the centuries. It had already been carried abroad by another indomitable woman from the ruling family of Tyre: Jezebel's own grandniece, Elitha. That name means "woman of God" in Phoenician, but the one by which Elitha is renowned is that given her in later Greek legend: Dido.

Just twenty years after Jezebel's assassination, Dido and her half-brother Pumayyaton, better known in Greek and thence English as Pygmalion, became the joint inheritors of the throne of Tyre. In a bitter outbreak of sibling rivalry, Pygmalion seized sole power for himself and murdered Dido's husband, the high priest of Melqart. Knowing that she was next, Dido moved quickly. That same night, she organized her supporters to seize the ships in the city's northern harbor—along with their cargoes of gold and silver—and set sail west across the Mediterranean to found a new Phoenician outpost at the northernmost tip of Africa, near the modern city of Tunis. She would call it the New City: Qart Hadath in Phoenician, or in English, Carthage.

The power of the new city rose as that of its mother city, Tyre, declined. Across the Mediterranean, the Greeks recognized Carthage by adopting Dido herself. Where Carthaginian legend has it that she threw herself onto a funeral pyre rather than submit to the demands of the native king that she marry him and so betray her dead husband, Virgil would adapt the legend and immortalize her by having her throw herself onto that same pyre in despairing love for his departed hero, Aeneas. Either way, dramatic death clearly ran in the female line of Jezebel's family.

Dido would live on not only in legend but also in the identities of countless women throughout the world. As the Carthaginian empire expanded across the north coast of Africa and up into Spain, it carried its culture and its language with it. And its names. Dido's Phoenician name, Elitha, was adopted in Spanish as Alicia and later in English as Eliza. And in the same way, the name of the greatest of her foremothers entered the Spanish language too. Jezebel's Phoenician name, Ithabaal, became Isabella, and in that form it would achieve its own notoriety. In the fifteenth century, Queen Isabella of Spain ensured her place in history not only by funding Columbus's voyage to the New World but also by authorizing the horrors of the Inquisition. Spanish Jews of the time were more accurate than they realized when they called her "the Catholic Jezebel."

The grandeur of Carthage would not survive much longer than that of its mother city of Tyre. Empires inexorably fade as new ones arise. After Hannibal's disastrous attempt to cross the Alps and take Rome, Carthage was absorbed into the Roman Empire, and the Phoenician language was all but forgotten. Yet Jezebel's name endures. Every Isabel and Isabella gives the lie to Jehu's vainglorious declaration that "they shall not say, This was Jezebel." Her life may have been stamped out, but her name lives on, and with her name, her spirit.

Despite the demeaned image created in the oldest smear campaign on record, the true spirit of Jezebel is indomitable. In this era of renewed militant prophecy, it lives not only in the pride and intelligence of every woman who bears her name, but in everyone who sees clear-eyed the dangers of blind zealotry and the terrible hypocrisy of those who kill in the name of God.

Three thousand years may have passed since Jezebel died, but her spirit cannot be repressed. On the contrary, it is as vital now as it was three millennia ago, standing tall and defiant in the face of fanaticism and intolerance. Courageous, unbowed, and magnificent, Jezebel lives.

Acknowledgments

As the bibliography makes clear, I am deeply indebted to the historians, archaeologists, and biblical scholars on whose work I have drawn in this book, and I trust they feel that their findings have been well used.

In the Middle East, particular thanks are due to Dr. Adel Yahya and his colleagues at the Palestinian Association for Cultural Exchange in Ramallah; to De'eb Hussein of Pella, Jordan; to Carol-Ann Bernheim in Jerusalem; to Amnon Beker of Kibbutz Jezreel; to Dr. Melila Helner of the Hebrew University; to Rabbi Adin Steinsaltz in Jerusalem; to Professor David Ussishkin of Tel Aviv University; and to Dorothy and Zvi Pantanowitz in Zichron Yaakov.

In the United States, I was fortunate to have the stimulating conversation of Jonathan Raban as I was thinking my way through the book; my friend and neighbor Olivier D'Hose was a sharp-eyed first reader and master of technology; Dr. Deborah Appler generously shared her research; and the University of Washington's outstanding library collections together with the interlibrary loan department of the Seattle Public Library made my work possible. At Doubleday, Andrew Corbin's knowledge and understanding made him a dream editor, while Darya Porat patiently guided me through prepublication. And as always, deepest thanks to my longtime friend and agent Gloria Loomis, who acts as my personal Mount Hermon.

Notes

Introduction

3 *"a creature both forceful and bold"*: Josephus, *Jewish Antiquities*.

3 *Theda Bara:* See Djikstra, *Evil Sisters*.

3 *"In the Bitch Hall of Fame"*: Robbins, *Skinny Legs and All*.

3 *"except for a single ruby glittering"*: Robins, *Jezebel*.

3 *"save for a tiny golden girdle"*: Slaughter, *Curse of Jezebel*.

4 *"he turns to gaze at her"*: Shoham, *Tyre and Jerusalem*. For a far more sympathetic dramatic portrayal of Jezebel, see Masefield, "King's Daughter."

4 *stereotype used to stigmatize and exploit black women:* See the Jim Crow Museum of Racist Memorabilia, curated by Ferris State University sociologist David Pilgrim, online at www.ferris.edu/jim-crow/jezebel.

4 *"Jezebel shall be eaten by dogs"*: 1 Kings 21:23.

5 *the last book of the New Testament:* Revelation 2:20–23 reads: "Thou sufferest that woman Jezebel, who calleth herself a prophetess, to teach and to seduce my servants to commit fornication, and to eat things sacrificed unto idols . . . Behold, I will cast her into a bed, and them that commit adultery with her into great tribulation, except they repent of their deeds. And I will kill her children with death." This Jezebel is Saint John of Patmos' contemptuous name for a popular Christian prophet of his time, Thyatira.

5 *it is told in Kings:* 1 Kings 16 through 2 Kings 10.

7 *"none more evil than Ahab"*: 1 Kings 16:30.

9 *"the virgin ironpants"*: Rushdie, *Shame*.

9 *Hillary Clinton was rumored:* Klein, *Truth About Hillary*.

9 *"the only one with balls"*: An endlessly repeated Israeli joke of the late 1960s.

9   *"Harlot!":* 2 Kings 9:22.

13   *"the historical imagination":* Collingwood, *Idea of History.*

14   *"I will cut off":* 1 Kings 21:21.

14   *elsewhere in the Bible:* Genesis 17:10, 12, 14, Leviticus 12:2, and Isaiah 66:7, where the Hebrew word used is *ʒakar,* "male," with specific reference to newborn boys.

1. Tyre

19   *rescued by his sister Anat:* the stories of Baal, Anat, Astarte, and El are the basis of the magnificent epic series of religious poems known as the *Baal Cycle* found on clay tablets at Ras Shamra, the site of the northern Phoenician city of Ugarit, from 1929 on. See Smith, *Ugaritic Baal Cycle.*

21   *The jewel of the Mediterranean:* Aubet, *Phoenicians and the West,* and Moscato, *Phoenicians,* are particularly good on Phoenician culture.

22   *"Haughty Tyre":* Chapters 26–28 of Ezekiel are devoted entirely to Tyre.

24   *"the Tyrian purple":* Legend had it that the dye was discovered by the god Melqart while he was strolling along the shore with his dog and the nymph Tyros. The dog picked up a murex shell and worried at it, then nuzzled Melqart's robe, leaving a purplish stain. It's a lovely story—what more could a man want than a nymph, a dog, and a beautiful stretch of sand?—but reality was a lot tougher. One hundred snails had to be gathered to produce just one gram of dye. Each shell had to be broken open, the snail's glands extracted, and the secretions boiled for ten days in large vats filled with salt water. The vats gave off a nauseating stench, which is why the facilities for producing the dye were well to the south of Tyre in Sarepta, the modern Lebanese town of Sarafand.

26   *"the ships of Tarshish":* Isaiah 2:16.

26   *Ahab was polygamous:* The Kings account doesn't state the number of wives, but 2 Kings 10:1 states that he had seventy sons, a number generally used in the Bible to indicate "many." Polygamy was standard in royal and elite society of the time.

27   *"All glorious is the king's daughter":* Psalm 45:13–16.

28   *"a land flowing with milk and honey":* Exodus 3:8.

28   *the story of Cadmus:* For an entrancing exploration of the legend, see Calasso, *Marriage of Cadmus and Harmony.*

30   *The face of the goddess:* Many of these plaques, dubbed "the woman at the window" plaques by archaeologists, were found in the excavations of Samaria. Similar plaques have been found at three Assyrian sites, where they had presumably been taken as part of the spoils of war after the Assyrian conquest of Samaria in 720 B.C.

30   *"As soon as El spied her":* Translation by Frank Moore Cross in *Canaanite Myth and Hebrew Epic.*

30   *Gula, the goddess of healing:* Ornan, "Goddess Gula and Her Dog."

2. Samaria

35   *Solomon had done the same:* 1 Kings 11:7–8.

35   *Ahab reigned in his name:* See Lang, *Monotheism and the Prophetic Minority.* Lang notes that the British coronation ceremony is modeled on that for the consecration of Israelite kings. When Elizabeth II was crowned in 1953, the Archbishop of Canterbury intoned these words: "As Solomon was anointed king by Zadok the priest and Nathan the prophet, so be thou anointed, blessed, and consecrated Queen over the peoples whom the Lord thy God hath given thee to rule and govern." Like the ancient Israelite ritual, the modern British one includes the presentation of the royal insignia, the new monarch's oath to maintain and defend the law of God, blares of trumpets and rolls of drums, and the people's shout of acclamation, "Long live the king/queen." The ceremony is intended to bestow the spirit of God—"the breath of Yahweh"—on the monarch, and dates from the idea of the "divine right of kings," when kings took on aspects of the divinity in whose name they reigned, so that king and god were often conflated.

36   *"Had the biblical authors and editors":* Finkelstein and Silberman, *The Bible Unearthed.*

37   *Monolith Inscription:* Text in Miller and Hayes, *History of Ancient Israel and Judah.*

37   *the Moabite Stone:* Ibid.

37   *Israel as* bit-Humri: e.g., on the Black Obelisk of Shalmanezer III, ibid.

38   *Like Rabin:* Yitzhak Rabin, chief of staff during Israel's victory in the Six-Day War of 1967, later became prime minister and the architect of a tentative agreement with the Palestinians. For this he was accused of treason by extreme right-wing Israelis and, in 1995, was assassinated by a fundamentalist fanatic.

41 *Ahab and Jezebel's palace:* See Reissner, Fisher, and Lyon, *Harvard Excavations.*

41 *"the house of ivory":* 1 Kings 22:39.

43 *four hundred priestesses:* 1 Kings 18:19.

43 *"Yahweh and his Asherah":* See Becking et al., *Only One God?* Both Astarte and Asherah are regional variations on the Mesopotamian Ishtar, also known as Ishara, for whom the wedding bed was laid in the Epic of Gilgamesh.

43 *"the queen of heaven":* Jeremiah 7:18.

43 *fertility cakes:* Ibid. The triangular poppy-seed-filled *haman taschen*—"Haman's ears"—baked for the Jewish festival of Purim in celebration of Esther's defeat of the evil Haman are clear descendants of these fertility cakes.

43–44 *"polytheistic Yahwism":* Smith, *Early History of God.*

45 *the* Baal Cycle: See Smith, *Ugaritic Baal Cycle.*

46 *a stand-alone chapter:* 1 Kings 20.

46 *"So may the gods do to me":* 1 Kings 20:10.

47 *"It is not the man who puts on armor":* 1 Kings 20:11.

48 *"like two herds of goats":* 1 Kings 20:27.

48 *"If we dress in sackcloth":* 1 Kings 20:31.

49 *"Your servant Ben-Hadad begs you":* 1 Kings 20:32.

49 *"He is my brother":* 1 Kings 20:32.

50 *"When Yahweh your god gives":* Deuteronomy 7:2.

50 *"smite Amalek":* 1 Samuel 15:3.

50 *"Because you have rejected":* 1 Samuel 15:23.

50 *"a man of blood":* 1 Chronicles 28:3.

51 *"I seized and killed":* Text of the Moabite Stone, a.k.a. the Mesha Inscription, in Miller and Hayes, *History of Ancient Israel and Judah.*

51 herem: For an in-depth discussion of this concept, see Niditch, *War in the Hebrew Bible.* Note that the concept was later softened in rabbinical Judaism to become excommunication, or a ban.

52 *"sold himself into evil":* 1 Kings 21:25.

52 *"incited by Jezebel his wife":* Ibid.

53 *"Because you have let go the man":* 1 Kings 20:42.

3. Gilead

58 *"Go up unto Gilead, and take balm":* Jeremiah 46:11.

58 *"Is there no balm in Gilead?":* Jeremiah 8:22.

59 *the* tel *of Master Elijah:* A *tel* is a low hill or mound created when a new city is repeatedly built on top of the ruins of a previous one, then is eventually abandoned so that it is covered over with dust and silt.

59 *"Elijah of Tishbi":* 1 Kings 17:1.

62 *an eternal lesson in atonement:* See Helner, "Zealous Spirit."

63 *"militant" or "opposition" prophecy:* See Uffenheimer, *Early Prophecy in Israel.*

63 *"the ẓealot may be outwardly motivated":* Krakauer, *Under the Banner of Heaven.*

64 *"he exhibits an intense, prurient disgust":* Raban, *My Holy War.*

65 *"The Believer from his height":* Qutb, *Milestones.*

66 *Think of argument as war:* Lakoff, *Don't Think of an Elephant.*

66 *"You have polluted the country":* Jeremiah 3:2.

66–67 *"playing the harlot":* The verb ẓana, meaning "to prostitute oneself" or "to play the harlot," is used to speak of apostasy in, among others, Exodus 34:15–16; Deuteronomy 31:16; throughout Leviticus; Numbers 15:39 and 25:1; Judges 2:17 and 8:27; 1 Chronicles 5:25; fifteen times in Ezekiel; throughout Jeremiah 2 and 3; Psalm 106:39; and Hosea 1:2, 4:5, 4:12, and 9:3.

67 *"sons of a sorceress":* Isaiah 57:3.

67 *"You have offered your services":* Ezekiel 16:28–29.

67 *"a lustful she-camel":* Jeremiah 2:23–24. The meaning is evaded in the King James translation; the Jerusalem Bible renders the passage this way: "A frantic she-camel running in all directions . . . snuffing the breeze in desire; who can control her when she is in heat?"

67 *"infatuated by profligates":* Ezekiel 23:20.

68 *"Let her rid her face of her whoring":* Hosea 2:2–3, 2:13, 2:16–17. The last four lines here involve a triple entendre on the word "Baal." The name used as "lord" for any foreign god also means both "owner" and "husband" and is still used in both these senses in modern Hebrew.

68–69 *"They will level your mound":* Ezekiel 16:39.

70 *"pagan queen":* In, for instance, Gloria Howe Bremkamp's novel *Merai: The Woman Who Challenged Queen Jeẓebel and the Pagan Gods* (Harper, 1986).

70 *the myth of orgy:* The phrase was coined by Frymer-Kensky in *In the Wake of the Goddesses.*

70 *"sacred prostitute":* See in particular Bird, *Missing Persons;* Oden, *Bible Without Theology;* Hooks, *Sacred Prostitution.*

71 *"The temples of the Semitic deities"*: Smith, *Lectures on the Religion of the Semites.*

71 *"voluptuous and dissolute"*: Budde, *Religion of Israel to the Exile.*

71 *"Immorality was nowhere so flagrant"*: Cumont, *Oriental Religions in Roman Paganism.*

71 *"all girls were obliged"*: Fraser, *Golden Bough,* vol. 1, pt. 4.

71 *"Sacred prostitution was apparently"*: Albright, *Archaeology and the Religion of Israel.*

72 *"There is, to be sure, a mounting hesitancy"*: Oden, *Bible Without Theology.*

72 *"The foulest Babylonian custom"*: Herodotus, *History,* vol. 1.

73 *women began to rise in the ranks:* See, most notably, Ackerman, *Under Every Green Tree*; Frymer-Kensky, *In the Wake of the Goddesses*; Bird, *Missing Persons and Mistaken Identities*; Yee, *Poor Banished Children of Eve.*

74 *Western image of the Middle East:* See Said, *Orientalism.*

75 *"As Yahweh the god of Israel lives"*: 1 Kings 17:1.

4. Carmel

78 *"You shall be cursed in the city"*: Deuteronomy 28:16.

79 *the advent of iron tools:* See Forbes, *Studies in Ancient Technology.*

79 *"Take heed that your heart be not deceived"*: Deuteronomy 11:16.

79 *"I will make a wilderness of her"*: Hosea 2:3.

82 *"internal jihad"*: In Stern, *Terror in the Name of God.*

82 *"because the true faith is in jeopardy"*: Ibid.

83 *"a cleansing force"*: Fanon, *Wretched of the Earth.*

84 *"Now I know that you are a man of god"*: 1 Kings 17:24.

84 *"Go show yourself to Ahab"*: 1 Kings 18:1.

85 *"Is it you, you troubler of Israel"*: 1 Kings 18:7.

85 *"It is not I who have afflicted Israel"*: 1 Kings 18:18.

85 *"Go gather all of Israel"*: 1 Kings 18:19.

86 *the highest point of Mount Carmel:* Geologists have in fact established that another part of the Upper Carmel, closer to Haifa, is a few feet higher than the Muhraka, but the Muhraka is nonetheless still known as the highest point, partly because of tradition and partly because it looks higher to the naked eye.

87 *"Then the prophet Elijah arose"*: Ben-Sirah/Ecclesiasticus, 48:1.

88 *"the site of Armageddon"*: The only reference in the Bible to Armaged-

don is in Revelation 16:16 ("And he gathered them together into a place called in the Hebrew tongue Armageddon"). The assumption is that this is a Greek corruption of the Hebrew Har Megiddo, meaning Mount Megiddo, though in fact there is no Mount Megiddo and never was. Megiddo was a city at the southwestern edge of the long, wide Valley of Jezreel. It was a ceremonial center in prebiblical times, an administrative center in Omride times, subsequently a fortified city, and currently an archaeological park. Today it is referred to as Tel Megiddo.

89 *thirty-four major battles:* See Cline, *Battles of Armageddon.*

90 *"Choose!" he yelled:* 1 Kings 18:21.

91 *"whichever god answers":* 1 Kings 18:24.

91 *"there was no voice, and none who answered":* 1 Kings 18:26.

91 *"They leaped around the altar":* Ibid.

92 *"They began to howl:"* Quoted in de Vaux, *Bible and the Ancient Near East.*

92 *Enheduanna:* Quoted in Frymer-Kensky, *In the Wake of the Goddesses.*

93 *"She cut her skin with a stone":* Translated by Ackerman in *Warrior, Dancer, Seductress, Queen.*

93 *"answering a call of nature":* 1 Kings 18:27. The King James translation evasively renders this as "gone aside."

94 *"Yahweh, the god of Abraham":* 1 Kings 18:36.

94 *"And then Yahweh's fire fell":* 1 Kings 18:38.

94 *"Take hold of the priests of Baal":* 1 Kings 18:40.

95–96 *a cloud "as small as a man's hand":* 1 Kings 18:44.

97 *"Whoever is on the side of Yahweh, to me":* Exodus 32:26.

99 *"So may the gods do to me":* 1 Kings 19:2.

100 *"If you are Elijah":* In Basileion C, Kings III 19:2 (1 Kings 19:2) of *Septuagint Version of the Old Testament,* tr. Brenton.

100 *"Her liver swelled with laughter":* Translated by Ackerman in *Warrior, Dancer, Seductress, Queen.*

101 *"He ran for his life":* 1 Kings 19:3.

5. The Vineyard

105 *A series of excavations:* See Ussishkin and Woodhead, "Excavations at Tel Jezreel."

106 *"Once there was a vineyard":* 1 Kings 21:1.

106 *"Give me your vineyard":* 1 Kings 21:2.

108 *Moses' spies from the land of Canaan:* Numbers 13:23.

109 *"Yahweh forbids me":* 1 Kings 21:3.

Notes

109   *"Land is a central . . . theme"*: Brueggemann, *Land.*

110   *charter of the ruling Hamas party:* The English translation of the 1988 text is online at www.palestinecenter.org/cpap/documents/charter.html.

110   *two mule-loads of Israelite soil:* 2 Kings 5:17.

111   *"sullen and displeased"*: 1 Kings 21:4.

111   *"Why are you so displeased"*: 1 Kings 21:5.

112   *Talmudist Adin Steinsaltz:* Personal communication to the author.

112   *"Ahab was so addicted to her"*: Wiesel, *Five Biblical Portraits.*

113   *"a coward in thine own esteem"*: Shakespeare, *Macbeth,* Act I, scene VII.

113   *"Come you spirits, unsex me here"*: Shakespeare, *Macbeth,* Act I, scene V.

113   *"She wrote letters in Ahab's name"*: 1 Kings 21:8.

113   *"a kind of lynch law of ancient times"*: Rofé, "Vineyard of Naboth."

114   *the Whitewater affair:* It is disconcerting to realize that nearly three thousand years after the episode of Naboth's vineyard, the Whitewater real estate scandal of the 1990s was manufactured by political opponents of the Clinton administration to discredit a sitting president and his outspoken wife, even down to malicious rumors that an aide who committed suicide had actually been murdered to ensure his silence. Those who drummed up the scandal may well have taken their cue from Kings, seeing Hillary Clinton as a modern Jezebel whose political outlook threatened the conservative agenda of orthodox Republicans.

114   *"Jezebel reveals the whole plot"*: Rofé, "Vineyard of Naboth."

116   *"cut off" the priests of Yahweh:* 1 Kings 18:4.

116   *two halves of a slaughtered animal:* Jeremiah 34:18, which reads "I will make the men who transgressed my covenant . . . like the calf which they cut in two and passed between its parts." For more, see Hillers, *Covenant.*

117   *"killed the priests of Yahweh"*: 1 Kings 18:13.

118   *"Get up and take possession"*: 1 Kings 21:15.

119   *"Have you found me, my enemy?"* 1 Kings 21:20.

119   *"Have you murdered"*: 1 Kings 21:19.

119   *"I want to ask you"*: Quoted in Ari Shavit, "The General: An Israeli Journalist's Six Years of Conversation with Ariel Sharon," *The New Yorker,* January 23 and 30, 2006.

121   *"Woe to those who are at ease"*: Amos 6:1.

121   *"Kings is the history of landed Israel"*: Brueggemann, *Land.*

122   *"I will bring evil upon you"*: 1 Kings 21:21.

122   *"And I will cut off from Ahab every one":* Ibid.

123   *"Ahab's people who die in the city":* 1 Kings 21:24.

123   *King Jeroboam and King Baasha:* 1 Kings 15:11 and 1 Kings 16:4.

124   *"And the dogs shall eat Jezebel":* 1 Kings 21:23.

6. Sinai

126   *"the God-trodden mountain":* Kazantzakis, *Journeying.*

127   *"And behold the Lord passed by":* 1 Kings 19:11.

127   *"What are you doing here, Elijah?":* 1 Kings 19:13.

128   *"I have been very zealous":* 1 Kings 19:14.

128   *"Go back by way of Damascus":* 1 Kings 19:15.

133   *creation of Adam and Eve:* "Male and female created he them" in Genesis 1:27, and "from the rib, he made a woman" in Genesis 2:22.

134   *he's plowing the fields of Abel Mehola:* 1 Kings 19:19.

137   *"As Yahweh lives":* 2 Kings 2:2.

138   *"May your spirit be doubled in me":* 2 Kings 2:9.

138   *a chariot of fire appears:* 2 Kings 2:12.

139   *"The spirit of Elijah rests on Elisha":* 2 Kings 2:15.

139   *merkaba (chariot) mysticism:* For an introduction to the subject, see Silberman, *Heavenly Powers.*

139   *eternal hero:* Campbell, *Hero With a Thousand Faces.*

140   *Moses died on Mount Nebo:* Deuteronomy 34:1.

141   *"heal the water":* 2 Kings 2:21.

142   *"Rise up thou bald one":* 2 Kings 2:23.

142   *calls into being two bears:* 2 Kings 2:24.

7. Damascus

146   *"he rent his clothes":* 1 Kings 21:27.

148   *"Go up to Ramot Gilead and prosper":* 1 Kings 22:15.

149   *"How many times do I have to make you swear":* 1 Kings 22:16.

149   *"Yahweh has put a lying spirit":* 1 Kings 22:22.

149   *"If you return at all in peace":* 1 Kings 22:28.

149   *"between the lower armor and the breastplate":* 1 Kings 22:34.

149   *"in innocence":* Ibid.

150   *"And the blood ran out of the wound":* 1 Kings 22:35.

150   *"washed by the pool, and the dogs":* 1 Kings 22:38.

151   *a deliberate contraction:* Gray, *I and II Kings.*

152 *"A land that devours its inhabitants":* Numbers 13:32.

152 *a full week of public mourning:* For details of mourning rituals, see Olyan, *Biblical Mourning.*

153 *"You have been called, O Ahab":* Adapted by me from a Phoenician funerary incantation in Pardee, *Ritual and Cult at Ugarit.*

153 *"drank tears like wine":* Ackerman, *Warrior, Dancer, Seductress, Queen.*

155 *"Well-being for Ahab":* Adapted by me from a Phoenician funerary incantation in Pardee, *Ritual and Cult at Ugarit.*

156 *the title of Great Lady or gevira:* For more on the role of the queen mother, see Ackerman, *Warrior, Dancer, Seductress, Queen.*

157 *visiting her husband and bowing down:* 1 Kings 1:16.

157 *her son, King Solomon, bows down to her:* 1 Kings 2:19.

158 *her younger son Joram:* Those referring back to Kings will find considerable confusion as to nomenclature. Joram and Jehoram are used interchangeably both for Jezebel's younger son and for her son-in-law (the son of the Judean king Jehoshaphat), while Ahaziah is the name both of Jezebel's elder son (the one who died after falling from a balcony) and of her grandson Ahaziah of Judea.

159 *"I am Mesha, son of Chemosh-Yat":* Text of the Mesha Inscription, a.k.a. the Moabite Stone, in Miller and Hayes, *History of Ancient Israel and Judah.*

160 *"What have I to do with you?":* 2 Kings 3:13.

160 *"Yahweh will deliver the Moabites":* 2 Kings 3:18.

160 *"took his eldest son, the heir":* 2 Kings 3:27.

161 *high infant mortality rate:* See Jackson, *Doctors and Diseases in the Roman Empire.*

164 *a senior Damascus general:* The story of Naaman and Elisha takes up most of 2 Kings 5.

164 *"every good thing of Damascus":* 2 Kings 8:9.

165 *"Your son Ben-Hadad, king of Damascus":* 2 Kings 8:8.

165 *"Go tell the king that he will certainly recover":* 2 Kings 8:10.

165 *"Why do you weep, my lord?":* 2 Kings 8:12.

165 *"Because I know the evil":* Ibid.

166 *"But who am I, your servant":* 2 Kings 8:13.

166 *"Yahweh has shown me":* Ibid.

166 *"Then the next day, he took a cloth":* 2 Kings 8:15.

167 *"Gird up your loins":* 2 Kings 9:1.

168 *"Thus says Yahweh the god":* 2 Kings 9:6.

168 *"they blew the horn":* 2 Kings 9:13.

8. Jezreel

170 *"The wild dogs of Najaf"*: Berenson, "After the Siege, a City of Ruins, Its Dead Rotting."

171 *"That you roar at the land"*: In Frymer-Kensky, *In the Wake of the Goddesses*.

171 *"When someone's javelin or sword"*: Homer, *Iliad*.

172 *yet modern chemical analysis:* Rozell, "Dog Saliva: The Next Wonder Drug?"

172 *dogs as effective as high-tech medical testing:* McNeil, "Dogs Excel on Smell Test to Find Cancer."

172 *hair of a dog placed on the forehead:* In Pardee, *Ritual and Cult in Ugarit*.

174 *"May the valley be filled with their bodies":* In Miller and Hayes, *History of Ancient Israel and Judah*.

174 *"Their corpses will be eaten by dogs":* In Pritchard, *Ancient Near Eastern Texts*.

174 *two Israelite kings:* Jeroboam and Baasha.

174 *"in madness":* 2 Kings 9:20.

175 *"Is it peace, Jehu?":* 2 Kings 9:22.

176 *"What peace, when your mother Jezebel's harlotries":* 2 Kings 9:22.

176 *"Treachery, Ahaziah!":* 2 Kings 9:23.

176 *"He drew his bow with his full strength":* 2 Kings 9:24.

176 *"Cut him down too":* 2 Kings 9:27.

177 *"She painted her eyes":* 2 Kings 9:30.

177 *"Show me, my women, like a queen":* Shakespeare, *Antony and Cleopatra*, Act V, scene II.

178 *white lead powder:* For details of makeup, see Forbes, *Studies in Ancient Technology*.

179 *"woman at the window" plaques:* Photos can be found in Isserlin, *Israelites*; Tubb, *Canaanites*; and on the cover of McKinlay, *Reframing Her*.

180 *"My life begins to dissolve like mist":* In Shulamit Kalugai, *Nashim* (Women) (Yavne, 1936). This is my own translation. The original Hebrew can also be found with a different translation in *Hebrew Feminist Poems from Antiquity to the Present*, ed. Kaufman, Hassan-Rokem, and Hess.

183 *"Is it peace, Zimri":* 2 Kings 9:31.

183 *Jehu takes on the role of the pruner:* Olyan, "2 Kings 9:31."

184   *"Throw her down":* 2 Kings 9:33.

184   *"And they threw her down":* Ibid.

185   *"Go see to this cursed woman":* 2 Kings 9:34.

185   *"Men feared death itself less":* Brichto, "Kin, Cult, Land, and Afterlife."

186   *"May they have no resting place among the shades":* Text of the sarcophagus of King Ezmunazar in Pritchard, *Ancient Near Eastern Texts.*

186   *"no more of her than her head and her feet":* 2 Kings 9:35.

187   *Today, henna is still used:* For a remarkable collection of information on henna, see the Encyclopedia of Henna, online at www.henna page.com/henna/encyclopedia/index.html.

187–88   *"This is the word of Yahweh when":* 2 Kings 9:37.

188   *"You shall bake barley cakes with human dung":* Ezekiel 4:12.

188   *"They shall be dung upon the face of the earth":* Jeremiah 8:12.

188   *"Behold I will corrupt your seed":* Malachi 2:13.

188   *"your houses shall be made into a dunghill":* Daniel 2:5.

189   *"The repugnance, the retching, thrusts":* Kristeva, *Powers of Horror.*

9. Babylon

191–92   *"king of multitudes of men":* Text of the Black Obelisk in Miller and Hayes, *History of Ancient Israel and Judah.*

193   *"If you are with me, cut off the heads":* 2 Kings 10:6.

193   *"You are righteous":* 2 Kings 10:9.

193   *"See my zealousness for Yahweh":* 2 Kings 10:16.

194   *"the priests and worshippers of Baal":* 2 Kings 10:19.

195   *"I killed Joram the son of Ahab":* Text of the Dan Stele, a.k.a. the King David Inscription since it contains the earliest nonbiblical reference to King David found so far, in Biran and Naveh, "Aramaic Stele."

196   *"They multiply falsehood and violence":* Hosea 7:11.

196   *"avenge the blood of Jezreel":* Hosea 1:4.

197   *"I built a pillar by the city gate":* Text of Sargon inscription in Pritchard, *Ancient Near Eastern Texts.*

197   *more than four million people were displaced:* See Oded, *Mass Deportations.*

200   *"By the rivers of Babylon":* Psalm 137:1.

200   *"Exiles cross borders":* Said, "The Mind in Winter."

200   *"no other gods before me":* Exodus 20:3.

201   *"there is no god but me":* Isaiah 44:6, also 43:10–11 and 45:5. Note that the later chapters of Isaiah, known as Deutero-Isaiah, were writ-

ten in exile in the sixth century B.C. and were added on to the prophetic text.

201 *"The text was substituted for the land"*: Smith, *Origins of Biblical Monotheism.*

203 *"a world full of gods"*: Hopkins, *World Full of Gods.*

204 *the Gnostic gospels:* These include a Gospel of Mary, written in the voice of Mary Magdalene. See King, *Gospel of Mary of Magdala.*

205 *Australia's aboriginal peoples:* See, for example, Chatwin, *Songlines.*

205 *golden spruce that was revered by the Haida:* See Vaillant, *Golden Spruce.*

205 *Peer Gynt's famous onion:* Cox, *Seduction of the Spirit.* The reference is to Act V, scene 5, of Henrik Ibsen's verse play *Peer Gynt,* in which the hero searches for the core of his identity by peeling an onion but finds only layer after layer.

10. Carthage

208 *rabbinic lore:* For more, see Wiener, *Prophet Elijah.*

208 *a kind of educational punishment:* Helner, "Zealous Spirit."

209 *"restore the tribes of Israel"*: Ben Sirah/Ecclesiasticus, 48:10.

209 *"I will send you Elijah"*: Malachi 4:5.

210 *John the Baptist:* Some Palestinian Christians celebrate Elijah in yet another guise, identifying him with Saint George, the horseback saint who slew his dragon at Ramle, on the coastal plain between Jerusalem and the Mediterranean, as the original Elijah fought the dragon of polytheism.

210 *"Elias truly shall come first"*: Matthew 17:10–13.

210 *"We also sent forth Ilyis"*: in *Koran,* tr. Dawood.

211 *El Khadr:* The mysterious figure of El Khadr, also known as Il-Khidr, acts as the guide to Moses in Sura 18 of the Koran. For more on his legend in Palestine, see Augustinovic, *El-Khadr and the Prophet Elijah.*

211 *"A whirlwind sweeps him up"*: Trible, "Odd Couple."

212 *the bombed-out rubble of war:* Tyre, still rebuilding after the destruction of the Lebanese civil war of 1975–90, was again bombed by the Israel Defense Forces in the summer of 2006 in an attempt to destroy the Hezbollah militias.

213 *Carthage:* See in particular Aubet, *Phoenicians and the West.*

Bibliography

Ackerman, Susan. "And the Women Knead Dough: The Worship of the Queen of Heaven in Sixth-Century Judah." In *Gender and Difference in Ancient Israel*, ed. Peggy L. Day. Minneapolis: Fortress Press, 1989.

————. *Under Every Green Tree: Popular Religion in Sixth-Century Judah*. Atlanta: Scholars Press, 1992.

————. *Warrior, Dancer, Seductress, Queen: Women in Judges and Biblical Israel*. New York: Doubleday, 1998.

Ackroyd, Peter. "Goddesses, Women, and Jezebel." In *Images of Women in Antiquity*, ed. Averil Cameron and Amélie Kuhrt. Detroit: Wayne State University Press, 1983.

Aguiar, Sarah Appleton. *The Bitch Is Back: Wicked Women in Literature*. Carbondale: Southern Illinois University Press, 2001.

Ahlström, Gösta. *Royal Administration and National Religion in Ancient Palestine*. Leiden, Netherlands: E. J. Brill, 1982.

Albertz, Rainer. *A History of Israelite Religion in the Old Testament Period*. Vol. 1. Louisville, Ky.: Westminster John Knox Press, 1994.

Albright, William F. *Archaeology and the Religion of Israel*. Baltimore: Johns Hopkins University Press, 1942.

Alfa, Cristina León. *Fantasies of Female Evil: The Dynamics of Gender and Power in Shakespearean Tragedy*. Newark, N.J.: University of Delaware Press, 2003.

Allen, Virginia M. *The Femme Fatale: Erotic Icon*. Troy, N.Y.: Whitston, 1983.

Almond, Gabriel A., R. Scott Appleby, and Emmanuel Sivan. *Strong Religion: The Rise of Fundamentalisms Around the World*. Chicago: University of Chicago Press, 2003.

Anderson, Francis I. "The Socio-juridical Background of the Naboth Incident." *Journal of Biblical Literature* 85 (1966).

Appler, Deborah. *A Queen Fit for a Feast*. Ph.D. diss., Vanderbilt University, 2004. Online at wwwlib.umi.com/dissertations/.

Bibliography

Armstrong, Karen. *A History of God: The 4,000-Year Quest of Judaism, Christianity and Islam*. New York: Ballantine, 1993.

Atwood, Margaret. "Spotty-Handed Villainesses: Problems of Female Bad Behavior in the Creation of Literature." Online at www.web.net/ow-toad/vlness.html. 1994.

Aubet, Maria Eugenia. *The Phoenicians and the West: Politics, Colonies and Trade*. New York: Cambridge University Press, 1993.

Augustinovic, Agostino. *El-Khadr and the Prophet Elijah*. Jerusalem: Franciscan Printing Press, 1972.

Avigad, N. "The Seal of Jezebel." *Israel Exploration Journal* 14 (1964).

Avi-Yonah, Michael. "Mount Carmel and the God of Baalbek." *Israel Exploration Journal* 2 (1952).

Bach, Alice. *Women, Seduction, and Betrayal in Biblical Narrative*. New York: Cambridge University Press, 1997.

Baly, Denis. "The Geography of Monotheism." In *Translating and Understanding the Old Testament*, ed. Harry Thomas Frank and William L. Reed. Nashville, Tenn.: Abingdon Press, 1970.

———. *The Geography of the Bible*. New York: Harper and Row, 1974.

Barkay, Gabriel. "The Iron Age II–III." In *The Archaeology of Ancient Israel*, ed. Amnon Ben-Tor. New Haven: Yale University Press, 1992.

Beach, Eleanor Ferris. "The Samaria Ivories, Marzeach, and Biblical Text." *Biblical Archaeologist* 56; no. 2 (1993).

———. "Transforming Goddess Iconography in Hebrew Narrative." In *Women and Goddess Traditions in Antiquity and Today*, ed. Karen L. King. Minneapolis: Fortress Press, 1997.

———. *The Jezebel Letters: Religion and Politics in Ninth-Century Israel*. Minneapolis: Fortress Press, 2005.

Becking, Bob. "Only One God: On Possible Implications of Biblical Theology." In *Only One God?: Mmonotheism in Ancient Israel and the Veneration of the Goddess Asherah*, ed. Bob Becking et al. Sheffield, U.K.: Sheffield Academic Press, 2001.

Bellis, Alice Ogden. *Helpmates, Harlots, Heroes: Women's Stories in the Hebrew Bible*. Louisville, Ky.: Westminster John Knox Press, 1994.

Ben-Barak, Zafira. "The Status and Rights of the Gebira." In *A Feminist Companion to Samuel and Kings*, ed. Athalya Brenner. Sheffield, U.K.: Sheffield Academic Press, 1994.

Berenson, Alex. "After the Siege, a City of Ruins, Its Dead Rotting." *New York Times*, August 28, 2004.

Bibliography

Bergen, Wesley J. "The Prophetic Alternative: Elisha and the Israelite Monarchy." In *Elijah and Elisha in Socioliterary Perspective,* ed. Robert B. Coote. Atlanta: Scholars Press, 1992.

Billinghurst, Jane. *Temptress: From the Original Bad Girls to Women on Top.* Vancouver, B.C.: Greystone, 2003.

Binger, Tilde. *Asherah: Goddesses in Ugarit, Israel, and the Old Testament.* Sheffield, U.K.: Sheffield Academic Press, 1997.

Biran, Avraham, and Joseph Naveh. "An Aramaic Stele Fragment from Tel Dan." *Israel Exploration Journal* 43 (1993).

Bird, Phyllis A. *Missing Persons and Mistaken Identities: Women and Gender in Ancient Israel.* Minneapolis: Fortress Press, 1997.

————. "The End of the Male Cult Prostitute: A Literary-Historical and Sociological Analysis of Hebrew Qades-Qedesim." In *Congress Volume, Cambridge 1995* (Fifteenth Congress of the International Organization for the Study of the Old Testament), ed. John Adney Emerton. Leiden, Netherlands: E. J. Brill, 1997.

Brenner, Athalya, ed. *The Feminist Companion to the Bible.* Sheffield, U.K.: Sheffield Academic Press, 1993.

————, ed. *A Feminist Companion to Samuel and Kings.* Sheffield, U.K.: Sheffield Academic Press, 1994.

Brichto, Herbert Chanan. "Kin, Cult, Land, and Afterlife—A Biblical Complex." *Hebrew Union College Annual* 44 (1974).

Bronner, Leah. *The Stories of Elijah and Elisha as Polemics Against Baal Worship.* Leiden, Netherlands: E. J. Brill, 1968.

Brueggemann, Walter. *The Land: Place as Gift, Promise, and Challenge in Biblical Faith.* Minneapolis: Fortress Press, 1977.

Budde, Karl. *Religion of Israel to the Exile.* New York: Putnam, 1899.

Burns, John Barclay. "Devotee or Deviate: The Dog (*keleb*) in Ancient Israel as a Symbol of Male Passivity and Perversion." *Journal of Religion and Society* 2 (2000).

Calasso, Roberto. *The Marriage of Cadmus and Harmony.* New York: Knopf, 1993.

Camp, Claudia V. "1 and 2 Kings." In *The Women's Bible Commentary,* ed. Carol A. Newsom and Sharon H. Ringe. Louisville, Ky.: Westminster Press, 1992.

————. "The Strange Woman of Proverbs: A Study in the Feminization and Divinization of Evil in Biblical Thought." In *Women and Goddess Traditions in Antiquity and Today,* ed. Karen L. King. Minneapolis: Fortress Press, 1997.

————. *Wise, Strange, and Holy: The Strange Woman and the Making of the Bible.* Sheffield, U.K.: Sheffield Academic Press, 2000.

Campbell, Joseph. *The Hero With a Thousand Faces.* New York: Pantheon, 1949.

Carmody, Denise Lardner. *Biblical Woman: Contemporary Reflections on Scriptural Texts.* Belleville, Mich.: Crossroad, 1988.

Cassuto, Umberto. *The Goddess Anath: Canaanite Epics of the Patriarchal Age.* Jerusalem: Magnes Press, 1971.

Cavendish, Richard. *The Powers of Evil in Western Religion, Magic and Folk Belief.* New York: Putnam, 1975.

Chatwin, Bruce. *The Songlines.* New York: Viking, 1987.

Clément, Catherine, and Julia Kristeva. *The Feminine and the Sacred.* New York: Columbia University Press, 2001.

Cline, Eric H. *The Battles of Armageddon: Megiddo and the Jezreel Valley from the Bronze Age to the Nuclear Age.* Chicago: University of Michigan Press, 2000.

Collingwood, R. G. *The Idea of History.* New York: Clarendon Press, 1946.

Coote, Robert. "Yahweh Recalls Elijah." In *Traditions in Transformation: Turning Points in Biblical Faith,* ed. Baruch Halpern and Jon D. Levenson. Winona Lake, Ind.: Eisenbrauns, 1981.

————. *Elijah and Elisha in Socioliterary Perspective.* Atlanta: Scholars Press, 1992.

Cox, Harvey. *The Seduction of the Spirit: The Use and Misuse of People's Religion.* New York: Simon and Schuster, 1973.

Cross, Frank Moore. *Canaanite Myth and Hebrew Epic: Essays in the History of the Religion of Israel.* Cambridge, Mass.: Harvard University Press, 1973.

Cumont, Franz. *The Oriental Religions in Roman Paganism.* New York: Dover, 1956.

Day, John. *Yahweh and the Gods and Goddesses of Canaan.* Sheffield, U.K.: Sheffield Academic Press, 2000.

Day, Peggy L., ed. *Gender and Difference in Ancient Israel.* Minneapolis: Fortress Press, 1989.

de Vaux, Roland. *The Bible and the Ancient Near East.* New York: Doubleday, 1971.

Djikstra, Bram. *Evil Sisters: The Threat of Female Sexuality and the Cult of Manhood.* New York: Knopf, 1996.

Djikstra, Meinart. "El, the God of Israel—Israel, the People of YHWH" and "Women and Religion in the Old Testament." In *Only One God?: Monothe-*

ism in Ancient Israel and the Veneration of the Goddess Asherah, ed. Bob Becking et al. Sheffield, U.K.: Sheffield Academic Press, 2001.

Eisenstadt, S. N., ed. *The Origins and Diversity of Axial Age Civilizations*. Albany: SUNY Press, 1986.

Eliade, Mircea. *The Sacred and the Profane: The Nature of Religion*. New York: Harper and Row, 1961.

Exum, J. Cheryl. *Plotted, Shot, and Painted: Cultural Representations of Biblical Women*. Sheffield, U.K.: Sheffield Academic Press, 1996.

Fanon, Frantz. *The Wretched of the Earth*. New York: Grove Press, 1965.

Fewell, Danna Nolan, and David M. Gunn. *Gender, Power, and Promise*. Nashville, Tenn.: Abingdon Press, 1993.

Finkelstein, Israel, and Neil Asher Silberman. *The Bible Unearthed: Archaeology's New Vision of Ancient Israel and the Origin of Its Sacred Texts*. New York: Simon and Schuster, 2001.

Fisher, E. J. "Cultic Prostitution in the Ancient Near East? A Reassessment." *Biblical Theology Bulletin* 6 (1976).

Fitzgerald, A. "The Mythological Background for the Presentation of Jerusalem as a Queen and False Worship as Adultery." *Catholic Biblical Quarterly* 34 (1972).

Fleming, Daniel E. *The Installation of Baal's High Priestess at Emar: A Window on Ancient Syrian Religion*. Atlanta: Scholars Press, 1992.

Fontaine, Carol. "A Heifer from Thy Stable: On Goddesses and the Status of Women in the Ancient Near East." In *The Pleasure of Her Text: Feminist Readings of Biblical and Historical Texts*, ed. Alice Bach. Philadelphia: Trinity Press, 1990.

Forbes, R. J. *Studies in Ancient Technology*. Vol. 3. Leiden, Netherlands: E. J. Brill, 1955.

Fraser, Sir James. *The Golden Bough: A Study in Comparative Religion*. New York: Macmillan, 1911.

Friedman, Richard Elliot. *Who Wrote the Bible?* New York: Summit Books, 1987.

Frost, Stanley B. "Judgment on Jezebel, Or a Woman Wronged." *Theology Today* 20, no. 4 (1964).

Frymer-Kensky, Tikva. *In the Wake of the Goddesses: Women, Culture, and the Biblical Transformation of Pagan Myth*. New York: Free Press, 1992.

———. *Reading the Women of the Bible*. New York: Schocken, 2002.

Gaines, Janet Howe. *Music in the Old Bones: Jezebel Through the Ages*. Carbondale: Southern Illinois University Press, 1999.

Bibliography

Girard, René. *Violence and the Sacred*. Baltimore: Johns Hopkins University Press, 1977.

————. "Generative Scapegoating." In *Violent Origins: Walter Burkert, René Girard and Jonathan Z. Smith on Ritual Killing and Cultural Formation*, ed. Robert G. Hamerton-Kelly. Stanford, Calif.: Stanford University Press, 1987.

Gnuse, Robert Karl. *No Other Gods: Emergent Monotheism in Israel*. Sheffield, U.K.: Sheffield Academic Press, 1997.

Goodfriend, Elaine Adler. "Could *keleb* in Deuteronomy 23:19 Actually Refer to a Canine?" In *Pomegranates and Golden Bells: Studies in Biblical, Jewish, and Near Eastern Ritual, Law, and Literature*, ed. David P. Wright, David Noel Freedman, and Avi Hurvitz. Winona Lake, Ind.: Eisenbrauns, 1995.

Gottwald, Norman K. *All the Kingdoms of the Earth: Israelite Prophecy and International Relations in the Ancient Near East*. New York: Harper and Row, 1964.

Gray, John. *I and II Kings: A Commentary*. Philadelphia: Westminster Press, 1970.

Greenberg, Moshe. "On the Political Use of the Bible in Modern Israel: An Engaged Critique." In *Pomegranates and Golden Bells: Studies in Biblical, Jewish, and Near Eastern Ritual, Law, and Literature*, ed. David P. Wright, David Noel Freedman, and Avi Hurvitz. Winona Lake, Ind.: Eisenbrauns, 1995.

Gross, Beverly. "Bitch." *Salmagundi* 162 (1994).

Gruber, Mayer I. "Women in the Ancient Levant." In *Women's Roles in Ancient Civilizations: A Reference Guide*, ed. Bella Vivante. Westport, Conn.: Greenwood Press, 1999.

Hackett, Jo Ann. "Can a Sexist Model Liberate Us?—Ancient Near Eastern 'Fertility' Goddesses." *Journal of Feminist Studies in Religion* 5 (1989).

Hadley, Judith. "From Goddess to Literary Construct." In *A Feminist Companion to Reading the Bible: Approaches, Methods and Strategies*, ed. Athalya Brenner and Carole Fontaine. Sheffield, U.K.: Sheffield Academic Press, 1997.

Halpern, Baruch. *David's Secret Demons: Messiah, Murderer, Traitor, King*. Grand Rapids, Mich.: Eerdmans, 2001.

————. *The First Historians: The Hebrew Bible and History*. San Francisco: Harper and Row, 1988.

————. "'Brisker Pipes Than Poetry': The Development of Israelite Monotheism." In *Judaic Perspectives on Ancient Israel*, ed. Jacob Neusner,

Baruch A. Levine, and Ernest S. Frerichs. Minneapolis: Fortress Press, 1987.

Hauser, Alan J., and Russell Gregory. *From Carmel to Horeb: Elijah in Crisis.* Sheffield, U.K.: Sheffield Academic Press, 1990.

Heider, George C. *The Cult of Molek: A Reassessment.* Sheffield, U.K.: JSOT Press, 1985.

Helner, Melila. "The Zealous Spirit in the Zohar" (in Hebrew). In *Elu v'Elu.* Center for Continuing Education of Progressive Judaism in Israel, 1996.

Herm, Gerhard. *The Phoenicians: The Purple Empire of the Ancient World.* London: Victor Gollancz, 1975.

Herodotus. *History.* Tr. A. D. Godley. Cambridge, Mass.: Harvard University Press, 1920.

Hill, Scott D. "The Local Hero in Palestine in Comparative Perspective." In *Elijah and Elisha in Socioliterary Perspective,* ed. Robert B. Coote. Atlanta: Scholars Press, 1992.

Hillers, Delbert R. *Covenant: The History of a Biblical Idea.* Baltimore: Johns Hopkins University Press, 1969.

Hillman, James. *On Paranoia.* Dallas: Spring Publications, 1986.

Holladay, John S., Jr. "Assyrian Statecraft and the Prophets of Israel." In *Prophecy in Israel,* ed. David L. Petersen. Minneapolis: Fortress Press, 1987.

Homer. *The Iliad.* Tr. Robert Fitzgerald. New York: Anchor, 1974.

Hooke, S. H., ed. *Myth and Ritual: Essays on the Myth and Ritual of the Hebrews in Relation to the Culture Pattern of the Ancient East.* New York: Oxford University Press, 1933.

Hooks, Stephen M. *Sacred Prostitution in Israel and the Ancient Near East.* Ph.D. diss., Hebrew Union College, Cincinnati, 1985.

Hopkins, Keith. *A World Full of Gods: The Strange Triumph of Christianity.* New York: Free Press, 2000.

Huntington, Samuel P. *The Clash of Civilizations and the Remaking of World Order.* New York: Simon and Schuster, 1996.

Isserlin, B.S.J. *The Israelites.* Minneapolis: Fortress Press, 2001.

Jackson, Ralph. *Doctors and Diseases in the Roman Empire.* Norman: University of Oklahoma Press, 1988.

Jewett, Robert, and John Shelton Lawrence. *Captain America and the Crusade Against Evil: The Dilemma of Zealous Nationalism.* Grand Rapids, Mich.: Eerdmans, 2003.

Josephus. *Jewish Antiquities.* Tr. H. St. J. Thackeray and Ralph Marcus. Cambridge, Mass.: Harvard University Press, 1998.

Bibliography

Kaufman, Shirley, Galit Hassan-Rokem, and Tamar S. Hess. *Hebrew Feminist Poems from Antiquity to the Present*. New York: Feminist Press at CUNY, 1999.

Kaufmann, Yehezkel. *The Religion of Israel*. Chicago: University of Chicago Press, 1960.

Kazantzakis, Nikos. *Journeying*. Tr. Themi Vasils and Theodora Vasils. Boston: Little, Brown, 1975.

King, Karen L. *The Gospel of Mary Magdala: Jesus and the First Woman Apostle*. Santa Rosa, Calif.: Polebridge, 2003.

Kirsch, Jonathan. *The Harlot by the Side of the Road: Forbidden Tales of the Bible*. New York: Ballantine, 1998.

————. *God Against the Gods: The History of the War Between Monotheism and Polytheism*. New York: Viking Compass, 2004.

Klein, Edward. *The Truth About Hillary*. New York: Sentinel, 2005.

Koch, Klaus. *The Prophets*, vol. 1: *The Assyrian Period*. Minneapolis: Fortress Press, 1983.

The Koran. Tr. N. J. Dawood. New York: Penguin, 1956.

Korpel, Marjo C. A. *A Rift in the Clouds: Ugarit and Hebrew Descriptions of the Divine*. Münster, Germany: Ugarit-Verlag, 1990.

————. "Asherah Outside Israel." In *Only One God?: Monotheism in Ancient Israel and the Veneration of the Goddess Asherah*, ed. Bob Becking et al. Sheffield, U.K.: Sheffield Academic Press, 2001.

Krakauer, Jon. *Under the Banner of Heaven: A Story of Violent Faith*. New York: Doubleday, 2003.

Kristeva, Julia. *Powers of Horror: An Essay on Abjection*. New York: Columbia University Press, 1982.

————. *New Maladies of the Soul*. New York: Columbia University Press, 1995.

Lakoff, George. *Moral Politics: How Liberals and Conservatives Think*. Chicago: University of Chicago Press, 1996.

————. *Don't Think of an Elephant*. White River Junction, Vt.: Chelsea Green, 2004.

Lakoff, George, and Mark Johnson. *Metaphors We Live By*. Chicago: University of Chicago Press, 1980.

Lang, Bernhard. *Monotheism and the Prophetic Minority: An Essay in Biblical History and Sociology*. Winona Lake, Ind.: Eisenbrauns, 1983.

————. "No God but Yahweh! The Origin and Character of Biblical Monotheism." In *Monotheism*, ed. Claude Geffré and Jean-Pierre Jossua. Concilium series. Edinburgh, Scotland: T&T Clark, 1985.

Bibliography

————. *Wisdom and the Book of Proverbs: A Hebrew Goddess Redefined.* Cleveland, Ohio: Pilgrim Press, 1986.

Lang, Graeme, and Vivienne Lee. "Fundamentalist Ideology, Institutions, and the State: A Formal Analysis." In *Religious Fundamentalism in the Contemporary World: Critical Social and Political Issues,* ed. Santosh C. Saha. New York: Lexington Books, 2004.

Leach, Edmund. *Genesis as Myth and Other Essays.* London: Jonathan Cape, 1969.

————. "Anthropological Approaches to the Study of the Bible During the Twentieth Century." In *Structuralist Interpretations of Biblical Myth* by Edmund Leach and D. Alan Aycock. New York: Cambridge University Press, 1983.

Leith, Mary Joan Winn. "Verse and Reverse: The Transformation of the Woman, Israel, in Hosea 1–3." In *Gender and Difference in Ancient Israel,* ed. Peggy L. Day. Minneapolis: Fortress Press, 1989.

Lipinski, E., ed. *Phoenicia and the Bible.* Leuven, Belgium: Peeters Press, 1991.

Loewenthal, L.J.A. "The Palms of Jezebel." *Folklore* 83 (1972).

MacNeill, William H. "Fundamentalism and the World of the 1990s." In *Fundamentalisms and Society,* ed. Martin E. Marty and Scott Appleby. Chicago: University of Chicago Press, 1993.

Margalit, Othniel. "The Kelabim of Ahab." *Vetus Testamentum* 34 (1984).

Markoe, Glenn E. *Phoenicians.* London: British Museum Press, 2000.

Marsman, Hennie J. *Women in Ugarit and Israel: Their Social and Religious Position in the Context of the Ancient Near East.* Leiden, Netherlands: E. J. Brill, 2003.

Marty, Martin E. "The Fundamentals of Fundamentalism." In *Fundamentalism in Comparative Perspective,* ed. Lawrence Kaplan. Amherst: University of Massachusetts Press, 1992.

Marty, Martin E., and F. Scott Appleby, eds. *Fundamentalisms and Society.* Chicago: University of Chicago Press, 1993.

Masefield, John. "A King's Daughter." In *Verse Plays.* New York: Macmillan, 1925.

McKinlay, Judith E. *Reframing Her: Biblical Women in Postcolonial Focus.* Sheffield, U.K.: Sheffield Phoenix Press, 2004.

McNeil, Donald G., Jr. "Dogs Excel on Smell Test to Find Cancer." *New York Times,* January 17, 2006.

Meyers, Carol. *Discovering Eve: Ancient Israelite Women in Context.* New York: Oxford University Press, 1988.

Miles, Jack. *God: A Biography.* New York: Knopf, 1995.

Miller, David L. *The New Polytheism: Rebirth of the Gods and Goddesses.* Dallas: Spring Publications, 1981.

Bibliography

Miller, J. Maxwell, and John H. Hayes. *A History of Ancient Israel and Judah.* Philadelphia: Westminster Press, 1986.

Mitchell, T. C. *The Bible in the British Museum: Interpreting the Evidence.* London: British Museum Publications, 1988.

Moscato, Sabatino, ed. *The Phoenicians.* New York: Rizzoli, 1999.

Na'aman, N. "Historical and Literary Notes on the Excavations of Tel Jezreel." *Tel Aviv* 24 (1997).

Napier, B. D. "The Omrides of Jezreel." *Vetus Testamentum* 9 (1959).

Niditch, Susan. *War in the Hebrew Bible: A Study in the Ethics of Violence.* New York: Oxford University Press, 1993.

————. *Oral World and Written Word: Ancient Israelite Literature.* Louisville, Ky.: Westminster John Knox Press, 1996.

Oded, Bustenay. *Mass Deportations and Deportees in the Neo-Assyrian Empire.* Wiesbaden, Germany: Ludwig Reichert Verlag, 1979.

Oden, Robert A., Jr. *The Bible Without Theology: The Theological Tradition and Alternatives to It.* San Francisco: Harper and Row, 1987.

Olyan, Saul M. "Hasalom." *Catholic Biblical Quarterly* 46 (1984).

————. "2 Kings 9:31—Jehu and Zimri." *Harvard Theological Review* 78 (1985).

————. *Asherah and the Cult of Yahweh in Israel.* Atlanta: Scholars Press, 1988.

————. *Biblical Mourning: Ritual and Social Dimensions.* New York: Oxford University Press, 2004.

Ornan, Tallay. "The Goddess Gula and Her Dog." *Israel Museum Studies in Archaeology* 3 (2004).

Otto, Rudolf. *The Idea of the Holy: An Inquiry into the Non-rational Factor in the Idea of the Divine and Its Relation to the Rational.* New York: Oxford University Press, 1970.

Pardee, Dennis. *Ritual and Cult at Ugarit.* Leiden, Netherlands: E. J. Brill, 2002.

Pardes, Ilana. *Countertraditions in the Bible: A Feminist Approach.* Cambridge, Mass.: Harvard University Press, 1992.

Parrot, André. *Samaria: The Capital of the Kingdom of Israel.* New York: Philosophical Library, 1955.

Pheterson, Gail. *The Prostitution Prism.* Amsterdam: Amsterdam University Press, 1996.

Pippin, Tina. *Death and Desire: The Rhetoric of Gender in the Apocalypse of John.* Louisville, Ky.: Westminster John Knox Press, 1992.

————. "Jezebel Re-Vamped." In *A Feminist Companion to Samuel and Kings,* ed. Athalya Brenner. Sheffield, U.K.: Sheffield Academic Press, 1994.

Bibliography

Pomeroy, Sarah B. *Goddesses, Whores, Wives, and Slaves: Women in Classical Antiquity.* New York: Schocken, 1975.

Pritchard, James B., ed. *Ancient Near Eastern Texts Relating to the Old Testament.* Princeton, N.J.: Princeton University Press, 1969.

Quick, Catherine S. "Jezebel's Last Laugh: The Rhetoric of Wicked Women." *Women and Language* 16 (1993).

Qutb, Sayyid. *Milestones.* Karachi: International Islamic Publishers, 1981.

Raban, Jonathan. *My Holy War: Dispatches from the Home Front.* New York: New York Review of Books, 2006.

Rabinovich, Abraham. "Chipping Away at the Past." *Jerusalem Post,* December 24, 1999.

Reissner, George Andrew, Clarence Stanley Fisher, and David Gordon Lyon. *Harvard Excavations at Samaria.* Cambridge, Mass.: Harvard University Press, 1924.

Renan, Ernest. *Mission de Phènicie.* Paris: Imprimerie Nationale, 1874.

Renteria, Tamis Hoover. "The Elijah/Elisha Stories: A Sociocultural Analysis of Prophets and People in Ninth-century BCE Israel." In *Elijah and Elisha in Socioliterary Perspective,* ed. Robert B. Coote. Atlanta: Scholars Press, 1992.

Richardson, Alan, ed. *A Theological Word Book of the Bible.* New York: Macmillan, 1951.

Riddle, Maxwell. *Dogs Through History.* Edgewater, Fla.: Denlinger's, 1987.

Ringdal, Nils Johan. *Love for Sale: A World History of Prostitution.* New York: Grove Press, 2004.

Robbins, Tom. *Skinny Legs and All.* New York: Bantam, 1990.

Robins, Denise. *Jezebel.* London: Hodder & Stoughton, 1977.

Rofé, Alexander. *The Prophetical Stories.* Jerusalem: Magnes Press, 1988.

———. "The Vineyard of Naboth: The Origin and Message of the Story." *Vetus Testamentum* 38 (1988).

Rollin, Sue. "Women and Witchcraft in Ancient Assyria." In *Images of Women in Antiquity,* ed. Averil Cameron and Amélie Kuhrt. Detroit: Wayne State University Press, 1983.

Rozell, Ned. "Dog Saliva: The Next Wonder Drug?" *Alaska Science Forum,* May 11, 1995; online at www.gi.alaska.edu/ScienceForum/ASF12/1234.html.

Rushdie, Salman. *Shame.* New York: Knopf, 1983.

Ruthven, Malise. *Fundamentalism: The Search for Meaning.* New York: Oxford University Press, 2004.

Said, Edward. *Orientalism.* New York: Vintage, 1979.

———. "The Mind in Winter: Reflections on Life in Exile." *Harper's,* September 1984.

Bibliography

Schwartz, Hans. *Evil: A Historical and Theological Perspective*. Minneapolis: Fortress Press, 1995.

Schwartz, Regina M. *The Curse of Cain: The Violent Legacy of Monotheism*. Chicago: University of Chicago Press, 1997.

The Septuagint Version of the Old Testament. Tr. Lancelot C. L. Brenton. London: Bagster, 1851.

Shoham, Mattitiyahu. *Tyre and Jerusalem* (in Hebrew). Israel: Dvir, 1933.

Silberman, Neil Asher. *Heavenly Powers: Unraveling the Secret History of the Kabbalah*. New York: Grosset/Putnam, 1998.

Silberman, Neil Asher, and David Small, eds. *The Archaeology of Israel: Constructing the Past, Interpreting the Present*. Sheffield, U.K.: Sheffield Academic Press, 1997.

Slaughter, Frank. *The Curse of Jezebel: A Novel of the Biblical Queen of Evil*. New York: Doubleday, 1961.

Slotki, I. W. *Kings: Hebrew Text and English Translation*. Brooklyn, N.Y.: Soncino Press, 1950.

Smith, Carol. "Queenship in Israel." In *King and Messiah in Israel and the Ancient Near East*, ed. John Day. Sheffield, U.K.: Sheffield Academic Press, 1998.

Smith, Daniel L. *The Religion of the Landless: The Social Context of the Babylonian Exile*. Bloomington, Ind.: Meyer-Stone, 1989.

Smith, George Adam. *The Historical Geography of the Holy Land*. London: Hodder and Stoughton, 1894.

Smith, Mark S. *The Early History of God: Yahweh and the Other Deities in Ancient Israel*. San Francisco: HarperSanFrancisco, 1990.

———. *The Ugaritic Baal Cycle*. Leiden, Netherlands: E. J. Brill, 1994.

———. *The Origins of Biblical Monotheism: Israel's Polytheistic Background and the Ugaritic Texts*. New York: Oxford University Press, 2001.

———. *The Memoirs of God: History, Memory, and the Experience of the Divine in Ancient Israel*. Minneapolis: Fortress Press, 2004.

Smith, Morton. *Palestinian Parties and Politics that Shaped the Old Testament*. New York: Columbia University Press, 1971.

Smith, W. Robertson. *Lectures on the Religion of the Semites*. Edinburgh, Scotland: Black, 1889.

Stern, Jessica. *Terror in the Name of God: Why Religious Militants Kill*. New York: HarperCollins, 2003.

Streete, Gail Corrington. *The Strange Woman: Power and Sex in the Bible*. Louisville, Ky.: Westminster John Knox Press, 1997.

Bibliography

Tappy, Ron E. *The Archaeology of Israelite Samaria*. Vol. 2. Harvard Semitic Studies #44. Atlanta: Scholars Press, 1992.

Tarlin, Jan. "Toward a 'Female' Reading of the Elijah Cycle: Ideology and Gender in the Interpretation of 1 Kings 17–19.21, and 2 Kings 1–2.18." In *A Feminist Companion to Samuel and Kings*, ed. Athalya Brenner. Sheffield, U.K.: Sheffield Academic Press, 1994.

Thubron, Colin. *The Hills of Adonis: A Quest in Lebanon*. Boston: Little, Brown, 1968.

Tiffany, Sharon, and Kathleen Adams. *The Wild Woman: An Inquiry into the Anthropology of an Idea*. New York: Schenkman, 1985.

Toombs, Lawrence E. "When Religions Collide: The Yahweh/Baal Confrontation." In *The Yahweh/Baal Confrontation and Other Studies in Biblical Literature and Archaeology*, ed. Julia M. O'Brien and Fred L. Horton, Jr. Lewiston, N.Y.: Mellen Biblical Press, 1995.

Trible, Phyllis. *God and the Rhetoric of Sexuality*. Minneapolis: Fortress Press, 1978.

———. "The Odd Couple: Elijah and Jezebel." In *Out of the Garden: Women Writers on the Bible*, ed. Christina Buchmann and Celina Spiegel. New York: Fawcett Columbine, 1994.

———. "Exegesis for Storytellers and Other Strangers." *Journal of Biblical Literature* 114, no. 1 (1995).

Tubb, Jonathan N. *Canaanites*. London: British Museum Press, 1998.

Uehlinger, Christoph. "Anthropomorphic Cult Statuary in Iron Age Palestine and the Search for Yahweh's Cult Images." In *The Image and the Book: Iconic Cults, Aniconism, and the Rise of Book Religion in Israel and the Ancient Near East*, ed. Karel van der Toorn. Leuven, Belgium: Uitgeverij Peeters, 1997.

Uffenheimer, Benjamin. "Myth and Reality in Ancient Israel." In *The Origins and Diversity of Axial Age Civilizations*, ed. S. N. Eisenstadt. Albany: SUNY Press, 1986.

———. *Early Prophecy in Israel*. Jerusalem: Magnes Press, 1999.

Ussishkin, David. "Jezreel, Samaria and Megiddo: Royal Centres of Omri and Ahab." in *Congress Volume, Cambridge 1995* (Fifteenth Congress of the International Organization for the Study of the Old Testament), ed. John Adney Emerton. Leiden, Netherlands: E. J. Brill, 1997.

Ussishkin, David, and John Woodhead. "Excavations at Tel Jezreel 1990–1991." *Tel Aviv* 19 (1992).

———. "Excavations at Tel Jezreel 1992–1993." *Levant* 26 (1994).

———. "Excavations at Tel Jezreel 1994–1996." *Tel Aviv* 24 (1997).

Bibliography

Vaillant, John. *The Golden Spruce: A True Story of Myth, Madness, and Greed.* New York: Norton, 2005.

van der Toorn, Karel. *From Her Cradle to the Grave: The Role of Religion in the Life of the Israelite and the Babylonian Woman.* Sheffield, U.K.: JSOT Press, 1994.

Vesey-Fitzgerald, Brian. *The Domestic Dog: An Introduction to Its History.* London: Routledge and Kegan Paul, 1957.

Vriezen, Karel J. H. "Archaeological Traces of Cult in Ancient Israel." In *Only One God?: Monotheism in Ancient Israel and the Veneration of the Goddess Asherah,* ed. Bob Becking et al. Sheffield, U.K.: Sheffield Academic Press, 2001.

White, Marsha C. *The Elijah Legends and Jehu's Coup.* Atlanta: Scholars Press, 1997.

Wiener, Aharon. *The Prophet Elijah in the Development of Judaism: A Depth-Psychological Study.* London: Routledge and Kegan Paul, 1978.

Wiesel, Elie. *Five Biblical Portraits.* Notre Dame, Ind.: University of Notre Dame Press, 1981.

Yee, Gale A. *Poor Banished Children of Eve: Women as Evil in the Hebrew Bible.* Minneapolis: Fortress Press, 2003.

Yerushalmi, Yoseph Hayim. *Zakhor: Jewish History and Jewish Memory.* Seattle: University of Washington Press, 1982.

Index

Index

Index

Printed in the United States
by Baker & Taylor Publisher Services